VE SEP 2007

SU SEPT 11
AR May 2014
LC Nov 17

Waltzing Again

Waltzing Again

New and Selected Conversations with
Margaret Atwood

Edited by Earl G. Ingersoll

Ontario Review Press ✦ Princeton, NJ

Ontario Review Press
9 Honey Brook Drive
Princeton, NJ 08540

Distributed by W. W. Norton & Co.
500 Fifth Avenue
New York, NY 10110

Library of Congress Cataloging-in-Publication Data

Atwood, Margaret Eleanor, 1939–
    Waltzing again : new and selected conversations with Margaret
Atwood / edited by Earl G. Ingersoll.— 1st ed.
        p. cm.
    ISBN 0-86538-117-8 (pbk. : alk. paper)
        1. Atwood, Margaret Eleanor, 1939 —Interviews. 2. Novelists,
Canadian—20th century—Interviews. 3. Fiction—Authorship. I.
Ingersoll, Earl G., 1938– II. Title.

    PR9199.3.A8Z46 2006
    818'.5409—dc22

                                                            2005055484

First Edition

Contents

Introduction

When *Margaret Atwood: Conversations* appeared in 1990, her novel *Cat's Eye* had been published over two years earlier. In those days before Google and other electronic search engines made it possible to find the texts of recent interviews with relative ease, a collection such as *Conversations* had a built-in sense of belatedness: other than my own brief interview concerning *Cat's Eye*, Atwood's remarks essentially ended with her responses to questions about *The Handmaid's Tale* (1985). With the appearance of *The Handmaid's Tale*, Atwood had moved into bestseller-dom and an increasingly international reputation. Indeed, Rebecca Garron, one of her younger interviewers, indicates that the first Atwood work she and her friends read was *The Handmaid's Tale*, in part because they had seen the film adaptation. In addition to a continuing productivity in poetry, the essay, and short fiction, Atwood has become best-known in the past decade and a half as the author of a series of major novels, including *The Robber Bride*, *Alias Grace*, *The Blind Assassin*, and most recently *Oryx and Crake*. *The Blind Assassin* finally gained her the elusive (she had been short-listed several times before) Booker Prize, awarded annually to a writer in English from the British Commonwealth or the Republic of Ireland. The time seems appropriate, then, for a collection to combine selected earlier interviews with a group of conversations conducted in the past two decades.

Waltzing Again: New and Selected Conversations with Margaret Atwood offers a sample of Atwood's remarks, ranging over more than four decades. It begins with probably the first major conversation, conducted by her novelist-husband Graeme Gibson, who asks her to generalize about her "major pre-occupations as a novelist." She responds: "We're talking as though I've written ten novels. I've written two, and one that didn't get published." By the time she sat down with Martin Halliwell over forty years later for the last of the New conversations, she *had* in fact published ten novels.

In addition to providing readers with comments on her own work published in the past two decades, the new conversations point up the distinctly international character of Atwood's artistic reputation. Although she may joke about her indefatigable efforts in traveling around the world to talk about her books and sign copies, her work is clearly no longer "Canadian" alone, but truly "global." That reputation is indicated in part by her conversation with Beryl Langer in Australia and with John Stone in Spain. At the same time, even though she bristles at such slick media soubriquets as the "Reigning Queen of Canadian Literature," she is without question Canada's leading writer and one of a handful of truly distinguished contemporary novelists. The announcement of a new Atwood novel creates a special excitement among her loyal readers, some of whom may wonder immediately, What will she do next? Much of that excitement is generated from the consensus that each new novel is a new departure and very often a very different novel from its immediate predecessor. Atwood is at the peak of her creative powers, as demonstrated by what may seem to many readers her "big" book—*The Blind Assassin*—but also by her witty and chilling speculative fiction—*Oryx and Crake*—which she herself has likened to a "bookend" to match the work of speculative fiction that launched her international reputation—*The Handmaid's Tale*.

By the time the work on *Waltzing Again* had begun, Atwood had already "submitted to" interviews numbering in the hundreds. (And by the time readers hold a copy of this collection in their hands, that number will probably have increased by a dozen or more.) Many of the interviews she has granted are of the "celebrity" variety in which she often speaks on the telephone to an individual from the media, after the awarding of a prize such as the Booker, but even more frequently following the appearance of a book. The interviewer may know little about Atwood's writing, or even care to, but has been assigned a "story" to produce and is searching for something "sexy" to bring at least as much attention to the interviewer's work as to Atwood's. Like book tours, these interviews are part of her professional responsibilities she has learned to tolerate. Although she may joke about having been trained to do her duty when she was a Brownie, she has a keen awareness that writers need to support the presses that publish their books. Similarly she seems much more aware of the need for patience with the media as well as academics. In being interviewed she now demonstrates somewhat more restraint than decades ago when she startled an interviewer with the announcement that the interviewer would be happier if Atwood were the writer of Harlequin Romances. She went on to indicate even more archly that the interviewer would have been even happier if Atwood not only revealed she was leaving her husband Graeme but was prepared to offer this interviewer exclusive rights to all the "dirt." Atwood has become well enough established now for journalists and academics to treat her with the respect her achievements as a writer deserve, and many years have passed since that early encounter in which an interviewer impatiently asked her, "When are you going to say something interesting?" At the same time, as the interviews to follow should indicate, Atwood still has an uneasy relationship with her "public," and her interviewers quickly learn that she is likely to force them to define terms and consider the implications of their questions before they pose them.

Why she continues to have a somewhat uneasy relationship with her interviewers strikes to the heart of her being as a writer. First, because the conversations in this collection are of the "literary" variety, i.e., the interviewers generally are familiar with her writing, Atwood demonstrates again and again her resistance to misreadings of her writing, the novels in particular. The unwary interviewer who quotes Iris of *The Blind Assassin* on the subject of writing, or particularly on the ability to write "the truth," is likely to get reminded very firmly that the words belong to Iris and are relevant to her character for that specific moment; thus, what *Iris* says should not be generalized for her character and even more importantly those remarks should never be attributed to Iris's *creator*. In a sense, Atwood is still struggling to establish the distance between her characters and herself evident in the earliest interviews: when, for example, Graeme Gibson asked her a question about characters in her second novel *Surfacing* she pointedly asked him: "Are you asking me or are you asking the book?" Atwood continues to express frustration with the limitations imposed on her imagination and creativity she finds implicit in autobiographical readings of her work. A favorite anecdote is her frustrated amusement in acknowledging her early failure to distance herself from Joan, the viewpoint character in *Lady Oracle*, who is also a writer, by making Joan obese and giving her red hair. After an introduction in which she stressed that Joan in this novel was not Margaret, the author, Atwood read from *Lady Oracle*. In the question-and-answer session that followed, a member of the audience asked Atwood how she had succeeded in losing so much weight.

Because many of her interviewers are academics, Atwood also struggles against continual questions that encourage her to interpret her own work. The situation resembles the listener who asks the teller of a joke to explain why it's funny: Atwood implies, if not states, that if you don't get it on your own, no explanation is likely to help. Although she has become more tolerant of "academics," she is still not entirely comfortable, for example, with the existence of a Margaret Atwood Society, founded two decades ago and from her point of view more than a bit premature because such organizations ought to be reserved for dead authors. Perhaps she has had similar reservations about the existence now of the two biographies that have been written about her. Undoubtedly she thought she had earlier discouraged such attempts by claiming that any biography of her, or other writers, would be boring: after all, she asks, what does she do but sit around and write? More likely, she is resistant to re-constructions of her life because they could seem the "happy hunting ground" of the "Nosy Parkers"—as she calls them—who will use her Life to read her Art.

What she often resists most is the assertions I am at this moment making about her and her work. Frequently she reminds her "public" that she was raised among Scientists, and it would be easy enough to misunderstand that association with Science as having produced a comfortable confidence in The Truth. Perhaps because, as she has made it clear, she continues to associate with scientists—they tend to run in her family—it would be tempting to "analyze" her creative being as a conflict between the "certainty" of the Scientist and the "indeterminacy" of the Poet. Nothing perhaps could be farther from "the truth" for the very reason that she seems to have learned the lesson of those scientists in her milieu exceedingly well: those with the highest respect for The Truth are most aware of its rarity and its insubstantiality. If Atwood is a "poetic" novelist it is not because she lards her fiction with "purple passages" but because she approaches the writing of fiction with the sensibility of the poet, and even the "uncertainty principle" of the scientist, who understands that The Truth is excruciatingly difficult to come by. Atwood reminds her "public" of her Puritan ancestors who emigrated to Nova Scotia after their Loyalist politics made the newly forged United States an uncomfortable home. One legacy of that faith may be a devotion to Truth that emerges in her characteristic squeamishness about over-simplifications, abstractions, and generalizations. Readers will note Atwood as the wary interviewee who challenges questioners—for example, those who want her to certify a single Canadian "voice" or to trade in attractive generalities about her own work.

Because her "fame" has moved her readership outside the groves of academe, a number of the interviews among the new conversations in this collection are transcripts of performances before a "live" audience. Although she may demur when asked about her "performance" at readings of her work, it quickly becomes evident that she is an enthusiastic and highly adept "performer" in the later conversations. It's very clear that she thoroughly enjoys these conversations, and what's more, she demonstrates that she is a very, very funny person. Which, of course, she has been telling us for years! She has been asked about the trend toward grimness in her recent novels. For example, Iris, as readers predict, will be dead by the end of *The Blind Assassin,* and so-called homo sapiens at the end of *Oryx and Crake* threatens to join the other species "Man" has hurried into extinction. Without denying a "grimness" that reflects a far from perfect · "real" world, Atwood reminds her readers of all the humor in both novels, without resorting to that old chestnut that we laugh so we don't have to weep.

So why continue to collect her interviews? The more recent conversations contribute to a growing awareness of Atwood's views for critics and scholars, as well as the "common reader." If readers will indulge my impulse to speak personally here, the appearance of *Margaret Atwood: Conversations* fifteen years ago has been a gratifying experience for me as an editor. A case in point is my colleague Shuli Barzilai at the University of Jerusalem, who has told me that she keeps a copy of the earlier collection on a shelf over her desk so that when she is reading Atwood's work, or more often when she is writing about it, she can quickly consult the index for references to Atwood's comments on a whole range of matters. In this way, if a reader is professionally curious about whether Atwood has ever mentioned J. M. Coetzee's *Foe* or Primo Levi's *The Periodic Table*, the collection can be of assistance. Probably most readers of *The Handmaid's Tale* would have assumed that she had read George Orwell's *1984*; her comments on that dystopian novel, however, confirm not only that she has read it but that she read it at a very young age when it had a huge impact on her. In addition, her remarks on Orwell's work help us to read *The Handmaid's Tale* anew as an intertext with *1984*.

Furthermore, these interviews have the power to bring readers to the table of Atwood's fiction and poetry—in one case, quite dramatically. In soliciting permissions for the (re)printing of these conversations, I had a fascinating response from John Stone. He wrote me that some years ago he had noticed a copy of *Margaret Atwood: Conversations* behind the bar of a restaurant in Barcelona and asked the bartender if he could borrow it to read. The bartender indicated that a patron had left it with him for safekeeping but agreed to loan it to Stone if he would return it promptly. Stone wrote that he was so impressed with the interviews that he began reading Atwood's work, encouraged his wife to, and they now have over a dozen of her books in their library. Eventually he himself interviewed Atwood, and his conversation appears in this collection. The serendipity of his encountering *Margaret Atwood: Conversations* speaks in part to what we have been telling ourselves for a generation now: we are indeed a global village of readers and writers. It speaks also to the hunger of readers to "hear the voice" of the author whose books they read, to "hear" in her own voice what *matters* to her, how she *feels* about environmental issues, what is her sense of the future.

The conversations that follow have been selected from well over 200 interviews in which Atwood participated. They appear in roughly chronological order, based on the date of the interview or its publication. This organization allows readers to explore the range of Atwood's interests and attitudes over the past four decades in which they were conducted. Readers are likely in this way to discover both changes and consistencies.

Most of the conversations have previously appeared in print. Some appeared in easily accessible journals such as the *Ontario Review* and *Paris Review*. Others, however, appeared in less accessible journals such as *Revista Española de Estudios Canadienses* and *Australian-Canadian Studies*. Every effort has been made to gain permission to reprint or print these materials; however, despite even the usefulness of Google and other search engines, at least one rights holder continues to have "gone missing."

The interviews have been edited to achieve consistency in matters of mechanics, such as American spelling conventions, and to remove redundant or unimportant material. Where such passages have been removed, their absence is generally denoted with the symbol "//." On some occasions passages that repeat material from other interviews have been allowed to stand in order to emphasize matters important enough to Atwood to bear her repeating them or to demonstrate how she characteristically responds to frequently asked questions–repeated questions and answers certainly being a problem endemic to interviews in general.

As I indicated at the end of the introduction to *Margaret Atwood: Conversations*, Atwood's interviews in a very meaningful sense represent her "biography." If some have become impatient with biography, it may be because that genre often drowns in its obsession with externals. Which of us has not wondered, for example, if it is really important to know, say, *which* hospital Atwood was born in? In many ways Atwood's own remarks in these conversations more pointedly indicate what she thinks is important in her life, in her experience as a writer, and in her work. Once again, these New and Selected Conversations offer a "life" of Margaret Atwood—a feast of her comments on her own work, on her nation, and on writing in general.

EARL G. INGERSOLL

October 2005

Chronology

1939   Born 18 November, in Ottawa, Ontario; parents, Carl Edmund Atwood and Margaret Killam Atwood. Her brother, Harold, was born in 1937; her sister, Ruth, in 1951.

1946–61   Moves with her family from Ottawa to live in Toronto, where her father, an entomologist, is a member of the University of Toronto faculty.

1952–57   Attends Leaside High School in Toronto and begins writing at sixteen.

1957–61   A student at Victoria College, University of Toronto. Publishes in *Acta Victoriana*, *The Canadian Forum*, and *The Strand*. Graduates in 1961 with honors in English. Her collection of poems, *Double Persephone* (Hawkshead Press), appears and receives the E. J. Pratt Medal for Poetry.

1961   Receives a Woodrow Wilson Fellowship and begins graduate work at Radcliffe, attracted by the reputation of Jerome Buckley, the Canadian specialist in 19th-century English literature.

1962   Granted a Master of Arts in English and continues work on a Ph.D.

1963   Leaves Harvard to work in market research in Toronto and begins work on the manuscript of a yet-unpublished novel.

1964–65   Moves to Vancouver to teach at the University of British Columbia and works on the manuscript of *The Edible Woman*, between April and August.

1965   Returns to graduate work at Harvard.

1966   *The Circle Game* (Contact Press; Anansi) appears.

1967   Receives the Governor-General's Award for Poetry for *The Circle Game*. *The Animals in That Country* wins first prize in the Centennial Commission Poetry Competition. Marries James Polk, whom she met at Harvard in 1963.

1967–68   Teaches Victorian literature and American literature at Sir George Williams University in Montreal. In 1968 *The Animals in That Country* (Oxford, Atlantic Little-Brown) appears.

1969–70   Teaches at the University of Alberta. In 1969 *The Edible Woman* (McClelland and Stewart, Andre Deutsch; Atlantic Little-Brown, 1970) appears, its publication delayed because the publisher misplaced the manuscript for two years. *Poetry* magazine awards her the Union Poetry Prize. In 1970 *The Journals of Susanna Moodie* (Oxford) and *Procedures for Underground* (Oxford, Atlantic Little-Brown) appear.

1971   *Power Politics* (Anansi; Harper and Row, 1973) appears.

1971–72   Teaches at York University, Toronto.

1972   *Surfacing* (McClelland and Stewart; Andre Deutsch, Simon & Schuster, 1973) and *Survival: A Thematic Guide to Canadian Literature* (Anansi) appear.

1972–73   Writer-in-Residence at the University of Toronto.

1973   James Polk and she get divorced, and she moves to Alliston, Ontario, with Graeme Gibson, whom she met in 1970. Trent University grants her a D. Litt.

1974   *You Are Happy* (Oxford; Harper and Row, 1975) appears. *Poetry* of Chicago awards the Bess Hopkins Prize; Queen's University, the L.L.D.

1976   *Selected Poems* (Oxford, Simon & Schuster) and *Lady Oracle* (McClelland and Stewart, Simon & Schuster; Andre Deutsch, 1977) appear. Daughter Eleanor Jess Atwood Gibson is born.

1977   *Dancing Girls* (McClelland and Stewart; Simon & Schuster, Cape, 1981) appears. *Lady Oracle* receives the City of Toronto Book Award and the Canadian Bookseller's Association Award.

1978   *Two-Headed Poems* (Oxford; Simon & Schuster, 1980) and *Up in the Tree* (McClelland and Stewart) appear. Recipient of the St. Lawrence Award for Fiction.

1979   *Life Before Man* (McClelland and Stewart; Simon & Schuster, 1980) appears.

1980   *Anna's Pet* (James Lorimer & Co.) appears. Moves to Toronto, receives the Radcliffe Graduate Medal and a D. Litt. from Concordia University.

1981   *True Stories* (Oxford; Simon & Schuster, 1982) and *Bodily Harm* (McClelland and Stewart; Simon & Schuster, Cape, 1982) appear. Awarded a Guggenheim Fellowship.

1982   *The Oxford Book of Canadian Verse in English* (Oxford) and *Second Words: Selected Critical Prose* (Anansi; Beacon Press, 1984) appear. Receives an honorary degree from Smith College.

1983   *Murder in the Dark* (Coachhouse Press) and *Bluebeard's Egg* (McClelland and Stewart; Houghton Mifflin, 1986) appear. Receives an honorary degree from the University of Toronto.

1984   *Interlunar* (Oxford) appears.

1985   *The Handmaid's Tale* (McClelland and Stewart; Houghton Mifflin, Cape, 1986) appears. Spends the spring semester at the University of Alabama as holder of the Endowed Chair in Creative Writing. Receives honorary degrees from Mount Holyoke, the University of Waterloo, and the University of Guelph.

1986   *Selected Poems II: Poems Selected and New 1976–1986*
(Oxford) appears. Holds the Berg Chair at New York University
for three months and receives the Toronto Arts Award; *Los Angeles
Times* Fiction Award; *Ms.* Magazine, Woman of the Year, 1986; Ida
Nudel Humanitarian Award; Governor General's Award, *The
Handmaid's Tale*.

1987   *Selected Poems II* and *Selected Poems I* (Houghton Mifflin)
appear. Shortlisted for the Booker Prize (England); shortlisted for
the Ritz Hemingway Prize (Paris); Arthur C. Clarke Award for
best Science Fiction, 1987; Commonwealth Literary Prize,
Regional winner, 1987; Council for Advancement and Support of
Education, Silver Medal, Best Article of the Year; Humanist of the
Year Award; Fellow of the Royal Society of Canada. Receives
honorary degree from Victoria College.

1988   *Cat's Eye* (McClelland and Stewart, Bloomsbury;
Doubleday, 1989) appears. YWCA Women of Distinction Award;
National Magazine Award for Environmental Journalism, First
Prize; American Academy of Arts and Science, Foreign Honorary
Member, Literature.

1989   *Cat's Eye*, City of Toronto Book Award; Coles Book of the
Year; Canadian Booksellers Association Author of the Year;
Foundation for the Advancement of Canadian Letters /
Periodical Marketers of Canada Book of the Year for *Cat's Eye*;
shortlisted for the Booker Prize (England).

1990 *Selected Poems 1966–1984* (Oxford). *For The Birds* (Douglas
& McIntyre). Order of Ontario; Centennial Medal, Harvard
University.

1991   *Margaret Atwood Poems 1965–1975* (Virago). *Wilderness
Tips* (McClelland and Stewart, Doubleday, Bloomsbury). Receives
honorary degree from Université de Montréal.

1992   *Good Bones* (Coach House, Bloomsbury; Doubleday, 1994).
Trillium Award for Excellence in Ontario writing, for *Wilderness*

Tips; John Hughes Prize, from the Welsh Development Board; Book of the Year Award from the Periodical Marketers of Canada, for *Wilderness Tips*; Commemorative Medal for the 125th Anniversary of Canadian Confederation.

1993 *The Robber Bride* (McClelland and Stewart, Bloomsbury, Doubleday). Canadian Authors' Association Novel of the Year.

1994 Trillium Award for Excellence in Ontario Writing (*The Robber Bride*). Commonwealth Writers' Prize for Canadian and Caribbean Region, (*The Robber Bride*); Government of France's Chevalier dans l'Ordre des Arts et des Lettres; *Sunday Times* Award for Literary Excellence (*The Robber Bride*), London. Receives honorary degree from University of Leeds.

1995 *Morning in the Burned House* (McClelland & Stewart, Houghton Mifflin, Virago). *Princess Prunella and the Purple Peanut* (Key Porter, Workman). Swedish Humour Association's International Humourous Writer Award (*The Robber Bride*); Best Local Author, *NOW* Magazine Readers' Poll; Trillium Award for Excellence in Ontario writing, for *Morning in the Burned House*.

1996 *Alias Grace* (McClelland and Stewart, Bloomsbury, Doubleday). Norwegian Order of Literary Merit; short-listed for the Booker Prize for *Alias Grace*; The Giller Prize for *Alias Grace*; Canadian Booksellers Association Author of the Year. Receives honorary degree from McMaster University.

1997 National Arts Club Medal of Honor for Literature; Premio Mondello for *Alias Grace*; Best Local Author, *NOW* Magazine Readers' Poll; *Salon* Magazine Best Fiction of the Year for *Alias Grace*.

1998 Best Local Author, *NOW* Magazine Readers' Poll, 1998. Receives honorary degrees from Oxford University and Lakehead University.

1999 London Literature Award; Best Local Author, *NOW* Magazine Readers' Poll.

2000   *The Blind Assassin* (McClelland and Stewart, Bloomsbury, Doubleday). Best Local Author, *NOW* Magazine Readers' Poll; The Booker Prize for *The Blind Assassin*.

2001   International Crimewriters Association Dashiell Hammett Award; Canadian Booksellers Association People's Choice Award. Receives honorary degrees from Cambridge University and Algoma University.

2003   *Oryx and Crake* (McClelland and Stewart, Bloomsbury, Doubleday). *Rude Ramsay and the Roaring Radishes* (Key Porter, Bloomsbury). *NOW* Magazine Readers' Poll; The Radcliffe Medal; Harold Washington Literary Award; short-listed for the Man Booker Prize for *Oryx and Crake*; shortlisted for the Giller Prize, for *Oryx and Crake*; shortlisted for the Governor General's Award for Fiction for *Oryx and Crake*.

2004   *Bashful Bob and Doleful Dorinda* (Key Porter, Bloomsbury). Shortlisted for the Orange Prize for *Oryx and Crake*; *NOW* Magazine Readers' Poll. Receives honorary degree from Harvard University.

2005   *The Penelopiad* (Canongate) appears. Banff Centre's National Arts Award; Edinburgh's International Book Festival Enlightenment Award; Chicago Tribune Literary Prize. Receives honorary degrees from Sorbonne Nouvelle and Literary and Historical Society, University College Dublin.

Waltzing Again

Dissecting the Way a Writer Works
Graeme Gibson

Gibson: What is it about the novel that is opposed, say, to poetry or the film script that you've done, what is it about the novel you like?
Atwood: I don't know. I don't think it's a positive attraction towards the novel—it's just that there are things you can't do in any other form. Things you can't do in poetry unless you want to be E. J. Pratt and write very long narrative poems. You can't have characters, you can't have very involved plots—it's a whole different thing. Poems are very condensed, and a film script isn't a primary form for a writer—it's a secondary form. It's a primary form for a director.
Gibson: Are novels less personal?
Atwood: No, no, it has very little to do with that. It's more a question of how much room you have. You have a lot more room in a novel to move around, and you can build a much more complex, I won't say "complex" because poems can be very complex, but you can build a larger structure.
Gibson: Perhaps you never think this way, but do you think of yourself differently as a poet than as a novelist, when you're working.
Atwood: I don't think of myself at all when I'm working. I think of the thing I'm doing, and obviously I think of the novel as a different kind of thing than a poem…it's a lot more hard work. It's physical labor in a way that poetry isn't. You can write a poem very quickly, and then it's done, and you've had everything, all possible satisfactions and engagements with the thing, condensed into a short period of time. The equivalent for that with a novel is when you get the idea or when you get a few of the key scenes. But the problem then is sustaining your interest long enough to actually sit down and work it out, and that is difficult for me

because I don't like work. I will do anything to avoid it, which means that in order to actually finish a novel I have to isolate myself from all distraction because if it's a question of a choice between the work and the distraction I'll take the distraction every time.

Gibson: What about a collection of poems, like *Susanna Moodie*, where in fact you do have a character?

Atwood: Yes. That assumes that I sat down with the conception of a character and wrote the thing through from chapter one through the middle to the end, but they came as separate poems and I had no idea when I began that I was going to end up with a book of that size. It wasn't planned that way. I wrote twelve at first and stopped and thought, You know, this is just sort of a long short poem, twelve short poems, that's it. And then I started writing more of them but I didn't know where it was going. I don't write books of poetry as books. I don't write them like novels.

Gibson: With a novel presumably you know where you are going when you begin?

Atwood: Not entirely, but I know there is enough of a skeleton so I'll end up with a book of a certain length.

Gibson: How do you write novels? I mean, you write quickly, I gather.

Atwood: I write them in longhand which is very bad. I wish I could write on a typewriter—it would save a lot of trouble. I do write very quickly, but under a lot of pressure. I try to work through something like ten pages a day, which of course never happens....

Gibson: Do you write the first draft of a novel pretty well in one spurt?

Atwood: Well, I don't know. I've only written two, actually I've written three, the first one didn't get published, and the first one took a long time because I had a job, I didn't have uninterrupted time, and it took me about three months. With *The Edible Woman* I went through the first draft in about a month and a half. And the other one, *Surfacing*—when did I finish it? last summer? there's no sense of time—it got interrupted; I wanted to write it through and I did get something like a first draft. But then I had to go off and work on the film script, and not until I was into something like the third draft did I have a straight period of time.

Gibson: You do a fair amount of rewriting then?

Atwood: Yes, a lot. I think the pressure is to get the thing down in some form or other so that it's out there and then can be worked with.

Gibson: Do you enjoy writing?

Atwood: Do I enjoy writing? I guess I would have to, wouldn't I, or I wouldn't do it. I don't like the physical thing, and I don't like the sort of willpower involved in making sure that your sentences are OK and that you haven't repeated the same word about nine times on one page. That sort of busy-work is editing. I enjoy the initial thing. I don't enjoy the tidying up very much because it's like work.

Gibson: What is the writer's role? Do you think he has a role?

Atwood: I don't know. I'm sure he has lots of roles, but I very much object to other people telling me what my role is in any area of life whatsoever. I think people define their own roles, and my "role as a writer" may be entirely different from somebody else's. Somebody else may feel that his role is to write a novel about being saved for Jesus Christ and the novel should convert people, or that what he should be writing is a novel about how to get rid of the Americans. I don't see writing as having that kind of function. I think if you are going to save souls or save the world, you should be a preacher or a politician, so I don't see my role in any one-to-one relationship with society. I think anybody who does is deluding himself. Books don't save the world.

Gibson: Does a writer have any responsibility to society?

Atwood: Does society have any responsibility to the writer? Once society decides it has responsibility to me as a writer, I'll start thinking about my responsibility to it. You know, I think its general attitude towards me when I started to be a writer was that I was crazy or somehow undecorous, and if society regards me like that, I don't see that I have any particular responsibility towards it. I think that's society's attitude towards anybody when he's first starting. But if you become successful, then it's an OK thing for you to be doing because, as we all know, this society pays a lot of attention to success. But that is not a respect for writing *per se* as a legitimate activity; that's a respect for success, which is a different thing. It would have the same respect for you if you were a successful used-car salesman.

Gibson: Do you think this is particularly Canadian, our response to writers?

Atwood: No, it's American. It's getting better, but one always sees things in terms of one's struggling youth to a certain extent, and that was certainly the case with mine. I could count on the fingers of one hand people whose attitude towards what I was doing was positive. The rest were either incredulous or negative.

Gibson: Do writers know something special, say, in the way physicists or astronomers or sociologists do?

Atwood: Do they have a body of knowledge that is transmittable? No. They have presumably a skill with words. Apart from that they can be very different from one another. They don't necessarily share any body of knowledge, any viewpoint, any psychological pattern, although sometimes they try to. There's a certain amount of pressure on them to see themselves in terms of society's idea of what the writer should be. You know, you should go to Paris and drink a lot, or you should kill yourself, you should be Lord Byron or T. S. Eliot or something like that. I think they have common problems, but that's different. That may shape you to a certain extent, having problems in common.

Gibson: Do you mean problems professionally or personally?

Atwood: Professionally. I mean, what they do entails a certain kind of problem, such as how do you write and make enough money to live? How do you get published? Are publishers fair to writers? How to get your books distributed? How do you deal with your audience, supposing you acquire one?

Gibson: Do you feel kinship with other writers?

Atwood: With some, yes, with others, no. Just because a person is a writer is no guarantee that I'm going to like them or like their work or have anything in common with them at all. I don't think people get a gold star on their forehead for being a writer. There seems to be no connection whatsoever between whether I like someone's work and whether I like them. //

Gibson: What do you like most about your own writing?

Atwood: Doing it. After it's done, you mean? Looking at it as an object? I don't know. I don't tend to like it very much after a certain point, and I think that's maybe a healthy sign; that is, if you get too stuck on your own earlier work it probably means there's nothing else new coming along that you're interested in. I think the book you always like best is the one you're about to write. And what you think about the ones you have written is what you did wrong, or how you would do it if you were going to do it over again, or whether you ever would do it over again.

Gibson: Who do you write for?

Atwood: Once upon a time I thought there was an old man with a gray beard somewhere who knew the truth, and if I was good enough, naturally he would tell me that this was it. That person doesn't exist, but that's who I write for. The great critic in the sky.

Gibson: This feeling you have—it presumes some standards?

Atwood: Oh yes, but I don't always know what they are. I would say that's a personification of some ideal which is unattainable, but various human beings can embody certain parts of that, and they'll come along and, if it's somebody whose opinion you really respect, that's part of it, and you never know where those people are. You may never meet them, but if you don't have the faith that they are out there somewhere, then you'd stop writing.

Gibson: Do you feel part of a tradition?

Atwood: Yes.

Gibson: Now is it particularly a Canadian tradition or...?

Atwood: Yes. I can only talk about poetry because the Canadian tradition in novels isn't old enough. It's there, but you have to go searching a lot more for it than for the poetry one. It has partly to do with when I was born and when I started writing. If I had been born in 1920 there wouldn't have been a tradition for me to feel part of, or it would have been one that was hopeless or inaccessible. // But when I did discover Canadian writing it was a tremendously exciting thing because it meant that people in the country were writing and not only that, they were publishing books. And if they could be publishing books, then so could I. // I was talking with P. K. Page a couple of years ago, and she said that when she was writing there wasn't any Canadian tradition, they were all turned on to people like W. H. Auden; their models, the people they were learning to write from, were all in other countries, and that isn't true of me. I learned to write from people in this country.

Gibson: And that carried over when you came to the novel?

Atwood: People have only started to write novels in the same way, with the same profusion and the same confidence, if you like, in this country during the last seven years, and they weren't doing it when I was learning to write and I always wrote both poetry and prose. It's just that the prose took a while longer to get published, and that says something too, because people weren't publishing novels either at that time. The novel is a much more recent development.

Gibson: Have you any idea why it's happened in the last ten years or seven years?

Atwood: There's always a connection between what people write and what they read; and what they read depends partly on the availability of publishing facilities; that is, if what they are reading are all imported novels about New York or about London, England, nobody in this country is going to feel that they can write a "real" book unless they go to those places, and even then they can't really write a real one because they aren't from those places. So when you don't have a publishing industry in your own country that is publishing fiction about the country, you are automatically defeated because you have no audience, you have no models. You are a kind of amputee and you have to either go away and write as an exile or you can go away and write as a fraud, but you can't stay there and write real books about a real place, because there's no input for it, and there's no outlet for it.

Gibson: There tended to be for the short story, didn't there, during the '20s and the '30s?

Atwood: Yes, there were magazines and the CBC, and a lot of people wrote short stories as a result, but novels were another thing. Very seldom was one published, and very seldom did it acquire an audience. Historical romance is another thing, and books like *Jalna* and *Anne of Green Gables*. Those were different; you could write those if you wanted, but if you had other ambitions you were doomed to paralysis.

Gibson: Perhaps that's why there were so many one-book people writing.

Atwood: Yes. Sure, they wrote their book, they put everything into it. They got no feedback, and they gave up, and I would too. The increase in the number of good novels has something to do with the growth of the Canadian publishing industry and places like Oberon and Anansi, if you like, and New Press.

Gibson: We were talking about advantages and disadvantages of being a writer in Canada; are there any advantages?

Atwood: Oh, tremendous. All that I've been saying about this is changing very rapidly, obviously. It's almost reached the stage where there are more publishing companies than there are good writers. Also, as I found when I lived in the States, because there is no longstanding tradition, because there are no huge giants hanging over you in Canada, you're very free. You don't feel you're competing with Herman Melville or William Shakespeare, you know; the thing is wide open. You can do anything, although I think the desirable thing to do is to find what in the tradition is usable and use it. //

There are two things. One is how good the book is and that's got nothing to do with your country or anything else. The other thing is what is in it? You can take any body of material—let's just take the Western as an example—and you can use the tradition and you can make a good one or you can make a bad one, using essentially the same kind of thing. You learn to write really from two directions; one is the formal direction and the other is the social mythology direction. The formal thing you can learn from anyone who happens to plug into your own formal direction. He could be from Mars. It wouldn't matter, if he was doing something you found formally interesting; but if you're trying to use somebody else's social mythology, you're doomed. If you try to write like an American or an Englishman, and you aren't one, you will just produce a piece of plastic. No matter how formally skillful you are.

We've been so cut off from our social mythology that we hardly know what it is; that's one thing that has to be discovered. The other thing you have to learn, and you don't learn it from "Canada" necessarily, is how to be a good writer, how to do the thing you're doing in the best way possible.

Gibson: Because we don't have within our own tradition

"giants," for want of a better word, is there a danger that it's too easy for us to make an impact or too easy for us to…

Atwood: You can be as good as everyone else fairly easily, but to be really better, that is harder. //

Gibson: Does writing demand a particular kind of selfishness?

Atwood: Everything demands a particular kind of selfishness. If you're asking is the kind that writing demands different from everybody else's kind, I don't know. There again, that assumes that writers have personalities in which you can identify an X factor common to all. And I'm not too sure that is true. Partly my suspicion of questions like that is the wish to avoid romantic stereotypes of the writer. You know, all writers are crazy, or they're all geniuses, or some nonsense like that; and to say that all writers have a peculiar kind of selfishness seems to me to fit in a bit with that. But you sort of have to go into a room and shut the door and say, "Go away everyone, because I'm going to write," and you get very annoyed at people who interrupt you, but I don't know whether that's selfish. It seems to be just a kind of condition. If you were a watchmaker and somebody interrupted you, you would probably be just as aggravated if you dropped your dial or whatever. //

Gibson: What sustained you as a writer?

Atwood: My next book. What keeps me going as a writer? That's a very mysterious area. I don't really want to find out. There are a lot of things that I just would rather not know about writing, because I think that if you get too curious about it and start dissecting the way you work and why you do it, you'd probably stop. Maybe not. Anyway that's one of my superstitions. //

Gibson: Have you encountered any particular problems as a woman writer?

Atwood: Sure. I don't think they are typical. At the time I started writing, since writing was such a freaky thing in itself and since very few men were doing it either, it wasn't that I was a woman who was writing that people found peculiar, it was that anybody at all was writing. For so long writing was regarded as a freak thing to be doing, and in a frontier society what is important is work and building houses and bridges and things like that. And writers are viewed as irrelevant or redundant. Men writers overreact to that and define writing as a really male thing to be doing. And if you're a woman doing it, that really threatens their position, considering they've gone to all this trouble to tell anybody who sort of scorns their activity that what they're doing is really very hairy-chested.

Reviewing is something else; there is no critical tradition that the reviewer or critic can draw on for treating the work of women seriously. It's better in this country than in the States, and looking back through *Letters in Canada*, you don't find much of that garbage about feminine sensibilities; but in your run-of-the-mill review it often comes up, though not so much in connection with my own work because they can't really do that easily. What you get instead is the other side of the coin. If people can't say you have a water-color feminine sensibility, they'll say something like she thinks like a man; they find it very hard, if they want to say something that's good, to say that it's good and also admit that the writer is female. They feel that they have to make you an honorary male if they're going to say you're good. So there's that.

What else? Certainly not with publishers. Publishers are in business to make money, and if your books do well they don't care whether you are male, female, or an elephant. I've seldom had any of that kind of thing from any of my publishers.

Gibson: What about the response of other women; do they try to categorize you or…

Atwood: Well of course, now that Women's Lib has come along, it's very curious. Back in the days when you were supposed to pay attention to the diapers and the washing of dishes, I was a threat to other women's life positions. Now I get made into a kind of hero, which is just as unreal. It makes me just as uncomfortable. It's turning me from what I am as a writer into something I'm not.

Gibson: Another general question, hopefully the last one: what do you think are your major preoccupations as a novelist?

Atwood: I don't know. We're talking as though I've written ten novels. I've only written two, and one that didn't get published.

Gibson: That's three and you're going to write another one.

Atwood: They're all so different from each other that I can't really talk about it. It's the sort of thing that critics do, and although I'm willing to talk about somebody else's preoccupations and do critical studies of them I'm not at all willing to do that on myself. Other people should do that if they're so disposed, but I don't want to make myself the subject of my own criticism.

Gibson: Let's talk about your two novels. There seem to be two kinds of problems, and each novel emphasizes one of them. The first one is the alternatives that are open to people, and specifically women, and that's in *The Edible Woman*; and the second is the destructiveness of society, or in some cases the mere banality of it or the irrelevance of it, but in *Surfacing*, your second book, it's the evil of it. In both novels there's the question of how to survive, given these two problems. Does that seem, generally, a relevant assumption?

Atwood: I guess so. The last thing you said, about how to survive, is certainly true.

Gibson: Marian in *The Edible Woman* is confronted with a frequently silly, irrelevant kind of social situation, like her fiancé is not up to her in any way, her job isn't up to her in any way, and there don't seem to be any alternatives in the lives around her, and what she's got to figure out is how to escape from this trap she finds herself in, survival in that way. The protagonist in the second book has a much more fundamental need to survive.

Atwood: Here we're getting into critical analysis. I can say certain formal things: *The Edible Woman* is an anti-comedy, and *Surfacing* is a ghost story. That sort of determines not only what happens in the book but the style.

Gibson: Let's pause here. What do you mean by an anti-comedy? *The Edible Woman* is an anti-comedy?

Atwood: In your standard 18th-century comedy you have a young couple faced with difficulty in the form of somebody who embodies the restrictive forces of society, and they trick or overcome this difficulty and end up getting married. The same thing happens in *The Edible Woman* except the wrong person gets married. And the person who embodies the restrictive forces of society is in fact the person Marian gets engaged to. In a standard comedy, he would be the defiant hero. As it is, he and the restrictive society are blended into one, and the comedy solution would be a tragic solution for Marian.

Gibson: In *The Edible Woman*, it seems to me that society is really unreal or irrelevant. It's the object of Marian's wit and her considerable kind of objective humor, which keeps coming through; but in *Surfacing*, it has become evil, society has become an evil force.

Atwood: Yes.

Gibson: The protagonist of *Surfacing*, who in a sense has gone through all of Marian's experiences, but has lived them out, the marriage...

Atwood: Oh no. The marriage isn't real. She made it up.

Gibson: But she's lived through it in her head, the implications of it, in a way that Marian hasn't. And there's another thing which I found in *Surfacing* which intrigues me, and that's guilt. That protagonist of *Surfacing* says at one point when she's talking about the dead heron: "The trouble some people have being German I have being human"; and she also, a bit later, talks about the cruelty of children, the cruelty that she partakes of...

Atwood: It all comes back to original sin, doesn't it? This is too complicated to talk about. // It depends on whether you define yourself as intrinsically innocent, and if you do, then you have a lot of problems, because in fact you aren't. She wishes to be not human, because being human inevitably involves being guilty, and if you define yourself as innocent, you can't accept that.

Gibson: Why does she define herself as innocent, or how does she define herself as innocent? Is it need because of...

Atwood: Ever since we all left the Roman Catholic Church we've defined ourselves as innocent in some way or another. But what I'm really into in that book is the great Canadian victim complex. If you define yourself as innocent then nothing is ever your fault—it is always somebody else doing it to you, and until you stop defining yourself as a victim that will always be true. It will always be somebody else's fault, and you will always be the object of that rather than somebody who has any choice or takes responsibility for their life. And that is not only the Canadian stance towards the world, but the usual female one. "Look what a mess I am and it's all their fault." And Canadians do that too. "Look at poor innocent us, we are morally better than they. We do not burn people in Vietnam, and those bastards are coming in and taking away our country." Well, the real truth of the matter is that Canadians are selling it.

Gibson: You seem to imply in the book that there are two kinds of people. There are the Americans, not based on nationality, but based upon a kind of approach—like hunters, because the people they mistake for Americans turn out to be Canadians and they're the ones that killed the heron. Is there a distinction? Are there the two types?

Atwood: Are you asking me or are you asking the book?

Gibson: I'm asking you about the book.

Atwood: In both of the books you have a choice of thinking the central character is crazy or thinking she is right. Or possibly thinking she is crazy and right. To a large extent the characters are creating the world which they inhabit, and I think we all do that to a certain extent, or we certainly do a lot of rearranging. There is an objective world out there, I'm far from being a solipsist. There are a lot of things out there, but towards any object in the world you can take a positive or a negative attitude or, let us say, you can turn it into a positive or a negative symbol, and that goes for everything. You can see a tree as the embodiment of natural beauty or you can see it as something menacing that's going to get you, and that depends partly on your realistic position towards it, what you were doing with the tree, admiring it or cutting it down; but it's also a matter of your symbolic orientation towards everything. Now I'm not denying the reality, the existence of evil; some things are very hard to see in a positive light. Evil obviously exists in the world, right? But you have a choice of how you can see yourself in relation to that. And if you define yourself always as a harmless victim, there's nothing you can ever do about it. You can simply suffer.

Gibson: And the protagonist of *Surfacing*, does she do more than identify herself as a victim?

Atwood: At the end she does. She refuses to identify herself as a victim, that's step one. Only if you stop identifying yourself as a victim, you know, fated by powers that be, can you act.

Gibson: Right. Then she says at one point too: "If I had turned out like the others with power, I would have been evil."

Atwood: Yes, but you have to think of where in the book she says that.

Gibson: Yes, it was at the beginning, yes.

Atwood: Yes. That's a refusal too. The other thing you do, if you are defining yourself as innocent, you refuse to accept power. You refuse to admit that you have it, then you refuse to exercise it, because the exercise of power is defined as evil, and that's like people who refuse to get involved in politics because it's dirty.

Gibson: So at the end when she says that she must be a survivor—is that her phrase? something to the effect that she mustn't be a victim?—is she accepting then the responsibility of some power?

Atwood: Of action.

Gibson: Of action, which is a kind of power.

Atwood: Sure. Every time you act you're exercising power in some form, and you cannot predict the consequences of your actions entirely. You may hurt someone, but the alternative is closing yourself up in a burrow somewhere and not doing anything ever at all.

Gibson: Which is what at one point she tries to do. Now is Marian's revolt against the situation she has found herself acquiescing to comparable? Is she asserting herself in the baking of the cake and offering it to Peter?

Atwood: I don't know, nobody's ever been able to figure that out. When writing the film script we had long conversations on just exactly what that means. Obviously she's acting, she's doing an action. Up until that point she has been evading, avoiding, running away, retreating, withdrawing.

Gibson: Hiding under the bed.

Atwood: Yes, to begin with; secondly in refusing to eat; and she commits an action, a preposterous one in a way, as all pieces of symbolism in a realistic context are, but what she is obviously making is a substitute for herself.

Gibson: Again in *Surfacing* the protagonist says: "but I was not prepared for the average, its needless cruelties and lies. My brother saw the danger early, to immerse oneself, join in the war or be destroyed. There ought to be other choices." Are there any other choices?

Atwood: We'll put it this way. You're standing on the edge of the lake, right, and you can do three things. You can stay standing on the edge of the lake, you can jump in and if you don't know how to swim you'll drown, or you can learn to swim, supposing you want to have anything to do with the lake at all. The other thing would be to just walk away, but we will suppose that this is the entire universe.

Gibson: One of the things that happens to both of them, but more clearly to the woman in the second book, in the popular phrase, is alienation or isolation, the deadening of sensibilities. I think it's towards the end of *Surfacing*, she says: "Language divides us into fragments: I wanted to be whole." Is this her attempt to be inhuman or to be nonhuman or to be like an animal or a plant?

Atwood: The ideal thing would be a whole human being. Now if your goal is to be whole, and you don't see the possibility of doing that and also being human, then you can try being something else…there are great advantages in being a vegetable, you know, except you lose certain other things, such as the ability to talk. Life is very much simplified. If you think you're a watermelon, you don't have to do anything, you can just sit around. The ideal, though, would be to integrate yourself as a human being, supposedly. And if you try that and fail, then you can try being something else for a while, which she does.

Gibson: By the end of both books, the women seem to have come a long way towards being human beings.

Atwood: Does anyone ever achieve it? If you define human beings as necessarily flawed, then anybody can be one. But if you define them as something which is potentially better, then it's always something that is just out of reach.

Gibson: In *Surfacing* there are the surveyors, the hunters, the // people who kill. One of the assumed definitions is that the Americans, not a nationality, but a state of mind, are the killers. And there are other people who aren't.

Atwood: OK, let's think of it this way. If the only two kinds of people are killers and victims, then although it may be morally preferable to be a victim, it is obviously preferable from the point of view of survival to be a killer. However, either alternative seems pretty hopeless; you can define yourself as innocent and get killed, or you can define yourself as a killer and kill others. The ideal would be somebody who would neither be a killer or a victim, who could achieve some kind of harmony with the world, which is a productive or creative harmony, rather than a destructive relationship towards the world. Now in neither book is that actualized, but in both it's seen as a possibility finally, whereas initially it is not.

Gibson: OK, just one more question, regarding the unacceptable roles open to your characters in both books. There aren't many things in society which give anybody enough, and in many cases they're filling in time. They're just doing things. It's a kind of busy-work living, and the men tend to be either pompous, like Peter, a kind of meticulous pomposity, or they're like Joe in the second book who is an observer. Then if you scratch them, beneath the surface you find a sense of failure and a sense of being threatened.

Atwood: Yes, I don't think that's very unrealistic. Let's say that I think of society in two ways; one is simply the kind of thing that Western Industrialism has done to people, and the other is the Canadian thing, where men particularly have been amputated. Women haven't been amputated as much relatively, because absolutely they've been amputated a lot more, but they didn't have as far down to go, and Western Industrialism hasn't changed their lives that much. They still have some kind of connection with their own bodies, and the celebrated woman's role, although many people may find it aggravating, still is something to do. If you can't think of what you are supposed to do you can always have a baby and that will keep you busy enough. But some guy who is doing nothing but punching little holes in cards all day, he has no connection with himself at all, and guys who sit around on their asses in an office all day have no contact with their own bodies, and they are really deprived, they're functions, functions of a machine.

Gibson: And they tend to feel themselves as failures, at least the characters in your books, well, particularly Joe. And David.

Atwood: In a way. They tend to blame that on other people.

Gibson: And they feel put down by women.

Atwood: Yes, sure. It's all true. That doesn't seem any great insight on my part. It just seems a state that is fairly widely acknowledged. And all the things that you've been talking about are really just the jam on the sandwich, because the interesting thing in that book is the ghost; and that's what I like. And the other stuff is there, it's quite true, but it is a condition; it isn't what the book is about.

Gibson: Your protagonist has returned, looking for her father, and at one point she says that one of the things about her father was his quite remarkable ability to give the illusion of peace. She grew up during the war, not knowing about the war, and her mother and father had been able to give this illusion of peace. And her return, and the whole ghost thing, seems tied in to that. Peace and being in touch with the land.

Atwood: That's all true, but it's much easier for me to talk about the formal problems involved in writing a ghost story, which I've always been fascinated by. You want to talk about ghost stories?

Gibson: She sees her own ghost, doesn't she?

Atwood: There are various kinds of ghosts you can see. You could have just a simple straightforward ghost story in which somebody sees a ghost which has no relation to them whatsoever. You could have a sort of primitive myth in which dead people are as alive as living people and they're just accepted. Nobody is too surprised by it because it happens all the time. Or you can have the Henry James kind, in which the ghost that one sees is in fact a fragment of one's own self which has split off, and that to me is the most interesting kind and that is obviously the tradition I'm working in. But I wanted to write a ghost story for the same reason that I'd like to make a good horror film. It's an interesting area which is too often done just as pulp.

Gibson: I'd like to relate the ghost, the fragment of self that is split off, to the society that is overwhelming her and isolating her, the victim thing. Because in some sense the father, the ghosts that she perceived, were not victims.

Atwood: That's true. And they aren't evil ghosts.

Gibson: And having perceived them, she is somehow stronger.

Atwood: I haven't worked this out. Again, it's like the cake in *The Edible Woman*; I just can't be that analytical about my own work. I could give you all kinds of theories as to what I think they're doing in there, but my guess is really as good as anybody else's. I know by the logic of the book what they are doing, but I don't have a whole lot of theories about it. They exist. You can make of it what you will.

Gibson: She's accused at one point of disliking men, this is in *Surfacing*, and for an instant she wonders, but then she says: "Then I realized it wasn't men I hated, it was the Americans, the human beings, men and women both. They'd had their chance, but they turned against their gods."

Atwood: Everybody has gods or a god, and it's what you pay attention to or what you worship. And they can be imported ones or they can be intrinsic ones, indigenous ones, and what we have done in this country is to use imported gods like imported everything else. And if you import a god from somewhere else, it's fake; it's like importing your culture from somewhere else. The only good, authentic thing is something that comes out of the place where you are, or the reality of your life. // Christianity in this country is imported religion. The assumption of the book, if there is one, is that there are gods that do exist here, but nobody knows about them. Anyway this gets us into metaphysical realms. The other thing that the imported gods will always tell you to do is to destroy what is there, to destroy what is in the place and to make a replica of the god's place, so that what you do is you cut down all the trees and you build a Gothic church, or imitation thereof. The authentic religion has been destroyed; you have to discover it in some other way. How that fits in with the book I don't know, but I'm sure it has something to do with it.

Gibson: We were talking about the irrelevance of society to the people living in it. In some sense, we're pushing it, but in some sense they're godless...

Atwood: They have gods. A kind of futile adjustment is probably the god. It used to be success. It used to be the individualist thing where you stomped on everyone and made a million dollars, but that isn't even the god anymore. The god is probably fitting into the machine.

Gibson: Somebody else's machine.

Atwood: Yes, somebody else's machine. People see two alternatives. You can be part of the machine or you can be something that gets run over by it. And I think there has to be a third thing.

A Question of Metamorphosis
Linda Sandler

Linda Sandler's interview was conducted at Margaret Atwood's farm outside Alliston, Ontario, during March and April 1976 and originally appeared in the special issue of *Malahat Review* 41 (1977), devoted to Margaret Atwood. Copyright © 1977 by *Malahat Review*. Reprinted by permission.

Sandler: Why do people believe you have to compromise your integrity to be successful? George Jonas believes that a writer who finds common ground with a large audience deserves all the glory she gets. But others are less generous.

Atwood: In the States, of course, you're supposed to be successful. Failure is in bad taste. In Canada, success is somehow considered vulgar...although Canadians go both ways. Say you write a good novel and it's not well received: there is a small cult who will say, "She's a real writer, the others are selling out." But others are contemptuous. They will say, "She's a failure, her book isn't selling."

I suppose I'm a successful writer. I don't know why, I don't know what the "common ground" is. But I do know that there are all kinds of people who read books, who aren't members of cliques, who don't care what Joe down the street says in his review. Someone in Lethbridge will write to me and say, "I read your book, it meant a lot to me, I wanted to tell you."

Sandler: How do you respond to the media images of yourself? In the *Survival* era you were portrayed as an inspired national prophet; more recently, the press favors the Circe image.

Atwood: You should know that a political image is invented by other people for their own convenience. They need a figurehead or they need a straw person to shoot down. It's that simple. I don't know about the Circe image. Alan Pearson believes I'm a Medusa, but that has more to do with the kind of hair I have than my writing.

What success means is that you become a cult figure for a whole lot of strangers. And since they don't know you personally, they're dealing with two-dimensional images, courtesy of the media. Eventually you become a target and you are attacked. This is the pattern.

But bad reviews in Toronto don't kill a book. Far from it. No matter how much people bitch about Toronto, the fact is the literary world in Canada is far less centralized than in the States. There are umpteen papers around the country and they all have a local audience. In the States, the success of a book depends on the author's status in New York.

And that is such a small world, a small number of influential people writing for a couple of "organs" which have undisputed authority.

Sandler: You've had a powerful impact on the cultural scene. I remember Frank Davey saying that writers with a different aesthetic are in danger of being driven underground.

Atwood: I am always amazed to find what powers and motives these people ascribe to me. Davey's remark reminds me of that caricature of me in *The Canadian Forum*: Here is this enormously powerful and malevolent female, and she is gonna getcha! It's an infantile projection.

What people fail to understand about poetry and novels and criticism is that they are hypothetical, and they are patterns of words and ideas. You can write just as convincing an opposite number, as Davey has tried to do. The fact that I prefer one pattern to another probably means that I'm better at that kind. If I wanted to propagate my vision of Canada, I'd be a philosopher. And if I wanted to impose it on everyone, I'd be a politician or a minister.

Sandler: Has it made any difference to you, getting the kind of recognition you have?

Atwood: Some people love this kind of attention, they revel in it. I don't. And I don't particularly like being a public figure. It's not something I set out to do; it's something I found happening to me. I was quite unprepared, and rather horrified by some of the results. I couldn't understand why people I had never met would go in for malicious personal attacks. Now I'm prepared for just about anything. What else can one do but laugh at it? //

Sandler: What about the scale of your audience? I think your writing has become more dramatic, less introverted than it was.

Atwood: Whether something is dramatic or not is a question of style, rather than anything else. *Susanna Moodie* is quite contemplative. *Power Politics* is epigrammatic, so it sounds more "intimate," and I think that people found it shocking for this reason. But I haven't really altered my approach to writing; I've always written all kinds of things. When I was in high school and college I was writing borderline literary material that people don't usually associate with me—musical comedies, commercial jingles, various things under pseudonyms. I even wrote an opera about synthetic fabrics for my Home Economics class. It was about that time I realized I didn't want to be a home economist; I wanted to be a writer. That was a great change, because I was supposed to be practical and sensible; that was my "image."

Sandler: *The Servant Girl* was one of the best TV plays the CBC has done. Are there more to come, aside from your screenplays?

Atwood: I do that kind of thing to support my other writing; it's what I do instead of teaching. If I do a television play I like to do it well, but the possibilities are limited. What you're really constructing is the skeleton of a play which the actors and directors will either foul up or flesh out. I can't take all the credit for *The Servant Girl*, because television is a group activity and the writer has least control over the final product.

Sandler: How do you see the relation of your art to popular art? Serious writers in Canada don't usually relate to it at all.

Atwood: "Popular" art is a collection of rigid patterns; "sophisticated" art varies the patterns. But popular art is material for serious art in the way that dreams are. In *Power Politics* I was using myths such as Bluebeard, Dracula, and horror comic material, to project certain images of men and women, and to examine them.

You could say that popular art is the dream of society; it does not examine itself. Fairy tales do not examine themselves. They just *are*, they exist. They are stories that people want to hear. Some of them sell hope; others sell disaster, which seems to be equally appealing. You can ask all sorts of questions about *why* people wish to hear these particular stories, but popular art itself does not ask these questions. It merely repeats the stories.

Sandler: You seem to pick up the right signals, because *The Edible Woman* pre-dates feminism, *Surfacing* is about the wilderness. *Lady*

Oracle is about a cult figure, and these are all stories people want to hear.

Atwood: I don't have any special clairvoyant gifts. As "prophecies," reading my books is rather like going to the fortune teller. She peers into her crystal and she says, "Babble, babble, babble." You forget most of it, but then you meet a dark stranger and you say, "Gee, what clairvoyance!"

Plugging into the popular sensibility, though, is not peculiar to me. A lot of women are writing sophisticated soap operas, for instance. I'm not putting them down, I'm saying that their material, although they deal with it in complex ways, is soap opera material. I use it myself. Iris Murdoch, after all, writes psychological Gothics—so did Henry James—and *Surfacing* has elements of the mystery story and the ghost story.

I once had a letter from a woman in the States, complaining that her book club was advertising *Surfacing* as a novel of suspense, and not only were there all these dirty words in it, but she couldn't tell who did the murder. Her response wasn't entirely dumb—at least she saw that it was a mystery story.

Sandler: What about the controversial ending of *Surfacing*? The bloodhounds say that according to the logic of the story the heroine should have killed herself.

Atwood: They could be trying to say that I should kill myself. Dead authors are easier to deal with than living ones. But *Surfacing* is a ghost story which follows a certain formula. The heroine should no more have killed herself than the protagonist in Henry James's story "The Jolly Corner" should have. She is obsessed with finding the ghosts, but once she's found them she is released from that obsession. The point is, my character can see the ghosts but they can't see her. This means that she can't enter the world of the dead, and she realizes, OK, I've learned something. Now I have to make my own life.

I was going through my papers recently and I came across an old paper on ghost stories that I'd written in university. I'd forgotten all about it, but it contains the "recipe" for the ghost story in *Surfacing*.

Sandler: What about the theory that you gave the novel a positive ending for ideological reasons?

Atwood: From the people who think I wrote *Surfacing* to illustrate *Survival*? They should get their dates straight. It's nice that she doesn't want to be a victim, but if you examine her situation and her society in the cold light of reason, how is she going to avoid it? I'd say the ending is ambiguous. People say to me, "What is she going to do? Will she marry Joe?" I don't know what she's going to do. I fill in what I know, and after that anybody's guess is as good as mine.

Ideas in fiction are closer to algebra than you might think. What the heroine does at the end of *Surfacing* results from taking a hypothesis and pushing it as far as it goes: what happens when you identify with the animals? And she concludes that she can't stay on the island, because that will mean death...which isn't necessarily so. There are ways of dealing with the wilderness.

Sandler: In his essay on you in *Open Letter*, Frank Davey suggests that you endorse the idea and perceptions of your heroine. Is he wrong?

Atwood: You would think a literary critic would distinguish between an author and a character, especially when he doesn't know the author. You have to regard everything my heroine says as the utterance of a fictional character. The reader who endorses the character suddenly finds out that she's been telling horrible lies. The reader ought to be more cautious.

We like to trust the person telling the story, especially when the novel is written in the first person. There's one of Agatha Christie's, *The Murder of Roger Ackroyd*, where you go along with the narrator only to find out that he is the murderer. You've been lied to, all the way through.

Sandler: Were you trying to create a positive heroine, the way George Eliot did in *Middlemarch*?

Atwood: Is Dorothea so positive? Look where she ends up. What you have in *Middlemarch* is an idealistic young woman living in a society which will not permit her to be so. Saint Theresa achieved sainthood, but what happens to somebody in the nineteenth century who has similar impulses? So Dorothea ends up marrying this rather simpy young man.

The question is, why did George Eliot not write about a successful female writer? Why did she kill off Maggie Tulliver and marry off Dorothea? Perhaps Eliot was attempting to portray the fate of the average woman in her society—the average intelligent woman with no options. You could ask the same question of me. Why am I not writing about a successful female writer? Which is what I am. Why is the woman in *Surfacing* not a writer? Why isn't she a poet? Instead she's a rather mediocre illustrator of children's books. What point is that making about my society?

Sandler: You could say that the woman in *Surfacing* performs a typical act of Canadian heroism. She works out her connection with the wilderness and with her past, and she *survives*.

Atwood: We would have to say what we mean by a hero, but most of the characters in twentieth-century fiction are not heroes in the traditional sense, and I would not use the term in connection with the woman in *Surfacing*: she was not a savior, actually or potentially.

Who are the Canadian heroes? We have figures like Norman Bethune and Louis Riel, who have an organic connection with some society and are killed in the process of trying to save it. You could ask, In what sense is Bethune a Canadian hero? Well, he was a Canadian hero who found it impossible to be heroic in Canada, so he died for somebody else's society. And Riel? Are the Métis any better off because of his actions? This is always the question: has the hero lived and died in vain? //

Sandler: Don't victims have the same function as romantic heroes—to make negative statements about society? Isn't that why you call *The Edible Woman* an anti-comedy?

Atwood: That's stretching the point, but the book does make a negative statement about society. In traditional comedy, boy meets girl, there are complications, the complications are resolved and the couple is united. In my book the couple is not united and the wrong couple gets married. The complications are resolved, but not in a way that reaffirms the social order. The tone of *The Edible Woman* is lighthearted, but in the end it's more pessimistic than *Surfacing*. The difference between them is that *The Edible Woman* is a circle and *Surfacing* is a spiral...the heroine of *Surfacing* does not end where she began.

Sandler: How did *Lady Oracle* start? She's the least doomed of all your heroines.

Atwood: I probably started with the Gothic romances, but that was a long time ago and my books tend to evolve into something quite unrelated to the original idea. *Lady Oracle* was more tragic to begin with—it was going to start with a fake suicide and end with a real one. As you know, it turned out differently...it's a question of metamorphosis. I started with one voice and one character, and she changed during the writing, she became a different person. There's no accounting for how that happens.

Sandler: You have some futuristic poems like that, "Eventual Proteus" and "At first I was given centuries," where the speaker goes through a series of evolutionary changes.

Atwood: It's been a constant interest of mine: change from one state into another, change from one thing into another.

Sandler: How come?

Atwood: Who knows? But my father is an entomologist and he used to bring home these "things" in one form; they would go through some mysterious process and emerge as something else. So metamorphosis was familiar to me from an early age. Later on I studied chemistry and botany and zoology, and if I hadn't been a writer I'd have gone on with that. The U.S. publisher of *The Animals in That Country* found it very significant that I'd grown up in a family of biologists. You might link it up with that, I don't know how credible that would be. Ovid's father wasn't an entomologist.

You could also link it with my childhood reading; most fairy tales and religious stories involve miraculous changes of shape. Grimm's tales, Greek and Celtic legends have them. North American Indian legends have people who are animals in one incarnation, or who can take on the shape of a bird at will. I would say that *Grimm's Fairy Tales* was the most influential book I ever read.

Sandler: Reversals and metamorphoses seem to be the key principles of your work, and they come together in "Speeches for Dr. Frankenstein." That's a mirror poem, isn't it?

Atwood: Yes. The monster is the narrator's other self, and the process of writing that poem involved separating the two selves.

Have you read Mary Shelley's *Frankenstein*? It's a creation parable, where God forsakes Adam: instead of taking care of the monster, Dr. Frankenstein deserts him because he can't face the grotesque creature that he's produced. But the monster's not evil—as the movie would have it—that's just Hollywood hokum. He's totally innocent, and he can't understand why people find him so horrible.

There's a marvelous "chase scene" in the original version, when Dr. Frankenstein decides to hunt him down. The monster leads him on a merry chase, and when they get to this Arctic setting Dr. Frankenstein collapses and dies. There's a peculiar finale where the monster comes back for his body and carries him off across the ice floes.

My setting comes from the original novel, but in my poem it's the monster who deserts his maker—not the other way around. Although I tend to be more interested in plots than in allegorical meanings.

Sandler: The plot of *Lady Oracle* is your most intricate, what with various time zones and the interlocking of real action with Gothic plot.

Atwood: *Lady Oracle* is the most rewritten of my books and it took about two years to write. *Surfacing* and *The Edible Woman* each took six months, approximately, although I'd been thinking about them for a long time before I started writing. With *Lady Oracle* the conception and the writing were much closer together.

Sandler: The heroine says that writing Gothics is like moving through a maze, and *Lady Oracle*'s plot is something like that.

Atwood: Mazes are interesting. Apparently they were originally built for two reasons, religious initiation or defense. Edinburgh Castle is constructed that way and it was never taken—except once, by treachery.

In Gothic tales the maze is just a scare device. You have an old mansion with winding passages and a monster at the center. But the maze I use is a descent into the underworld. There's a passage in Virgil's *Aeneid* which I found very useful, where Aeneas goes to the underworld to learn about his future. He's guided by the Sibyl and he learns what he has to from his dead father, and then he returns home. It's a very ambiguous passage and scholars have spent a lot of energy analyzing it.

Sandler: Are people going to assume that *Lady Oracle* is just another version of your life?

Atwood: Undoubtedly. People are always asking me if I'm vegetarian and when my parents died. And they are astonished when I tell them that I am carnivorous and my parents are very much alive.

With *Lady Oracle* I was determined to make the character physically unidentifiable with myself, so I made her very fat and I gave her red hair—I had a friend with marvelous red hair that I always envied, so I took her hair and stuck it onto this character. What happens when I read these chapters to an audience? Someone immediately sticks up a hand and says, "How did you manage to lose all that weight?"

This probably wouldn't happen in England, where readers are more sophisticated. But even in Canada, where fiction is a fairly recent phenomenon, writers of escape literature are exempt—nobody would suggest that because Agatha Christie wrote eighty thousand murder mysteries she must have murdered at least one person, to find out how.

But if you write a "serious" book, everybody wants it to be autobiographical. You can protest till you're blue in the face, it doesn't make any difference...as my fat-lady story illustrates.

Shakespeare is in an enviable position. Nobody knows a thing about him, and they can speculate all they like, but what they have to deal with is his poems and his plays. And that's what counts. You don't need biographical information unless the work is unintelligible without it. It's most unfortunate that Dorothy Wordsworth kept a diary. I don't care whether William Wordsworth ever saw a field of golden daffodils, and I certainly don't care to know that he saw them on the seventeenth of March, or whenever it was.

Sandler: That's fair enough. But you must be interested in the way a poem or a novel is written, because there's a running parody of the creative process in *Lady Oracle*. Her writing is more or less automatic, dreams and nightmares.

Atwood: Parody, well...I'm reading the galleys now, and you don't really know what you've done until a couple of years later. But there's certainly some parody going on.

The trouble with dreams is that they're fragments and they're incoherent, most of them. And the unfortunate thing about the creative process is that you can have a wonderfully inspiring experience and still turn out a rotten poem. You soon find that out if you have anything to do with creative writing classes.

In my experience, writing is not like having dreams. It's not that unconscious. It's much more deliberate. You can add or subtract anything, and you can shape your material into a coherent pattern. When I write a poem or a novel I'm not interested in transcribing my dreams or "expressing myself." If I want to express myself I can go out in the back field and scream. It takes a lot less time.

Sandler: Susanna Moodie appeared to you in a dream, didn't she?

Atwood: Yes. I hadn't read her books, but I remembered quite vividly a winter scene with a house burning down; eventually I tracked it down in a Grade Five reader, I think it was. But I also remembered a scene with a child shrouded in a primitive oxygen tent. I thought it was Moodie, but in fact it had nothing to do with her.

I read her two books, *Roughing It in the Bush* and *Life in the Clearings*, after dreaming I had written an opera about her. They were very disappointing, but she interested me. I wrote poems about her, and I thought that was that. But six months later the other poems started happening. These things are always unpredictable.

After the radio broadcast of Susanna Moodie the CBC came to me and said, "Could you do one about Sir John A. Macdonald now?" They thought it would be nice for me to write a poem cycle about a really famous Canadian, and I had to explain that I didn't work that way; I didn't pick a likely candidate and then make up suitable poems.

Sandler: The business of dreams is interesting, because the dreamer is an *involuntary* poet who lies there and watches the show. But there's also the idea of the poet as an inspired dreamer.

Atwood: It's worth looking at poets in different ages to see where they think the inspiration is coming from. There's Milton saying, "Descend, O Dove!" and right up to the eighteenth century, poets were looking "up there" for inspiration. Then it got reversed. With Blake it's definitely coming from below, and this sterile, controlling figure sits upstairs. Shelley has lots of caves, he's invoking dark powers. Keats has an early poem where the narrator goes under the sea and there he finds Proteus, the shape-changer.

One of the few poems I've written about the creative process is "Procedures for Underground," and I do see it as a descent to the underworld. But—I repeat—having that inspired feeling doesn't guarantee that you'll write a good poem.

Sandler: What's your opinion of the West Coast people's view of your poetry? George Bowering, reviewing *Power Politics*, said you'd arranged your material like a bowl of fruit, and there were things he wanted to know that you didn't tell him.

Atwood: You could say that about your next door neighbor! There are things I want to know that George would never tell me! Is "spontaneous" versus "arranged" a real issue? Everybody thinks of Jay Macpherson's poems as "finely crafted," but she hardly ever revises them; and in fact, it's much easier to write spontaneously if you're firmly grounded in metrics and rhyme.

My poems in *Double Persephone* are metrically formal, but there's no way of knowing whether I "crafted" them. If you look at my worksheets you'll see that some poems write themselves and some, like Circe's poem about the suicides, are quite hard to write. And I suspect it's like that for every poet. The finished version of "Tricks with Mirrors" is basically what I scribbled on this sheet of paper. The same with "Threes." I wrote it down and that was it. It's the poem that counts. I don't care how it was written, and I distrust people who give out prizes according to extra-poetic factors. If you wanted to join the club you'd have to include or exclude poems in your canon according to their "spontaneity." Or you could arrange them that way, because once the style is established it's easy to imitate. Lots of white spaces, shrugs and asides and awkward spots, no punctuation. What does that prove? Some of them are very good. Others are very bad.

Sandler: Do you remember the origin of the Circe sequence in *You Are Happy*?

Atwood: Nobody really knows where poems come from, and it's not something I want to know. I would probably be disappointed if I knew where I got my ideas. I do know that I could never write anything like *Geneve*, where George Bowering turned up a Tarot card every day and wrote a poem about it. I would find that too formal, too deliberate.

What happened with "Circe" was that fragments started appearing before I had any idea that I was writing a connected sequence. This is generally the case; you accumulate a couple of poems and that acts as a priming agent, and you write more. You could stretch a point and say that it's the same process as writing a novel or a short story; incidents accumulate, details and phrases accumulate.

Sandler: Is it possible to talk about the difference between conceiving a poem and conceiving a novel?

Atwood: You can talk about it, but not very successfully. A poem is something you hear, and the primary focus of interest is words. A novel is something you see, and the primary focus of interest is people. But that's a huge generalization, it probably means nothing.

It's hard to talk about this process, because you can't observe it. It's not ultra-mysterious. The brain just works in a certain way, and if you're a poet you turn out poems rather than recipes for apple pie. But if you started observing it while it was happening, you would kill it. And I'm not too interested in observing it after the fact. It's too much like picking pieces of apple out of your teeth. I will say this: you can't write poetry unless you're willing to immerse yourself in language—not just in words, but in words of a certain potency. It's like learning a foreign language.

There was a time when I couldn't understand any poetry beyond simple narrative verse. I remember reading modern poems and being completely baffled by them, not knowing what they meant or how they worked. You try and try and all of a sudden you know how they work. It's like learning to ride a bicycle. How can you explain it? What is a sense of balance?

Sandler: The foreign language analogy might explain why people reacted so oddly to your presentation of sexual politics in *Power Politics*.

Atwood: Well, it's a question of what people find acceptable. Poems by men about the wicked behavior of women are part of a venerable tradition going back at least as far as the Elizabethans' Cruel Mistress, and few people bother to analyze conventional modes. We don't bat an eyelid when we read about bitch goddesses or when we see portraits of women with big tits and no heads. But women aren't supposed to say nasty things about men. It's not nice, and it's not conventional.

Sandler: When *Power Politics* was published, people started thinking of you as an Ice Maiden. What do you think of Susan Sontag's idea that coolness and distance usually conceal a passionate intensity?

Atwood: It's partly a matter of style, because every culture sets its own distances. Think of your reactions when you meet people. If a stranger taps you on the ass and says, "How's the little lady today," you will probably cringe. But if he's an American, he's only being friendly. If you're sitting next to him on a plane trip he will take out the family photos, and within five minutes he'll be telling you the story of his life. In Nova Scotia, you can have endless conversations with people about genealogy, which is not regarded as "personal," but they will not get around to asking you what you do for a living or whether you're married. Canadians are like the English, in this respect.

Sandler: If Canadians tend to be distant, *Power Politics* shouldn't have bothered them. But I don't know anyone who finds the hook-and-eye epigram amusing.

Atwood: There are people who won't laugh unless you flash an orange neon sign that says LAUGH NOW. You have to accept that. And the usual response to that epigram is horror—as I found out when I started reading these poems in public. The shock value is what gets across. Here again it's a question of what is and is not acceptable. Irving Layton could read his extremely nasty poems about women, and his audience would find them hilarious. My poems about men are not received that way although I've never written a poem about a male academic who has pimples on his bum. I don't go in for explicit personal attacks like that. I don't know why. Maybe I have a lingering feeling that ladies should be polite.

Sandler: How much of the impact of *Power Politics* has to do with its cutoff lines and rhythms? I remember Robert Weaver saying that the poems are like sharp pieces of glass.

Atwood: I don't think there's anything formally distinguishing about my writing as a whole. Much of *Power Politics* is epigrammatic, and the line is just about as short as you can get without disappearing altogether. In *You Are Happy* the line gets longer again, and it will probably go on changing. What you're doing is finding out how to write the poem while you're actually writing it. Once you know how to do that poem or that kind of poem, that's the moment when you should stop and go on to something else. Otherwise you become an imitator of yourself.

Sandler: A permanent self-parody, like Mary Tyler Moore? Do people expect continuity?

Atwood: Not usually. I think, though, that critics are always reviewing the book before last. They've assimilated your previous books and they have an idea about the kind of poet you are, and if you do something different it takes them a while to see what is happening in the new book. A lot of people were so obsessed with *Power Politics* that when *You Are Happy* appeared they went on reviewing *Power Politics*.

Sandler: There's another reviewer's heresy surrounding your guide to Canadian literature: people have said that *Survival* is an extension of *Surfacing*—of your interest in victims and your view of nature.

Atwood: It's unfortunate that the two books were published around the same time, because people make that connection. But in fact, *Surfacing* was finished and at the publisher by the time I started working on *Survival*. Some time before that I had begun to notice certain common themes in my own writing and in other people's, and I thought, Isn't it funny that such and such happens in all these books? Some people think that I deliberately invented these themes in order to write a book about them, but that's not the way it happened. The themes were there; I noticed them.

Survival was a hard book to write. It was too close to home. I'd much rather write about somebody else's culture. That's why I enjoy teaching Victorian literature. That's not my country, that's not my time. I'm not involved and I can have nice aesthetic reactions. The literature of one's own country is not escape literature. It tells truths, some of them hard. //

I tend to be shy of theories because I know their limits, but theories are useful for teaching. You can draw diagrams on the blackboard, and they will provide partial illumination; they are easy to react to, and to react against. And *Survival* is basically a diagram of Canadian literature.

Sandler: What's striking about *Survival* is the coherence of vision underlying it. It s a writer's book and it has a point of view.

Atwood: I'm not an academic, so I don't have to worry about my colleagues saying, "Tut tut, this will not do. Why don't you qualify all your statements and hedge all your bets?" I can write what I believe to be true, and I don't have to be plausible to professors; they're not hiring me. Eli Mandel, of course, feels that all works of criticism are novels, and in a way he's right. They are imaginative constructs.

Sandler: I guess it's also the the only literary survey around that has political overtones.

Atwood: For me, it's axiomatic that art has its roots in social realities; when you see an Aztec statue you don't doubt that it had an essential social function. People believed in that god and made sacrifice to it. I don't know why literature should be any different.

Sandler: You mean that literature is an index of popular faith? I wonder.

Atwood: Not exactly...but it does influence belief. Take nineteenth-century America which is handy for these purposes. You get Fenimore Cooper writing about huge primeval forests and noble redmen, giving them mythical and even moral dimensions. People accepted these myths; the myths multiplied and became "truths."

Sinclair Ross didn't invent the Depression, but what could have been more useful to him than the Depression? And once it was over you could read *As For Me and My House* to find out about it. The Depression became part of the social mythology.

Sandler: Is that the function of art? To be folk history?

Atwood: Must art have a specific "function"? Human societies have always produced art. Almost as far back as we know, people have been painting pictures; we assume they have also been singing songs and telling stories. Therefore, art must be an essential human activity. People create art for ostensibly different reasons from age to age. You can say that originally the impulse was magical, or religious, as with the Aztec statue. But what does that mean? It could mean that art is a way of explaining or controlling the environment.

Sandler: Does that mean your art could be an agent of change—as you said in your notes on *Power Politics*?

Atwood: As I said before, I'm not a politician, and it's wrong to suppose that the artist is a vanguard revolutionary. A literary work may have some political content, but it's not a book of political theory. It isn't a book of metaphysics, it's not a book on economics. It can include these ideas because they exist in the real world, because they are filtered through people's minds; they come up in conversation and they influence people's behavior.

Sandler: It's kind of ironic that feminists saw you as a leading proponent of their cause.

Atwood: A few years ago Women's Lib was looking for any woman writer who seemed to be dealing with "feminist" issues. The writings of Margaret Laurence, Marian Engel, Alice Munro were all enlisted as supporting evidence. A lot of women, though, have been writing about "special" women's problems: she's trapped in the home, three small kids, where is her identity, et cetera. In those terms, *Surfacing* fails as a feminist novel because it doesn't say whether you can marry Joe and still have a career. My characters are not role models. I don't try to resolve the problems of living, deal out the answers, and I'm not dealing with my female characters as members of a separate species. However, I probably am a feminist, in the broad sense of the term.

Sandler: I wanted to ask you about the satiric side of your work.

Atwood: A lot of things that may seem to be satiric are quotations from real life. Americans say to me, "What about this horrible anti-Americanism that David expresses in *Surfacing*? Does that mean you hate Americans?" And I have to say, "Number One, I'm not David. Number Two, if you think I invented him, why don't you go spend a weekend in Canada?"

Sandler: But once David is in your book, you've put a frame around him; he can't have a neutral value. Likewise, Arthur in *Lady Oracle*, plotting to blow up the Peace Bridge.

Atwood: The principle of selection is important, of course, and I try to select characters who are outgrowths of their society. But my writing is closer to caricature than to satire—distortion rather than scathing attack—and as I say, it's largely realism. The market research scenes in *The Edible Woman* are an example of realism verging on caricature, they are very slightly exaggerated. Arthur is probably some facet of myself, distorted and carried to an extreme.

Sandler: Wyndham Lewis insisted that satire is realism, a kind of mirror.

Atwood: Literature *can* be a mirror, and people can recognize themselves in it and this may lead to change. But in order to write satire in the traditional sense, you must have certain axioms in common with your audience. When something happens in the book that outrages common sense your audience must agree that it is in fact outrageous. That's the problem with the century we live in. There's almost nothing you can write about which has not been outdone in absurdity or ghastliness by real events. People see so many horrible and grotesque things that they become deadened. They have to deaden themselves; otherwise, they'd be in a constant state of psychic disturbance. In theory, satire is impossible but in fact, satire is being written. Canadian satire tends to be quite vicious, particularly in the earlier poetry. *The Harvard Lampoon*, you know, is run largely by Canadians, and its edge is much sharper than *Mad* magazine's. And Robertson Davies's early novels are all quite cutting.

Sandler: But as you said in your essay on Canadian humor, contempt for the uncultivated locals is the usual source of satire in novels.

Atwood: Possibly, but you have to try to visualize what it was like for Davies or Mordecai Richler, living in a society which was so hostile to art. People tend to forget what it was like. But using all one's imagination and charity, one has to say that Mordecai Richler had to leave the country when he did. There was no place for him here.

Sandler: Did you go to Harvard for similar reasons? One theory is that you went there because America was generally regarded as the country of light.

Atwood: Not at all. Not at all. I'm of a later generation, remember. // My cultural roots are in Nova Scotia, and if you want to see cultural nationalism, that's the place to go. It's not nationalism—

it's regionalism. But I certainly didn't grow up regarding America as the land of light. Even Ontario was *deeply* suspect. I remember that in the '50s *everybody else* regarded America as the land of light, and *Saturday Night* was publishing articles extolling the glories of baseball and the American Dream. I didn't have an image of Canada to counter that, but that was never my view.

Sandler: Tell me about your association with the House of Anansi. Did you see the press as Dennis Lee did, as the source of a literary renaissance?

Atwood: Anansi was certainly part of a literary renaissance, but I wasn't involved in it. I was in Montreal in 1967 when Dennis published *Kingdom of Absence* and then in Edmonton and then in Europe. I wasn't back in Toronto until 1971, and by that time the Anansi revolution had already happened. Dave Godfrey had left, Dennis was on the verge of leaving, and the press was embroiled in internal warfare. I was called in to infuse some new blood into its veins. I got a letter when I was in Italy, asking if I would sit on the Board of Directors, and I'd been making all these noises about an indigenous literature so I thought I should put my money where my mouth was. I didn't envisage becoming an editor for two years. I thought I was going to be an unpaid and marginal participant, mainly lending my name. I was wrong. It was a whirlpool. Lots of people got sucked in and down. But now it's on its feet again.

Sandler: You've been less active politically since the *Survival* days. Does activism get in the way of your writing?

Atwood: Activism isn't very good for the writer, and I'm not very good at it. I believe in saying what I think, and that's no way to be a politician. But I still think my analysis of the country was essentially correct. And despite the literary renaissance, and despite the level of national consciousness, things seem to be getting worse economically. It's a process of erosion.

Sandler: What are your politics?

Atwood: I don't have party loyalties as such. What's important to me is how human beings ought to live and behave. I doubt, for instance, that I would have gone along with Stalin, no matter how faithful he was to Karl Marx's theories. If people end up behaving in anti-human ways, their ideology will not redeem them.

All you can do is opt for the society that seems most humane. People don't seem to function well in very large groups, and that's why I prefer Canada to the States. It's more intimate, and people can still involve themselves in the political process. If you get enough people together, you can stop the Spadina Expressway from cutting through Toronto. You can stop the politicians from building an airport in Pickering...by the skin of your teeth.

In the States they have Citizens' Action groups too, but the machinery of government is out of control. It's too big, it doesn't respond. You can throw your body in front of it and it runs right over you. America is a tragic country because it has great democratic ideals and rigid social machinery. //But Canada is not tragic, in the classical sense, because it doesn't have a Utopian vision. Our constitution promises "peace, order and good government"—and that's quite different from "life, liberty and the pursuit of happiness." It doesn't suggest that you will be *happy* if you have peace, order and good government—nor does it say that you will be *free*. It just says that the government will take care of everything. //

My Mother Would Rather Skate Than Scrub Floors

Joyce Carol Oates

Joyce Carol Oates's interview was conducted by mail and telephone in February 1978 and originally appeared in the *New York Times Book Review*, May 21, 1978. Copyright © 1978 by Joyce Carol Oates. Reprinted by permission.

Oates: Are you interested primarily in a poetry of "music" or a poetry of "statement"?

Atwood: I don't think of poetry as a "rational" activity but as an aural one. My poems usually begin with words or phrases which appeal more because of their sound than their meaning, and the movement and phrasing of a poem are very important to me. But like many modern poets I tend to conceal rhymes by placing them in the middle of lines, and to avoid immediate alliteration and assonance in favor of echoes placed later in the poems. For me, every poem has a texture of sound which is at least as important to me as the "argument." This is not to minimize "statement." But it does annoy me when students, prompted by the approach of their teacher, ask, "What is the poet trying to say?" It implies that the poet is some kind of verbal cripple who can't quite "say" what he "means" and has to resort to a lot of round-the-mulberry-bush, thereby putting the student to a great deal of trouble extracting his "meaning," like a prize out of a box of Cracker Jack.

Oates: After the spare, rather sardonic exploration of the relationship between the sexes in *Power Politics*, *You Are Happy*, your recent book of poems, seems to have marked a radical transformation of vision. Could you comment? And what are you working on at the present time?

Atwood: At the moment, and in my most recent poems, I seem to be less concerned about the relationships between men and women than I am about those among women (grandmother-mother-daughter, sisters) and those between cultures. I am in the process of editing a new volume of poems to be called *Two-Headed*

Poems and Others, and I'm working on some stories which I hope to include in the American edition of *Dancing Girls*. I have two novels in my head, and I hope to start one this summer.

Oates: What is your background? Did your family encourage your writing?

Atwood: I was born in the Ottawa General Hospital right after the Gray Cup Football Game in 1939. Six months later I was backpacked into the Quebec bush. I grew up in and out of the bush, in and out of Ottawa, Sault Ste. Marie, and Toronto. I did not attend a full year of school until I was in grade eight. This was a definite advantage. My parents are both from Nova Scotia, and my "extended family" lives there. I have one brother who became a neurophysiologist and lives in Toronto and one sister who was born when I was eleven.

I began writing at the age of five, but there was a dark period between the ages of eight and sixteen when I didn't write. I started again at sixteen and have no idea why, but it was suddenly the only thing I wanted to do. My parents were great readers. They didn't encourage me to become a writer, exactly, but they gave me a more important kind of support; that is, they expected me to make use of my intelligence and abilities, and they did not pressure me into getting married. My mother is rather exceptional in this respect, from what I can tell from the experiences of other women my own age. Remember that all this was taking place in the '50s, when marriage was seen as the only desirable goal. My mother is a very lively person who would rather skate than scrub floors; she was a tomboy in youth and still is one. My father is a scientist who reads a great deal of history and has a mind like Leopold Bloom's. But as far as I know, the only poems he ever composes are long doggerel verses, filled with puns, which he writes when he has the flu.

Oates: Have fairy tales, Gothic romances, and other fantasies played a significant part in your reading background?

Atwood: The Gothic, the supernatural fantasy, and related forms have interested me for some time; in fact, my uncompleted Ph.D. thesis is called "The English Metaphysical Romance." This may or may not have something to do with the fact that in childhood—I think I was about six—we were given the complete *Grimm's Fairy Tales*, unexpurgated. My sister was terrified of it, but I loved it. These are, of course, not "children's stories"; they were originally told by adults to anyone who happened to be there, and there is quite a lot of material that we wouldn't consider suitable for children today. It was not the gore—being rolled downhill in barrels full of spikes and so forth—that caught my attention, but the transformations. "The Juniper Tree" was and remains my favorite, followed closely by a story called "Pitcher's Bird." The other interesting thing about these stories is that, unlike the heroines of the more conventional and re-done stories, such as "Cinderella" and "Little Red Riding Hood," the heroines of these stories show considerable wit and resourceful-ness and usually win, not just by being pretty virtuous, but by using their brains. And there are wicked wizards as well as wicked witches. I would like to write about this sometime. I have an article on this exact subject in a book which was just published by Harvard University Press. The book is called *The Canadian Imagination*, and the article is called "Canadian Monsters: Some Aspects of the Supernatural in Canadian Fiction."

Oates: You work with a number of different "voices" in your poetry and prose. Have you ever felt that the discipline of prose evokes a somewhat different "personality" (or consciousness) than the discipline of poetry?

Atwood: Not just a "somewhat different" personality, an almost totally different one. Though readers and critics, of course, make connections because the same name appears on these different forms. I'd make a bet that I could invent a pseudonym for a reviewer and that no one would guess it was me.

If you think of writing as expressing "itself" rather than "the writer," this makes total sense. For me, reviewing and criticism are the most difficult forms, because of the duty they involve, a duty to the book being talked about as well as to the reader. Poetry is the most joyful form, and prose fiction—the personality I feel there is a curious, often bemused, sometimes disheartened observer of society. The "public speaking"—there again it depends on whether I'm reading poetry, reading prose, or merely speaking. Making speeches is not something I like to do. I suppose, like many fiction and poetry writers, I don't like being in the position of pontificating about the truth. When I taught in universities I was a great diagram-on-the-board person, partly because you could draw arrows to indicate more than one thing at a time.

Oates: I am often astonished, and at times rather dismayed, by the habit that presumably intelligent readers have of assuming that most writing, especially that in the first person, is autobiographical. And I know that you have been frequently misread as well. How do you account for the extraordinary naiveté of so many readers?

Atwood: As far as I know, this is a North American problem. It doesn't happen much in England, I think, because England with its long literary tradition, is quite used to having writers around. And it doesn't happen as much (in my experience) in the United States as it does in Canada. And it doesn't happen as much to men as it does to women, probably because women are viewed as more subjective and less capable of invention.

I think it's the result of several factors. First, it may be a tribute to the writing. The book convinces the reader, therefore it must be "true," and who is it more likely to be "true" about than the author? Readers sometimes feel cheated when I tell them that a book is not "autobiographical," that is, the events as described did not happen to me. (Of course, every book is "autobiographical" in that the images and characters have passed through the author's head and in that he or she has selected them.) These readers want it all to be true.

Also, we have a somewhat romantic notion on this side of the Atlantic about what an author is. We think of "writing" not as something you do but as something you are. The writer is seen as "expressing" herself; therefore, her books must be autobiographical. If the book were seen as something made, like a pot, we probably wouldn't have this difficulty. But the idea is remarkably tenacious. I was talking about this at a reading one time. I explained that my work was not autobiographical, that the central character was not "me," and so on. Then I read a chapter from *Lady Oracle*, the chapter in which the fat little girl attends dancing school. The first question after the reading was over was, "How did you manage to lose so much weight?"

After saying all that, though, I'll have to add that I find it necessary, in order to write about a place, to have actually been there. I can invent characters, but I am absolutely dependent on the details of the material world to make a space for my characters to move around in.

Oates: In recent years Americans have become aware, at times to their chagrin, that Canadian nationalists are extremely anti-American and very much resent American "influence" in Canada as well as American economic exploitation. Apart from your nonfiction writing, your novel *Surfacing* deals with this feeling most explicitly. When some particularly brutal hunters in the novel turn out to be, not Americans, as the heroine believes, but Canadians, the heroine nevertheless thinks: "It doesn't matter what country they're from, they're still Americans, they're what's in store for us." Could you comment on this statement?

Atwood: It's dangerous to lift a statement out of context and take it as "the view" of the character and especially of the author. Cultural attitudes in novels are not usually invented by the novelist; they are reflections of something the novelist sees in the society around her.

But if you're saying that Canadians have no reason to resent the foreign and trade policies of the United States, I'd have to disagree. No one likes being dominated to this extent, whether it's women, blacks, Quebecois or Canadians. But each group—including Canadians—should have a good look at their past and present behavior to see to what extent they have contributed to their plight. In the case of Canada, I'd say the extent is considerable.

Oates: Finally, Yeats once said that the solitary imagination "makes and unmakes mankind, and even the world itself, for does not the 'eye alter all'?" What is your feeling about the function of poetry? Why, in effect, do you write?

Atwood: I'm not sure what the function of poetry is. That is, I know what it does for me, but I don't know what it does for other people. Probably many things, since each reader is different. We talk a great deal about the subjectivity of the reader. I sometimes say that poetry acts like a lens, or like a thread dipped in a supersaturated solution, causing a crystallization, but I'm not sure that's it either. Perhaps because of my earlier scientific background, I like things that can't ever be quite pinned down. But I know we're in trouble when we start talking about what poetry "ought" to do, about the supposedly good social effects of it. I don't feel that all art is a consequence of neurosis. I tend to see it as the opposite. Not that some artists aren't neurotic—but that art, the making or creating, is done in spite of the neurosis, is a triumph over it. Anne Sexton, for instance, was obviously "neurotic," whatever that is—unhappy and self-limiting, let's say. But even when she's writing about that the impulse to write at all seems to me a positive one. A defiance if you like. If all art were pearls secreted by the miseries of the oysters the totally healthy human being would be the one without a creative or joyful bone in her body. Can this be true? (Sorry to use words like "creative," but they're hard to avoid.)

Why do I write? I guess I've never felt the necessity of thinking up a really convincing answer to that one, although I get asked it a lot. I suppose I think it's a redundant question, like "Why does the sun shine?" As you say, it's a human activity. I think the real question is, "Why doesn't everyone?" But when you ask a roomful of people whether there's anyone who, at some time or other, hasn't written something, very few hands go up.

wood: A good poetry reading is a delightful and exhilarating
perience. A bad one is awful. It depends on the audience, on
our mood at the time, on whether you and the audience "like"
each other. I guess we've all run into the resident madman and
the faculty member who thinks he can put a notch in his gun by
being gratuitously rude to you at the little luncheon or whatever
thrown in your honor. Mostly I just get colds.

Oates: Your sense of the absurd—and of the essential playfulness
of the absurd—is one of the elements in your writing that I particularly admire. What inspired your novel *The Edible Woman*—
especially that surreal scene—and *Lady Oracle*?

Atwood: *The Edible Woman* was written in 1965, before the
Women's Liberation Movement had begun. It was still very much
the model pattern, in Canada anyway, to take a crummy job and
then marry to get away from it. I was writing about an object of
consumption (namely, my bright but otherwise ordinary girl) in a
consumer society. Appropriately, she works for a market research
company. Even in 1969, when the book was finally published,
some critics saw the view as essentially "young" or "neurotic." I
would mature, they felt, and things (i.e., marriage and kids)
would fall into place.

About the cake in the shape of a woman—all I can tell you is
that I used to be a very good cake decorator and was often asked
to reproduce various objects in pastry and icing. Also, in my
walks past pastry stores, I always wondered why people made
replicas of things—brides and grooms, for instance, or Mickey
Mice—and then ate them. It seems a mysterious thing to do. But
for my heroine to make a false image of herself and then consume
it was entirely appropriate, given the story—don't you think?

Lady Oracle was written much later—almost ten years later.
Again, I'm not sure where it began, but the central character is a
writer of Gothic romances partly because I've always wondered
what it was about these books that appealed—do so many
women think of themselves as menaced on all sides, and of their
husbands as potential murderers? And what about that "Mad
Wife" left over from *Jane Eyre*? Are these our secret plots?

The hypothesis of the book, insofar as there is one, is: what
happens to someone who lives in the "real" world but does it as

Dancing on the Edge of the I .

Joyce

Joyce Carol Oates's interview was conducted by mail ᵢ
in February 1978 and originally appeared in *The Ontar.*
(Fall-Winter 1978-9). Copyright © 1978 by *The Ontari*
Reprinted by permission.

Oates: Your books of poetry—*The Circle Game* (which was awarᵈ
the Governor-General's Award in 1966), *The Animals in Th*
Country, The Journals of Susanna Moodie, Procedures for Underground,
Power Politics, and *You Are Happy*—differ a great deal in content,
yet there is a remarkable similarity of tone, of rhythm, of "texture."
Your earlier poems, for instance "Journey to the Interior" and
"The Circle Game" itself, show a mastery of craftsmanship that
is rather unusual in first books. From whom did you learn,
consciously or unconsciously?

Atwood: When I first started writing I was sixteen and in high
school, in Toronto, in the '50s, and I knew nothing about either
modern poetry or Canadian poetry. So my first influences were
Poe and Shelley! When I got to university, I began discovering
modern and Canadian poetry, chiefly the latter. I read my way
through the library of a faculty member who, being a poet herself,
had an extensive collection. I might mention such names as P. K.
Page, Margaret Avison, whose *Winter Sun* I reviewed when I
was in university, James Reaney, D. G. Jones, and certain poems
of Douglas Le Pan. These poets were important to me not only
as poets but as examples of the fact that you could get a book
published. You would have to have known the situation in
Canada at the time to realize how important this was to me.

It's kind of you to say that you found my first book
accomplished, but by the time it came out, I'd been writing for ten
years. Also, *The Circle Game* isn't my real "first book"; there was
another one, seven poems long, which appeared in 1961, for
which I set the type and designed and printed the cover. I doubt
that you would find it quite so unusual!

Oates: Do you enjoy reading your poetry, in general?

though this "other" world is the real one? This may be the plight of many more of us than we care to admit.

Oates: Your novel *Surfacing* has been related to James Dickey's *Deliverance*. I see only a superficial, rather misleading relationship. Could you comment?

Atwood: There is a relationship of sorts, but for me it's one of opposites. For the central figure in Dickey's book, as I recall, nature is something wild, untamed, feminine, dangerous and mysterious, that he must struggle with, confront, conquer, overcome. Doing this involves killing. For me, the works cognate with Dickey's are Mailer's *Why We Are in Vietnam*, Faulkner's *Bear*, Hemingway's "Short Happy Life of Francis Macomber," and, if you like, *Moby-Dick*, though Ahab was not seen by Melville as having chosen the right path. The books cognate with mine are Canadian and probably unknown in the United States; Howard O'Hagan's *Tay John* is one of them.

Oates: "The Man From Mars," which appeared in *Ontario Review*, is a delightful story, and drew a great deal of favorable comments from our readers. Were your hapless heroine and indefatigable suitor based on "real" people? And is there any political significance to the title?

Atwood: I've found over the years that I can never explain or account for any reader response to my work. It constantly amazes me—and this isn't false modesty—that my work sells as well as it does. I consider it rather quirky and eccentric.

Real people? In a way. The situation was real, the characters are fictional.

The title...I'm not sure whether the significance is "political" or not; what it means to me is that we all have a way of de-humanizing anything which is strange or exotic to us. In our arrogance, we take ourselves to be the norm, and measure everyone else against it. The man, of course, is not from Mars; he is from Earth, like everyone else. But there's no way of accounting for the atrocities that people perform on other people except by the "Martian" factor, the failure to see one's victims as fully human.

Oates: I believe you're one of the few Canadian writers who is not associated with any university, and I assume this is deliberate.

Atwood: Yes, I enjoyed students when I taught in 1967–68, but I could not handle faculty meetings and departmental politics. I don't understand it. I'm not good in those situations. The reason I don't teach is the same reason I don't wait on tables, which I also used to do: right now I don't have to. If I have to do either again, I will. If it's a choice, I'd take teaching, which is less physically exhausting and doesn't put you off your food so much.

Oates: You have drawn upon your student days at Harvard quite infrequently in your writing. Did you enjoy your stay there?

Atwood: Well...Harvard is sort of like anchovies. An acquired taste. But in my case, one that I could never truly acquire, because at that time—early and mid-'60s—they wouldn't let women into Lamont Library, and that was where they kept all the modern poetry and records. So I always felt a little like a wart or wen on the great male academic skin. I felt as if I was there on sufferance. Harvard, you know, didn't hire women to teach in it, so the male professors were all very nice. We ladies were no threat. There was a joke among the woman students that the best way to pass your orals was to stuff a pillow up your dress, because they would all be so terrified of having parturition take place on the Persian rug that they would just ask you your name and give you a pass. One of my female colleagues was almost expelled for dressing like a woman of loose virtue. Actually she was a Latvian Shakespearian scholar with somewhat different ideas of dress than the rest of us tweedy, buttoned types.

So I enjoyed it, yes, in a nervous sort of way. There were some fine lecturers, and Widener Library is wonderful. And little madnesses go on there which seem unlike those of any other place. I often wondered what happened to the man who was rumored to have broken into Houghton Library (Rare Books) in order to expose himself to the Gutenberg Bible. I do have two "Harvard" stories, which are in *Dancing Girls*.

The most important things about the experience for me were: it was the place where I first learned urban fear. (Before I went there, I always walked around at night, didn't bother about locked doors, etc. If you behaved that way in Cambridge you were dead.) And, for various reasons, it was the place where I started thinking seriously about Canada as having a shape and a culture of its own. Partly because I was studying the literature of the American Puritans, which was not notable for its purely literary values—if one can study this in a university, I thought, why not Canadian literature? (You must understand that at that time Canadian literature was simply not taught in high schools and universities in Canada)—and partly because Boston was, in certain ways, so similar, in climate and landscape, to parts of Canada. One began to look for differences.

Oates: Did you discover any odd or upsetting attitudes toward Canada while living at Cambridge?

Atwood: It's not that anyone in Boston—few in the Graduate School were from that area in any case; they came from all over the U.S. and from non-North American countries as well—it's not that the Americans I met had any odd or "upsetting" attitudes towards Canada. They simply didn't have any attitudes at all. They had a vague idea that such a place existed—it was that blank area north of the map where the bad weather came from—but if they thought about it at all they found it boring. They seemed to want to believe that my father was a Mounted Policeman and that we lived in igloos all year round, and I must admit that after a while I took a certain pleasure in encouraging these beliefs. (Recall that this was before the Vietnam crisis, during which many Americans came to regard Canada as the Great Good Place or game refuge to which they might escape.) I met a number of Southerners and got to know some of them; they seemed to resent "the North" in some of the same ways as did the handful of Canadians there, though for different reasons.

Oates: Why had you gone to Harvard in the first place?

Atwood: Because—to trace it back—Canada had not hired one Jerome H. Buckley back in the Depression when he was looking for work. He had gone to the States and had become a leading Victorianist. The Victorian period was "my period," and I had won a Woodrow Wilson Fellowship, so I went to Harvard to study with Dr. Buckley. There is, you know, a kind of Canadian Mafia at Harvard and elsewhere in the States. Quite a few of the well-known professors at Harvard were closet Canadians. However, they kept their identities secret, for the most part, except when talking with other Canadians. They'd learned by experience that Americans found a revelation of one's Canadian-ness, dropped, for instance, into the middle of a sherry party, about as interesting as the announcement that one had had mashed potatoes for lunch. The beginning of Canadian cultural nationalism was not "Am I really that oppressed?" but "Am I really that boring?" You see, we had never been taught much about our own history or culture—but that's another whole story.

Oates: Is there a very distinctive difference between American "literary" responses and Canadian?

Atwood: I feel that American literary responses are, quite simply, more literary—at least in the groups of people with whom I'm likely to come in contact. I think the difference is that in the States there is a "literary" culture and a largely non-literary one, whereas in Canada these overlap a great deal more. I'm saying this only on the basis of who is likely to turn up at a poetry reading. But my experience isn't really wide enough to justify such general statements.

I always enjoy going to the States; it's an escape for me, from my own demanding culture. People there are polite to me, as they would be to a visiting foreigner (which I am), and, though interested, disinterested. Americans have such enthusiasms. It's a change from the gloom here, the suspicion. But of course, Canada is where I really live. That's why I can enjoy the States so much for brief periods of time.

Oates: What sort of working habits have you?

Atwood: My working habits have changed over the years, according to the circumstances of my life. I started writing seriously—though this may seem ludicrous—when I was sixteen and in fourth-year high school. At that time I wrote in the evenings when I was supposed to be doing homework, on weekends and occasionally during school hours. After that, I was in university for four years and wrote between classes, after hours, etc.—a haphazard pattern. I didn't have very regular habits as a student, either; I was a procrastinator and still am, so it helps me to set myself deadlines. (This applies only to prose, of course. Poetry does not get written, by me at least, as a matter of will.) During my years as a graduate student, odd-job-holder, university lecturer of the lowest order—up till the age of about twenty-seven or so—I almost had to write at night, and would stay up quite late. I'm not sure how I wrote at all the first year I spent as a "real" university teacher (1967-68, in Montreal). I was very busy and exhausted, and lost a lot of weight. But I seem to have been writing some then, too. I can't remember when I did it.

I became an afternoon writer when I had afternoons. When I was able to write full time, I used to spend the morning procrastinating and worrying, then plunge into the manuscript in a frenzy of anxiety around 3:00 when it looked as though I might not get anything done. Since the birth of my daughter, I've had to cut down on the procrastination. I still try to spend the afternoons writing, though the preliminary period of anxiety is somewhat shorter. I suppose this is a more efficient use of time. The fact is that blank pages inspire me with terror. What will I put on them? Will it be good enough? Will I have to throw it out? And so forth. I suspect most writers are like this.

Oates: Do you work on more than one project at a time?

Atwood: One project at a time, ideally. I am by nature lazy, sluggish, and of low energy. It constantly amazes me that I do anything at all.

Oates: How long, approximately, did it take you to write each of your three novels?

Atwood: I wrote *The Edible Woman* in unused University of British Columbia exam books from April to August of 1965. I revised in the fall. For reasons I won't go into, the publisher lost the manuscript, and I was so naive about the process that I thought it normal for them to take two years to tell me anything about it. The book was finally published in 1969. I had written another unpublished novel before this, and wrote another unpublished, unfinished one after it. Then I wrote *Surfacing* from about December 1969 to August 1970. There were only minor revisions and some retyping, though the handwritten version was extensively revised. *Lady Oracle* took much longer, partly because I was living a life filled with more interruptions, partly because it changed a lot while I was writing it. It took about two and one-half years, off and on.

Oates: I've enjoyed the cartoons of yours I've seen. Is drawing another of your talents?

Atwood: I paint a little and draw, for my own amusement I've been drawing a political cartoon strip for a Canadian magazine— *This Magazine*—for some years, under the pseudonym of "Bart Gerrard" (it's nice to get hate mail when they don't even know it's you) and I have a children's book coming out in Canada, in March, for the smallest age group, written, hand-lettered, and illustrated by myself. I hesitate to call this a "talent," since I know I'm not very good; that is, I have to rub out a lot in order to get the heads the same size and I have difficulty drawing owls flying sideways.

Oates: You must be disturbed by literary journalists' efforts to categorize you—to package you as "The Reigning Queen of Canadian Literature," or a national prophetess, or even a Medusa. What have your reactions been?

Atwood: I dislike the kinds of titles you mention; I find "Reigning Queen" a particularly offensive one, implying as it does that literature as practiced by women anyway, is either a monarchy or a beehive. In any case, there's only room for one "reigning queen," who will presumably be stung to death later on when she can't lay any more eggs. Such titles are insulting to the many fine women writers in this country (Marian Engel, Alice Munro, Margaret Laurence, to name three) and threatening to me. Anyone who takes language seriously would never use such a metaphor without being aware of its sinister range of meanings.

I suppose Canada is hungry for a few visible "stars," having been without any for so long. The danger to the writer is early stellification—one may become a vaporous ball of gas. But only if captivated by one's image. Luckily, my image here, as reflected in the press, has not been very captivating, at least to me. I can do without "Medusa." (It's one of the hazards of naturally curly hair.)

Oates: Do you think that reviewers and critics have, on the whole, been "fair" to you? Has there been any sort of backlash, as an inevitable consequence of your "rise to fame"?

Atwood: Of course, there has been a "backlash"; there always is, but vicious attacks in Canada tend to be much more open and personal than in the United States, partly because of the Celtic, blackly satiric literary tradition and partly because it's much more like a small town. We live in each other's pockets here, and the dust and gloom is therefore more intense. There are mixed feelings about small-town boys and girls making good, as you know. On the one hand, we're proud of them because they're ours; on the other hand, we don't like them getting too big for their boots, so we cut them down whenever possible; on the other hand (Canada, like Kali, has more than two hands), we can't quite believe that one of ours can really be any good—surely it's all some kind of hype or fraud; and on yet another hand, the success of one of our members is a reproach to us. If he could do it, why can't we?

There's that; but also, there have been a number of fairminded, objectively critical pieces which have dealt genuinely with the shape and characteristics of my work and its strengths and weaknesses. Canadian critics are always more close-mouthed than American ones; they seldom go overboard, and they look with great suspicion upon cult figures, especially their own. This has definite advantages. I think American writers are often made dizzy by a sudden rocket-like stellification, then confused when they are just as enthusiastically banished to outer darkness. Canadian writers are (to put it mildly) seldom permitted to get swelled heads.

Oates: An entire issue of *The Malahat Review* was devoted to you in Winter 1977. I remember being rather surprised by a photographic essay called "Anima," and wonder what your reactions to it, and to the volume as a whole, were.

Atwood: I also was rather surprised. But then, my capacity to be surprised by other people's reactions to me is, I have discovered, infinite. I don't really see myself as a sort of buttock coming out of an egg (or was it the other way around?), and as I recall there were quite a few naked ladies with large breasts. But I think the collage sequence was supposed to have been inspired by my work rather than by my finite personal being, which in this climate is usually swathed in wool. Even so???

The truth is that I am not a very glamorous person. Writers aren't, really. All they do is sit around and write, which I suppose is as commendable as sitting around painting your toenails, but will never make it into the fashion magazines. So when I see myself being glamorized or idealized, it makes me squirm somewhat. Of course, I'm as vain as most people. I'd rather see a picture of myself looking good than one of myself looking awful. But I've seen so many of both by now, some taken minutes apart....A photo is only a view. //

Oates: Do you think there are any problems inherent in the fact that so many of the arts are state-supported in Canada? As an American I am impressed with the generosity of the Canadian government, but as a reader and critic I am frequently disturbed by the kinds of publications funded by the Canada Council and the various arts councils. Small presses do not seem to offer much editing advice, with the consequence that books tumble from presses, are "distributed" minimally, and allowed to go out of print almost at once. Without wanting to discourage young writers, I must say that the sheer quantity of hurried and slovenly writing published in Canada is rather demoralizing. (Of course, the same thing is rapidly becoming true in the States.) There seems to be no tradition any longer of apprenticeship; student writers are being "published"—or at least printed—and in the long run premature publication will have a deleterious effect on their craft. What is your opinion?—or is this too dangerous an enquiry?

Atwood: This is not at all a dangerous enquiry. There are several different questions here, though, and I will try to deal with them one at a time. The Canadian literary scene has been likened (by myself, in fact) to a group of figures dancing with considerable vigor and some grace on the edge of a precipice. The precipice was always there, though it's become more visible recently. I'm referring, of course, to the Quebec situation and the potential splitting-up of Canada. But the group of figures was not always there—not so long ago there were only a few solitary writers who, in the field of fiction anyway, didn't know each other—and they did not always dance, with or without grace and vigor.

When I began writing, in the late '50s and early '60s, there were five or so literary magazines in the entire country. The number of books of poetry that came out in a year—including small press books and privately printed ones—was under twenty. The new Canadian novels published in a year could usually be counted on the fingers of one hand. Canadian literature was not recognized as a legitimate field of study. Canadian books were not taught in schools. The epithet "Canadian writer" was a term of derision, even to Canadian writers. Almost every writer's ambition was to get out of the country to some place "real" in a literary sense, or at least some place where he could get his books published. Canadian writers were not known in their own country, and even when published were rarely bought or reviewed. (Mordecai Richler's first novel sold three copies in Canada. The press run of even a respectable book of poetry was considered good at 200. The publishers of *The Circle Game* initially printed 450, and were worried that they had done too many. Even now, Canadian paperbacks account for maybe three percent of total paperback sales in Canada, and that includes Harlequin Romances.)

We can't take the publishing industry for granted, as one can in the States. It is always tottering on the brink of collapse. We can't take our own existence as writers for granted. True, there has been about a 1,000 percent growth in the publishing industry in the last twenty years, but remember that started from near zero. So what is viewed by an American as "generosity" is seen by us simply as necessity. If the government support that publishers currently receive were to be withdrawn, the industry, by and large, would collapse. The "Canadian Renaissance" in the arts was made possible, in large part, by the Canada Council. None of us like this situation. But none of us want to be back in 1961, either.

Now...editing in small presses. As an ex-editor for a small press, Anansi, I have to protest. Editorial time by the bucketful was poured into our books. Our chief editor at that time was Dennis Lee, who is renowned here as an absolutely devoted editor. So it isn't universal. I'd say you get about the same mix as you might in the States: some presses serious about the writing, some existing only to get their members and friends into print. I think you see the bad writing here because more of it makes its way across your desk. You couldn't possibly even read all of it that comes out in the States; the sheer volume is so high.

But to me, small presses, good or bad, are a necessity. They're like all those Elizabethan melodramas. Without them, Shakespeare would have had no milieu. They were a place where a writer could, as it were, "try out." Same with "little" magazines. I guess I have a certain belief in the reader, the intelligent reader. I think books will eventually find their own level. This may be overly optimistic.

Oates: I am often annoyed by critics' attempts to reduce complex works of art to simple "thematic" statements. Why are Canadian critics in particular so obsessed with statement and theme at the expense of a thoughtful consideration of technique?

Atwood: I'm probably one of those critics who has annoyed you, since my only critical work, *Survival: A Thematic Guide to Canadian Literature*, is concerned almost exclusively to demonstrate that there are such things as Canadian themes, which differ either in substance or in emphasis from their counterparts in English and American literature. Would it help if I told you that, even after I had written this book—which caused rather a furor here, almost as if I'd said that the Emperor was naked—many critics resolutely continued to deny that there was any such thing as a "Canadian" literature?

We've tried very hard over the past few decades to demonstrate our own existence, our own right to exist. Usually we ourselves— the writers, that is—don't doubt it; the voices of denial come from elsewhere. But this may explain, a little anyway, the concern with "theme." One can only afford "a thoughtful consideration of technique" when the question of mere existence is no longer a question.

Defying Distinctions

Karla Hammond

Hammond: In a *New York Times* interview, you spoke of your parents' support in expecting you to put to use your skills and intelligence and in not urging you to marry. What myths of patriarchy specifically did they work against?

Atwood: They didn't work specifically against any, because no one in the '40s thought in terms of patriarchal systems. Their attitude was that of Maritimers from Nova Scotia. Maritimers have a large number of universities per capita, and people tend to be readers there. For instance, my aunt, my mother's sister, was the first woman to get an M.A. in History from the University of Toronto. On the other hand, my grandfather felt that my mother was too frivolous to be sent to college. It wasn't that she was a girl; he just felt that she was too frivolous. So she ended up sending herself to college. My parents' attitude, then, was a Maritimers' one: use your intelligence. Indeed, it was a moral injunction; if you don't use your intelligence you're doing something wrong. Specifically and quite practically it was use your intelligence to get a scholarship to university, because you can do that and we'll feel affronted if you don't.

The orientation of my entire extended family was scientific rather than literary, except for my other aunt, who wrote children's stories and encouraged me when I first began writing. So while the society around me in the '50s was very bent on having girls collect china, become cheerleaders, and get married, my parents were from a different culture. They weren't consciously women's lib. They just believed that it was incumbent on me to become as educated as possible.

Hammond: You didn't attend a full year of school until you were in grade eight. How was this an advantage?

Atwood: I'm very glad that I grew up that way We spent six to eight months of the year in the bush, and the rest of the time in cities, where I attended school. At that time no one seemed to object to the fact that children were pulled out of school early in spring and didn't return until late fall. No one thought in terms of "peer groups," or "socialization."

School was still lessons and material that you learned. We were able to cover the school course, although we weren't attending the school, because our mother used to be a schoolteacher. She'd taught school in order to earn the money to put herself through college. So she taught us in the mornings and we were able to cover the material in a much shorter period of time than we otherwise would have spent on it. We got the afternoons off. So that was one advantage. The other advantage was that learning wasn't something that you did because you had to do it. I also escaped much of that peer group pressure on girls to be dumb–the idea that it wasn't chic to be intelligent.

The best learning situation for anyone is one-to-one, being taught something that you want to learn because you need the information and being taught by someone whom you love. Even Plato knew that. My brother regularly taught me the things that he himself was learning. The most extreme example of this occurred when he was in high school learning Greek. He attempted to teach me Greek, but it wasn't a success. My father also had a very instructive personality. He taught us informally–just what he happened to be doing at the moment. We learned by observation. We probably spent considerably more time with our father than other children would because he didn't go to an office. He was an entomologist and collected insects in the summer. He would take the family along. He'd put a rubber sheet under a tree, hit the tree with the back of an ax, and the caterpillars and other insects would fall down onto the rubber sheet. Then everyone would pick them up. He was a well-versed naturalist, too. So we learned a number of things informally that we would not otherwise have known. The main advantage was that I didn't feel learning was something that was imposed on me, by a system, from the outside. When I entered fully into the educational system, I resented having to sit in a chair all the time and all the other rules and restraints.

Hammond: You've taught in the "system" yourself–on the college level. How has this affected your writing?

Atwood: I haven't taught since 1972 and before then only sporadically. It affected my writing by giving me less time to write. I couldn't write prose because I couldn't block out those large portions of time that you need for prose. If I teach I prefer to teach a subject which is at some distance from my own concerns, like Victorian literature–the subject I know best.

Hammond: You've mentioned graduate school. Did you get a Ph.D. from Harvard?

Atwood: I've done everything except about a quarter of the thesis. Somehow things came along that I had to write and I did that instead. Also since teaching isn't my life's work, what would be the value of my finishing my thesis? It wouldn't have any monetary or practical value. I will, however, eventually finish it because I like finishing things. But I'd never turn down the chance to write a novel for the chance to finish my thesis. I'll do it sometime in a moment of emptiness or despair. //

Hammond: Did you teach creative writing?

Atwood: I have attempted to do that, and it was quite enjoyable. I set up exercises, almost like experiments, to see what would come out. My students enjoyed that because they got things out of themselves that they never thought possible.

But if you're teaching subjects in which you're really heavily involved that you find painful, then teaching becomes an energy drainer. Teaching Canadian literature is painful. I didn't really enjoy writing *Survival*, but I felt that I had to write it because no one else had. If I teach I'd want it to be something unconnected with what I myself do. It's unlikely that I'll ever have that choice again.

Hammond: Earlier you mentioned escaping "peer group pressure," by virtue of your own liberal education, and you've spoken of teaching. As a writer, who are some of the women poets today whose poetry presents women with choices for self-definition in a largely male-defined world?

Atwood: I'm too ignorant to be able to name poets in any kind of categorizing way, but some of the women whose work I read and admire are: Anne Hébert, P. K. Page, Jay Macpherson, Margaret

Avison, Phyllis Webb, Gwendolyn MacEwen (the preceding are all Canadian poets)...Adrienne Rich, Marge Piercy, Rosellen Brown, Annie Dillard...any list I could give would be incomplete at best. I'm sure there are many, many more. This has been a hotly debated issue in the United States. In the United States you can say "feminism" and you can draw a line around it and go inside it and there you are. There are so many people in your country that you can form a fairly isolated subculture. In Canada it's much harder to do that because everyone's so saturated with the problems of Canada at the moment that it's difficult to pull away from that and say, "That doesn't concern me. I'm going to do nothing but feminism." I see the two issues as similar. In fact, I see feminism as part of a large issue: human dignity. That's what Canadian nationalism is about, what feminism is about, and what Black power is about. They're all part of the same vision.

Hammond: How do you respond to feminist critics' conviction that men are knowers and women are practical doers?

Atwood: I've never run across that one. I would think that most feminists would object to that distinction. Women have been practical doers in many societies, as have men. They've also been knowers. Anything that states, Thus shall you be because of your set of genitals—whether it's said by feminists or others—is going to be limiting. No society is above making these distinctions. Earlier this year, I heard Margaret Mead give a lecture in which she said that this is the first attempt that has ever been made in the history of human society to say that everyone can do everything; roles in previous societies have always been divided according to sex. It wasn't always women who cooked and men who were merchants. She did say, however, that few societies have given weapons to women and sent them out to war. The division is there partly so that men can say they're men. It's very easy to say that you're a woman. People use the term "real woman," but it doesn't have the same connotation as "real man." If you're not a "real man" you're not a man. If you're not a "real woman"—that is, someone's idea of desirable femininity—you're still a woman. No one says that you're a non-woman. "Real woman" may mean good woman or acceptable woman. But if you're not a "real man," something's missing. Men worry much more about their maleness than women worry about their female-ness. We all know we've got femaleness. The question is what to do with it. Many of these distinctions have been made by men.

Hammond: "Backdrop Addresses Cowboy" raises an interesting concept of woman as space desecrated.

Atwood: That poem is about Canada. What is being desecrated may in fact be female, but it's also a particular place. The cowboy is a familiar symbol. The poem was written in the era of Lyndon Johnson, and the border is more than just a decorative frame in the poem. It's an actual border between one place and another as well as a metaphor. So it isn't just about women. //

Hammond: "Marrying the Hangman" is a poem which many people familiar with your work frequently cite and are excited about. Could you tell me something about the origin of this poem, how you came to write it, how long it took to be written, etc.?

Atwood: It's coming out in my new book, *Two-Headed Poems*, in the fall (1978) in Canada. It will be published later in the States. It will also be appearing in the October (1978) issue of *Ms.* Magazine. It's based on an actual historical event. In the eighteenth century, in Quebec, there were only two ways to avoid being hanged if you'd been condemned to death by hanging. One was to take the position of the hangman, if the position was vacant and if you were a man. The second was to marry the hangman, if you were a woman and the hangman was unmarried. You could not, however, become the hangman if you were a woman. There was a woman who was lodged next to a man in prison. She had been condemned to death by hanging for the offense of petty theft. The man, however, had not been condemned to death. He was only incarcerated for dueling. But she talked him into taking the position of hangman, which was vacant, and then into marrying her. So the poem is based on that event and it takes off from there.

A friend of mine saw the story in *The Dictionary of Canadian Biography* and sent it to me. I didn't do anything with it for a long time, but then one day a number of other things came together and I just wrote the poem in one fell swoop! It took me about an afternoon. I didn't revise it much. I added a couple of little clarifying details and I added one word to one of the catalogs, but apart from that it stayed the same.

Hammond: In *Survival* you've explained that Canadian poets prefer drowning as a "natural" means of dispatching their victims because it is useful "as a metaphor for a descent into the unconscious." Both your fiction and your poetry is characterized by drowning scenes, i.e., in *Surfacing* and in "This Is a Photograph of Me." Is it a way of cutting through false memories?

Atwood: Too complex a question. Canadian poets have used quite a few drownings. They also like freezings to death. Drowning and freezing. In Quebec they prefer people to burn up. It's just a very, very general statement. It doesn't really mean anything except in that general manner of critical statement that causes people to react and contradict you. I'd have to take each poem and point out the differences. //

Hammond: You've spoken of Poe as an influence?

Atwood: That's a joke. I usually say that in speaking of this high school period, when we weren't taught any Canadian literature or any modern literature. In writing poetry your idea of a poem is defined by what you've read, what has been given to you. So, in saying Poe, I also mean Byron, Shelley, Tennyson, and others whom we read at that time. I didn't get to T. S. Eliot until college. My early poems are all rhythmically regular. They rhyme. A number of them have the galloping rhythms of "The Destruction of Sennacharib."

Hammond: You've said, "I don't think of poetry as a 'rational' activity but as an aural one." Does the aural quality of a line alone determine line length and line breaks?

Atwood: Poetry is primarily oral in that it was oral first in human societies, and it's oral first when a child is learning language. Children learn to recite, chant, and make up their own verse long before they learn to read. While speed reading may be very helpful for reading business reports, it's impossible to speed read poetry because you have to do the equivalent of moving your lips when you read. You're sounding out the poem and anyone who just scans it visually is missing the whole point. If you can't get the aural quality right, then the poem will be wrong; not that the play between the visual line, as it appears on the page, and how you hear it, isn't important—it is! //

Hammond: In any given poem are style and meaning inseparable–that is, if one changes, the other inevitably changes?

Atwood: Yes, that's why it's annoying to find that people, teaching our work in high school, say, "Make a précis of this poem, twenty-five words or less: 'What does it mean?'" That antagonizes the students because they think, If all it meant was that love is difficult, spring is nice, or war is hell, why did the poet go to all this trouble to hide it from us? Anyone who teaches that way doesn't take language seriously. They believe in abstractions.

Hammond: Does your work incorporate elements of surrealism, i.e., dream imagery, obscure humor, anti-rhetoric statements, fantasy landscapes, obscure abstractions, a non-repressive vision of reality?

Atwood: You can have all these characteristics that you mention in work that's not necessarily surrealistic in the classic sense. Literature itself does these things. I try to avoid obscure abstractions when I can. Of course, every poet thinks they're being clear. But I would certainly never deliberately be obscure. That's cheating. It's mannerist.

Hammond: In your Afterword to *The Journals of Susanna Moodie*, you explained that these poems were "generated by a dream." Have any other poems come to you in dreams or evolved out of dreams?

Atwood: Yes, I have several. I could tell you what they were if you felt it would be of interest; but it's not really very useful because it doesn't make the difference between a good poem and a bad one. Dreams, in themselves, are usually quite incoherent.

Hammond: Through what means other than dream have poems come to you, i.e., conversations overheard, dialogue, correspondence, research, pure observation?

Atwood: Those factors are more related to the way in which I write prose. I'm a magpie with prose. I collect little pieces of information, overheard conversations. A poem, however, is generated by a word or a phrase. I've said this before, but I'll repeat my metaphor. It's like dipping a thread into a supersaturated solution. If you do that, the supersaturated solution will form crystals on the thread. From the language the poem condenses. All these other bits and pieces, you mentioned, are floating in the language. So if they happen to attach themselves to that thread, yes. But that isn't what has generated the poem and it isn't what generates the novel. For me, a novel is generated by a certain vision, which may be a scene or a character. The things you mentioned are what I write down on scraps of paper and put at the side of my desk because they may come in useful sometime…road signs, brand names, lettering on people's tee shirts. They're of linguistic interest. There's a man here who has a tee shirt that says, "Occam's Razor."

Hammond: Stanley Kunitz has spoken of the originality of a poem determined by that individual discovering his or her own "key images." Would you agree that mirrors/glass, snow, green, maps, blood, totems, games are key images for you?

Atwood: They certainly recur. I don't ever talk about that because it's too determining of the future. Also since you've stated "key images," people are always using them against you. Once a statement to that effect has appeared in print you can never get rid of it. It follows you around forever.

Hammond: Is the poet, by virtue of the craft, part theoretician and part philosopher?

Atwood: I don't know. I try to avoid defining what the poet is. As soon as you define what the poet is, someone else comes along and contradicts it.

Hammond: When I asked Nancy Willard whether the advent of the prose poem had made it more difficult to discern what is prose and what is poetry, she said you'd given a good criterion.

Atwood: The unit of the poem is the syllable. The unit in a prose work—a short story or a novel—is something much larger. It may be the character or the paragraph. Formally it may be the paragraph, but then you're working with very large building blocks—things that may appear on page fifty and again on page one hundred. It's a very large structure. With the prose poem, the unit is still the syllable, but the difference between a prose poem and a short story for me is that the prose poem is still concerned with that rhythmical syllabic structure You're as meticulous about the syllables in a prose poem as you are in a poem. If the syllables aren't right, then the whole thing is wrong. In prose fiction the effects that are occurring are different. You may have someone saying something quite ugly that sounds ugly because that's the way people speak.

Hammond: What are some of the striking differences in approach to poetry and prose? Can one of the dangers of being both novelist and poet be that one may tend to write a poetic prose?

Atwood: I don't work on poetry when I'm writing novels. The verbal energy that would otherwise go into poetry goes into the novel. I have working habits when I'm writing a novel, but not when I'm writing poetry. I can't talk about theme and style generally.

As to the dangers, there's greater danger in being reviewed in a certain way. If reviewers know you write poetry, then they say, "This is poetic prose"; whereas, if you don't write poetry, they may never say that. For example, I can't remember ever reading that about *Ulysses*, in which Joyce used prose in a very rhythmic way. Unfortunately, you can't prevent the way in which your work is reviewed. If you're writing as a novelist when you're self-editing you'll delete passages that don't fit the novel.

As for writing habits, my ideal place for writing is an isolated place. If I'm writing a novel I like to have at least two hours a day, hopefully four. Late in the life of the book, six to eight hours. I use pieces of paper, a writing implement which can be a pencil or a ball-point pen and a typewriter. That's why people don't think that poets and novelists need very large grants. They don't have to buy paint. I write on scrap paper in longhand. The first step in revision is typing it. I'm a poor typist. Still, if I were a good touch typist, I'd miss a lot of things. As it is, I'm very involved in the texture of what I'm typing and have to look at it all the time.

Hammond: You've said that *Surfacing* "does not exist for the sake of making a statement but to tell a story." Is this true of your poetry as well?

Atwood: What I was trying to say was that it is a novel and not a sermon. The same applies to poetry.

Hammond: The characters in your novels have frequently been labeled as victims and survivors. Would it be accurate to ascribe such categorization to the speakers of your poems—in a volume such as *Power Politics*?

Atwood: People have taken *Survival* and applied it to my work. This can sometimes be bothersome because one doesn't always like one's insights as a critic being applied to one's work, from which they weren't drawn. They were drawn from reading books by other people.

For instance, take the woman in *Lady Oracle*; I don't think that she's either of those. She's not particularly a victim. Although she's a survivor, I wouldn't say that that's what categorizes her. Certainly many of her complicated problems are caused, not by her victim-hood or her survivor-hood, but by her romanticism. She's someone who is attempting to act out a romantic myth we're all handed as women in a non-romantic world. I'm interested in the Gothic novel because it's very much a woman's form. Why is there such a wide readership for books that essentially say, "Your husband is trying to kill you"? People aren't interested in pop culture books out of pure random selection. They connect with something real in people's lives.

Hammond: Science fiction, too.

Atwood: It's true of science fiction which is not particularly an inarticulate form anymore; it's become a fairly rarefied form. But it's certainly true of *True Romance* magazines which are–although sometimes in a more dramatic and bizarre form–about what happens in the lives of those who are reading them. There's usually an area of reality in popular literature that's hooking into the reality in the lives of the readers. Even Harlequin Romances. Those books are about the dream that we all secretly have–that everything can work out, that everything can be happy, that there is a Mr. Wonderful who does exist. The Gothic form centers on *My husband is trying to kill me*, and that's of great interest when you think about it. The story of *Jane Eyre* is really still with us, as are the four characters in it. The mad wife is still with us. The question is at what point does the orphan turn into the mad wife? How long does she have to he married to Mr. Rochester before she turns into the mad wife?

Hammond: Would you comment on the theme of appearance and reality in your work?

Atwood: I'd prefer not to say anything about that because some poor teacher is going to have to wade through a number of badly written term papers that take off from whatever I might say. It's too general a statement. From my work and the remarks that I've made about it, you probably realize that I don't necessarily think there's only one appearance vs. only one reality. It's fun to write about Henry James's novels that way because people are always putting on social fronts in them; then you discover that what's really occurring is horrifying and appalling. But in our society people don't put on social fronts very much. They're likely to reveal their whole life to you in about the first half hour of sitting beside you on a bus. So it isn't that they're hiding anything; it's just that the true story of their life is used as a defense. No longer do we have those closets with skeletons in them which we had in the Victorian period. Everyone is quite fond of their skeletons. They take them out and parade them around so that everyone can commiserate with them.

Hammond: In what genre other than prose and poetry or critical articles reviews, etc., have your written?

Atwood: Just about everything that you've mentioned except plays. I've never written a play set in modern times. I wrote them as a child. Nor have I written one of those factual nonfiction books like *How My Leg Fell Off and I Learned to Talk Again*, or a biography, or an autobiography. Don't know that I ever will.

Articulating the Mute

Karla Hammond

Karla Hammond's interview was conducted July 8, 1978, and originally appeared in *The American Poetry Review* 8 (1979). Copyright © 1979 by Karla Hammond. Reprinted by permission.

Hammond: You've mentioned in another interview a dark period between the ages of eight and sixteen when you didn't write.

Atwood: When I said a "dark period" between the ages of eight and sixteen when I didn't write, it was partly a joke. At four, five, six, and seven years of age, I was just writing comic strips, little poems, stories and plays. Between eight and sixteen I was interested in other careers. First, I wanted to be a painter. Next I wanted to be a dress designer. Then I went to high school and got hit with the concept of having to earn my own living. My extra option at school was Home Economics. I chose Home Economics because the guidance book presented five possible careers for women: airline stewardess, school teacher—preferably public— nurse, secretary, and home economist. Of the five, home economist was the least distasteful and the most sensible financially to me. It didn't occur to me that I might be a writer. In fact, at the time, I didn't really write anything except for school essays. At sixteen I started writing poetry. I don't know why I wrote; there certainly weren't any role models around.

Hammond: Did your early work come out of "nationalistic consciousness"?

Atwood: There was no nationalistic consciousness in Canada at that time. It didn't arise until the mid-'60s. We were taught very little Canadian writing or history in school. This is why nationalistic consciousness emerged. It's often difficult for Americans to understand because they've had the opposite experience. They've been so inculcated with the American ethic that their deepest wish is to become international. But, as Canadians, we were inter- national already and still are. We receive more world news and more publications from different countries than you do. We're much more eclectic in our total behavior, so that a shortage of internationalism for us isn't the problem. The problem is nationalism. It isn't a question of dominating other countries; it's impossible given Canada's size. Someone who hasn't seen how close we came to extinction and how close we are to it now, just can't understand. They think we're being narrow or belligerent; whereas all we're saying is, "We exist." Not that we're better, just that we're different. Similarly women have been saying, "We exist. We don't wish particularly to be defined by you."

Hammond: Has life in the Ontario and Quebec northland given you a distinct sense of a personal mythology?

Atwood: The main thrust of Canadian poetry over the last fifteen or twenty years has been to articulate the mute; so I'm really not very interested in a personal mythology. If you were put down in a place where you'd never been before you'd probably be more interested in figuring out the place than you would be in figuring out yourself. You can only indulge in the luxury of figuring out yourself when you're oriented in space and time. Canada was a country that lacked such orientation.

Hammond: Winter is a frequent landscape in your poems. Is it because, as you explain in *Survival*, winter is the "real" season?

Atwood: Although it's not true in Vancouver, in the part of Canada in which I live and over most of the country, there are only three months of the year when it almost definitely won't snow: June, July and August. Most of the time the snow stops in April and doesn't start until October or November. But it may stop as late as May. It snowed on May 20th in 1976. Winter is the real season because it's the prevalent season in Canada. When I was in India the people there asked me why green was so important a color in my poetry. I asked them what the opposite of green was for them and we concluded that brown was the opposite of green. When the foliage ceases being green it becomes brown. But when the landscape ceases being green in Canada it becomes white. So the visual alternation in Canada is not green/brown (or green/blue as it is in Hawaii), but green/white. Winter is important in my work because winter is important in the place where I write. Water is important in my work because if you look at an aerial map of Canada, you will see that there is more water per square mile there than in almost any other country on earth. Therefore, the key element for Canada is water. I suspect that the key element for the United States is fire.

Hammond: You have a number of references to maps. But do you have any interest in cartography apart from poetry?

Atwood: From what I've said about Canada you should be able to figure out why I have an interest in maps. The map is a usable metaphor for locating where you are. I suspect maps will become less important in my present and future work because of my past usage of them. I'm interested in ecology and geography apart from poetry—not just the drawing of maps but looking at maps and seeing where places are in relation to each other. That's often more important than you realize. For instance, if you look at Afghanistan (where Graeme and I were just before the coup) and if you can think of Afghanistan by itself that's one thing. But if you see that it adjoins Russia to the North, China to the East, the Indian subcontinent to the South, and Iran to the West, you'll realize that in fact, it's a very strategically located country. I enjoy visiting places where historical events of significance have happened. I liked going to Kabul because one of the greatest military disasters of the nineteenth century, or indeed of modern times, took place there. Namely the retreat of the British from Kabul in 1842. Sixteen thousand men set out and one arrived. The rest were all killed.

Hammond: You speak of poetry as a lens—indeed, you use images of glass and mirrors in your work. How is your work a reflection of Canadian culture or consciousness?

Atwood: A lens isn't a mirror. A lens can be a magnifying or focusing lens, but it doesn't merely give a reflection. It gives a condensation. Mirrors are, in fact, quite tricky because they give a backwards reflection; whereas a lens does something else. So I think of my poetry as a lens rather than as a mirror, although the literary culture, as a whole, often acts like a mirror of the society. I recognize my work more as a distillation or a focusing. But that isn't the only level on which art should function, the national level. A novel, in order to be successful, has to first hold the attention of the reader; second, it has to function on the level of the language in which it's composed. If the use of the language is terrible you're going to have a poor novel regardless of the consciousness it's reflecting or focusing. The same is true for women's work.

No culture exists apart from the ground in which it's rooted, but it doesn't stay there. "Universal" literature is always rooted in the particular. Russian novels come out of Russia. Canadian ones come out of Canada! It seems very simple to say.

Hammond: In *Words and Women,* Casey Miller and Kate Swift have a chapter entitled "The Specter of Unisex," in which they are speaking of an unsexed tongue. Miller and Swift speak of a book such as *Charlotte's Web* which by its "male orientation and use of subsuming masculine terms" no longer reflects reality. Miller and Swift are arguing that women want a tongue that includes them as well.

Atwood: Unfortunately, we're stuck with language and, by and large, it determines our categories. Poets generally are working with the expansion and elaboration of the language. When the Anglo-Saxons didn't have a word for something they made one up. That's not outside the English tradition. It's also a matter of word arrangement. A word isn't separate from its context. That's why I say language is a solution, something in which you're immersed, rather than a dictionary. There are little constellations of language here and there, and the meaning of a word changes according to its context in its constellation. The word *woman* already has changed because of the different constellations that have been made around it. Language changes within our lifetime. As a writer you're part of that process—using an old language, but making new patterns with it. Your choices are numerous.

Hammond: Have any women influenced your consciousness of a poetics?

Atwood: Yes. Influences occur in your first ten formative years. In Canada, some of the most interesting and prominent writers are women, and this has always been true. It's impossible to teach Canadian literature and ignore women. I first read a Quebec poet, Anne Hébert in French and in English translation. Her poetry is wonderful—and very unEnglish. It's highly surrealistic, characterized by marvelous condensed imagery. I recommend it—particularly a poem called "The Tomb of the Kings." Another poet whom I read was P. K. Page. If you could see her poems, you'd understand why she was an influence. Jay Macpherson, a personal friend of mine, influenced me in that she was there; she was visible. It's all very well to have Elizabeth Barrett Browning and Charlotte Brontë kicking around in the nineteenth century, but to actually be able to look at someone and say, that person has published a book. You can't imagine how important that was to a Canadian living at that time because of the dearth of poets and books available. Jay had a library, and I read poetry that I probably otherwise wouldn't have been able to read or have known about. Margaret Avison published a book, *Winter Sun*, which I reviewed in 1960 when I was in college. She's a very accomplished poet. I should mention Phyllis Webb and Gwendolyn MacEwen, another contemporary. You notice they're all Canadian.

Hammond: Is there a particular woman poet with whom you feel any affinity?

Atwood: Tends to be Adrienne Rich. Partly because everyone in the entire universe seems to have decided that whenever Adrienne Rich publishes a book I must review it. I don't know why this has happened. But I've reviewed her frequently in Canada and in the States, most recently in *The New York Times*. I have all her books and I've followed her through the years. She's very good. But my reading of American poetry tends to be accidental—whatever comes through the mail. For obvious reasons I know more about the women than about the men. I've read and reviewed Marge Piercy's work. But I do read American male poets, for instance, Robert Bly.

Hammond: Has your work been compared to Marge Piercy's or Colette Inez's?

Atwood: No. It's been compared to Sylvia Plath's. For a while Sylvia Plath took the place of Emily Dickinson. You could tell when someone had read only one or two women poets. They would either say that you were like Emily Dickinson or you weren't like Emily Dickinson. Then they were saying that you were like Sylvia Plath or that you weren't like Sylvia Plath.

Hammond: When I interviewed Karen Swenson we both agreed that women are more aware of their personal relationships as daughter, wife, sister, mother. Karen said that men, on the other

hand, are always writing about their relationship with Nature. //
Is "Dream 2: Brian the Still-Hunter": "but every time I aim, I feel
/ my skin grow fur / my head heavy with antlers" meant to
suggest male identification with Nature?

Atwood: Men don't have to write about Nature either. They
could always say, "blood flows through my toes. I'm part of
the lunar cycle." Many women write about their relationship
to Nature. Women might be more likely to say, "I am like the
pumpkin" rather than "I am like the porcupine." The only way
that you would ever prove something like that is by taking all the
poems written by men and women and running them through a
computer. General statements should only be made so that other
people can agree with them.

In the "Arctic Syndrome: dream fox" poem, "arctic syndrome"
is the name of a specific kind of madness that occurs only north
of the Arctic Circle, in which the person becomes a fox or a wolf.
It's indulged in by men and women. Ways of going crazy are
culturally determined. This happens to be an Inuit form of insanity.

"Dream 2: Brian the Still-Hunter" grew out of an anecdote in
Susanna Moodie's first book. A man named Brian the Still-Hunter
used to come and talk to Susanna Moodie every once in a while
and he said this, although not exactly in those words. He said that
whenever he was aiming at a deer he felt that he was, in fact,
related to the deer. // So "Brian the Still-Hunter" isn't about male
identification with nature, necessarily; it's from a real anecdote.
This man was suicidal. He was always trying to kill himself by
cutting his throat with a knife.

Hammond: "The Explorers" and "The Settlers" suggest the
transformation that occurred in *Surfacing* in a passage such as
"The animals have no need for speech, why talk when you are a
word I lean against a tree, I am a tree leaning." "Resurrection"
suggests a final vision of this: "at the last / judgment we will all
be trees."

Atwood: "The Explorers" and "The Settlers" were written around
1964. I wrote *Surfacing* in about 1970. So they're spaced in time.
The relationships to the landscape are very different in "The
Explorers" and "The Settlers"—when the people have become
part of the landscape by being buried in it. The same is true for

"Resurrection." The only way the speaker could actually get into the landscape was by dying. In *Surfacing* it's a visionary experience in which language is transformed. There was some Indian influence on *Surfacing* at that point. //

Hammond: Has Indian myth or folklore influenced your poetic vision?

Atwood: Yes, I'm interested in it. It's one of the ways of viewing woman and nature now available to us. The view previously available was the Biblical relation between man, woman, and nature. That certainly dominated Western society for many years. Now, living where we do, there's another perspective, but it isn't the only other perspective.

Hammond: Is there anything that you'd like to say about female literary myths?

Atwood: Myths mean stories, and traditional myths mean traditional stories that have been repeated frequently. The term doesn't pertain to Greek myths alone. *Grimm's Fairy Tales* are just as much myth or story as anything else. But some get repeated so often in the society that they become definitive, i.e., myths of that society. Certainly Biblical ones have been very important in our society. We all know what the Bible's attitude toward women is. However, I wasn't brought up a Christian so I wasn't deeply affected by those beliefs, except insofar as they were held by the general culture. If I were going to convert to any religion I would probably choose Catholicism because it at least has female saints and the Virgin Mary. It does have a visible set of sacred female objects, whereas Calvinistic Protestantism doesn't. It is monolithically male.

When I was visiting Mexico, sometime ago, I visited a church there. In this church there were about six Virgin Marys—one for every occasion: one dressed in white for when you're feeling happy, one wearing blue. You'd pray to each for a different reason. Then there was one in black and you prayed to her when all the others had failed. They all had little tin arms, legs, pigs, and cows pinned on them, which were offerings that people had made when the Virgin had saved something of theirs.

The other alternative would be to become a Quaker because you're not given any images: you're given a relationship to the divine. While there is a God the Father, women do participate in the religion.

Really I'm a pantheist.

The unexpurgated *Grimm's Fairy Tales* contain a number of fairy tales in which women are not only the central characters but win by using their own intelligence. Some people feel fairy tales are bad for women. This is true if the only ones they're referring to are those tarted-up French versions of "Cinderella" and "Bluebeard," in which the female protagonist gets rescued by her brothers. But in many of them, women rather than men have the magic powers.

Hammond: In *Signs* you've explained that you're not a theologian and yet your poetry as well as your fiction is imbued with a sense of mysticism. If you feel any affinity to religion is it more a sense of ritualistic/tribal/primitive incantation than institutional allegiance?

Atwood: Yes, by default. I have no institutional allegiance. My background is scientific. Much of what you may interpret as mysticism is simply science translated into a literary form. In other words if you take a physicist and push him far enough he will get to something that is pretty close to what you might call mysticism. If you take a crystallographer, working in the higher reaches of crystallography, you'll arrive at the same resolution where the difference between matter and energy ceases to exist; ergo, mysticism—if you wish! I could call it science and you would probably feel that's the opposite of mysticism, but if you went far enough left and far enough right you would probably meet because you'd have a circle. Still, no one knows whether the universe is circular or not.

Hammond: What bearing does the preceding question and answer have on your lines: "there is nothing for us to worship" and "my wooden fossil God"? Is this an indictment of patriarchal religion? What beliefs of a matriarchal religious consciousness might serve as a basis for a future feminist theology?

Atwood: The subject of matriarchal religions interests me, but it isn't something with which I'm preoccupied because I'm just not a theologian. These forms appeal to me mythologically. With a male theology you had an exaltation of men, placing women in a secondary position. Would a matriarchal theology exalt women and give men a secondary place? If so, I'm not interested because it would be the same problem in reverse. It wouldn't interest me to have all the priests be women and all the altar boys be men. I'd prefer an egalitarian or human religion. Women are interested in female religious figures now simply because we've starved for them, but that doesn't mean that we should desacralize men and that women should be made sacred. There's no point in destroying a male child instead of a female one.

Hammond: Suzanne Juhasz in *Modern American Poetry by Women: A New Tradition* writes: "To be a woman poet in our society is a double-bind situation, one of conflict and strain. For the words 'woman' and 'poet' denote opposite and contradictory qualities and roles. Traditionally, the poet is a man, and 'poetry' is the poems that men write." Could you comment?

Atwood: It's part of the American tradition. I can see why an American woman would say that, because I'm familiar with those university courses: Romantic writers, all men. Then they'd include Emily Dickinson. Even now American universities habitually ignore women writers in favor of men. It isn't that Canadian men are nicer or less sexist. They would have done that in Canada, too, if they could have. But they couldn't because the tradition was already fairly heavily populated by women. So while they might sneer, they couldn't ignore them. When you look at a Canadian anthology, it's usually a quarter to a third women. Now that's not a half, but it's a quarter to a third. It was similar in the nineteenth-century English literature that I studied. You couldn't teach the nineteenth-century English novel without putting in Jane Austen, the Brontës, and George Eliot. So I never had the feeling that women were excluded from literature by necessity or fate. I did, however, feel that there was a conflict in the woman writer's own life. You would come to a fork in the road where you'd be forced to make a decision: "woman" or "writer." I chose being writer, because I was very determined, even though it was very painful for me then (the late '50s and early '60s), but I m very glad that I made that decision because the other alternative would have been ultimately much more painful: it's more painful to renounce your gifts or your direction in life than it is to renounce an individual.

People a little bit older than myself wrote in cupboards at night because they didn't want anyone to know that they were writing or criticize them for taking that time away from their family. They tried to fulfill all their roles. When they gained recognition, they would immediately have marital difficulties because their husbands couldn't deal with their success. So I felt that if I were going to marry or form a permanent relationship that individual had to know, from the beginning, who I was and what I was doing. I wasn't going to conceal it. Many people thought I was really quite cold and perhaps I am in a very specific way. It's a necessary protective device.

Hammond: You said *Surfacing* was reviewed in the United States "almost exclusively as a feminist or ecological treatise. In Canada it was reviewed almost exclusively as a nationalistic one." Has this been true of the poetry as well? How does the Canadian reviewer's consciousness of poetic issues differ from the American's?

Atwood: A Canadian reviewer is reviewing my work from within the culture in which it was written. An American reviewer is reviewing it from outside that culture. The difficulty arises when the American reviewer doesn't recognize that. Americans have a tendency to regard anything written in English, on the North American continent, as being essentially American, or even "universal." In encountering various cultures that write but don't necessarily speak English, you realize that there isn't only one literature being written in English. There's nearly thirteen. (Canadian English literature is written in English, but it's also written in Canada. Although Canadian poets deal with so-called universal themes, our literature has a shape and direction of its own. When you have an American reviewer who is conscious of that, then you get an intelligent, informed review. When you get an American reviewer who doesn't know that you may get an intelligent review but an uninformed one. Many American reviewers mistake poems that are, in fact, about the culture or about nationalistic consciousness for poems that are written as personal or confessional revelations.

In Canada you have a technology that comes into the country from the outside and is essentially a foreign technology. Not that

Canada doesn't have a technology of its own, but not much of it originates there. There are many influences and physical objects introduced or generated by foreigners. It isn't that we aren't good at messing up our own landscape—we can do that adequately, given the opportunity—much of that is being done for us.

But to get back to being reviewed...I've been reviewed in the most viciously sexist ways—more so in Canada than in the States because American reviewers are suaver about the way they attack people. I've been called a Medusa, an Octopus, etc. The attack being: here is a woman who doesn't use words in a soft, compliant way; therefore, she is an evil witch. And I'm tired of it; but it's impossible to educate them. You're getting someone who really has a tremendous fear of women.

Hammond: You have written: "The duty of the critic is to society, but the primary duty of the writer is to the thing being made." Can you elaborate?

Atwood: It's a statement about writing derived from my own background and the fact that Canada is a very political country where people frequently indicate what they feel writers ought to be doing. You always have to say first that a writer is a writer. A writer isn't a preacher, a politician, or a lawyer. If they're a bad writer—regardless of the attractiveness of their ideas—they're still a bad writer.

Hammond: In *Survival* you mention novels which deal with the situation of the artist attempting "to function in Canadian society." In each case the artist is portrayed as a handicapped individual. What changes in the last decade or so have made it possible for the artist in Canada to function more effectively or is exile still necessary for survival?

Atwood: There's been a tremendous change in the past fifteen years. The works I covered in *Survival* were written or conceived before that change took place. Before, writers lived in isolation and were ignored. Generally, they were one-book writers. Everything that Tillie Olsen discusses in her forthcoming book, *Silences*, happened not only to women in Canada but to all Canadian writers. With a large reading public now, that has changed. Writers know each other. Prose writers have a Union.

Poets have a League. They get together once yearly. The country is small enough so that you can have them all in an organization and get them all into a room. It's now possible to have a sense of literary community. The artist isn't the isolated, invisible person whom I described in that chapter.

Society, however, although it has seen the possibility for change, has not effectively changed. Canada is still a colony, although now it has recognized its own colonialism. The parallel with the Women's Movement is pretty accurate. Now we've had all the definitions, but the wage difference between men and women is still very large. Canadians have had the books on colonialization, but most of their industry is still owned by the United States. The power is held by people other than those having the realization. In the case of women, it's men; in the case of Canada it's Americans. //

Hammond: Is poetry a means of translating power into social and political forms?

Atwood: No, it's the reverse. Social and political forms get translated into poetry. If you want to change the world, you do not choose poetry as the means for accomplishing it. In Latin America, however, writing a poem can be an act of enormous courage because the penalty for doing so could be death. But let's not delude ourselves about the nature of the society in which we live. Here one doesn't get killed for writing poetry. As for "Poetry must be a weapon in the hands of the people," that's true only in certain countries where speech is controlled. Writing a poem against the government and circulating it is, in fact, an explosive act because it allows people to think differently. In our society everyone has numerous forms of thought available to them; thus, thought itself is not taken very seriously. Essentially, the government doesn't care what you write. It doesn't care about poetry. Canadian society, however, cares about poetry more per capita than American society does. American poets are often voices in a desert, shouting at the tops of their lungs, convinced that no one can hear them. Such a conviction affects what they shout. Certain women poets and Black poets are different. They believe people are listening to them. In fact, people are listening to them. You can articulate change, but it's already happening.

You can make change a possibility in the imagination, but you can't effect change the way a law can effect change.

Hammond: Carol P. Christ has asked you: "Is the traditional identification of women and nature a legacy of oppression or a potential source of power and vision?" Comment?

Atwood: It's a potential source of power and vision. The oppression isn't in Nature; it's in what people have done to Nature. To ask that question is to also ask, Is being a woman necessarily to be oppressed? The oppression doesn't come from within the fact of being a woman. It comes from outside that fact. Of course that separation is only theoretical. The oppression is in people's attitudes towards Nature. You aren't and can't be apart from Nature. We're all part of the biological universe: men as well as women.

So my answer would be that it's a potential source of power and vision—partly because the alternative is to lock yourself away or become a machine. And that isn't practical or plausible for anyone—men or women.

Using What You're Given

Jo Brans

Jo Brans's interview was conducted at Southern Methodist University where Margaret Atwood appeared as part of the University's eighth annual Literary Festival in 1982. The interview first appeared in *Southwest Review* and also appeared in Jo Brans's collection *Listen to the Voices: Conversations with Contemporary Writers* (Southern Methodist University Press, 1988). Copyright © 1988 by Jo Brans. Reprinted by permission.

Brans: Are you a feminist writer?

Atwood: "Feminist" is now one of the all-purpose words. It really can mean anything from people who think men should be pushed off cliffs to people who think it's OK for women to read and write. All those could be called feminist positions. Thinking that it's OK for women to read and write would be a radically feminist position in Afghanistan. So what do you mean?

Brans: Let me try again. What I meant by asking that question was whether you think that you espouse a feminist position or propaganda in your writing.

Atwood: I don't think that any novelist is inherently that kind of a creature. Novelists work from observations of life. A lot of the things that one observes as a novelist looking at life indicate that women are not treated equally. But that comes from observation. It doesn't come from ideology. I started writing in 1956. There wasn't any women's movement during my writing life until 1970. That's fourteen years of writing. Now, on the other hand—and you have to try to define this very clearly—I'm not one of those women who would say, "Well, I made it; therefore anybody should be able to do it, and what are they whining about." That's not the point. Nor am I against the Women's Movement. I think it's been a very good thing, and I was happy to see it. But it's very different from saying that what you write is embodying somebody's party line. It isn't. And none of the women writers that I know, including ones who are regularly defined as feminists, would say that they are embodying somebody's party line. It's not how they see what they're doing.

Brans: You have gotten crossways with some feminist groups, particularly with *Surfacing*, where a woman character wants to undo the effects of an abortion.

Atwood: To me that is just what that character would do. The abortion was coerced—it was forced. That's not an "anti-abortion" stand. It's an anti-coercion stand. I don't think even women who are in favor of freedom of choice would say abortion is a good thing that should be forced on everyone. And if they've read the book—you sometimes feel these people haven't or they don't know how to read—that is what they would see, the negative effects that happen to the character are connected with the fact that the thing is forced on her by the circumstances.

Brans: What does pregnancy mean in your writing? There are so many places, for example, in *Life Before Man*, and then the little story called "Giving Birth,"where pregnancy seems to mean something profound and various.

Atwood: Well, girls can have babies and boys can't. The fact has been noticed by more people than me. In the story "Giving Birth," giving birth is wonderful for the woman from whose point of view the story is told but she mentions this other shadow figure for whom it's not wonderful. It's awful. I think one of the things the story says is that there is no word for forced pregnancy in the language. We don't have that concept, although the fact itself exists. So, there again I wouldn't say that pregnancy is wonderful for everybody. We know that it isn't. It can be wonderful for a person who wants to go through it. But you could say that of every act in life.

Brans: What about a girl like Lesje, for example, in *Life Before Man*, who becomes pregnant in order to prove a point?

Atwood: Once upon a time more women than we would like to admit got pregnant to prove a point. In fact, they got pregnant to get married. Remember shotgun weddings? I'm sure that still happens. I don't think it's tiptop for the children who are involved. //

Brans: Yes. But Lesje doesn't have that in mind.

Atwood: No, no. She's tired of being put down for not being the mother. You can't say that pregnancy is one thing. It's many things, like making love. I mean, it's not just one thing that ought to have one meaning. It's one of those profoundly meaningful human activities which can be very multifaceted and resonant. It can have a very positive meaning for some people and a very negative meaning for others.

Brans: Which is the point of the extra woman in "Giving Birth."

Atwood: Remember that I'm old enough to remember the time when women were told they had to get pregnant and have babies in order to "fulfill their femininity." And I didn't like that either. Nor do I like women being told that they oughtn't to get pregnant, they can't get pregnant, that it's anti-feminist to get pregnant. I don't like that line either.

Brans: So you're really defining your feminism for me, I think, right now.

Atwood: Yes, I'm defining my feminism as human equality and freedom of choice.

Brans: What do you think an ideal relationship between a man and a woman would be?

Atwood: A happy one.

Brans: I was thinking of your poem "Power Politics."

Atwood: That talks about all kinds of different ways in which marriage isn't happy. You may often define a positive by defining negatives.

Brans: What I like most in "Power Politics" is the wit. It is the sharpest and wittiest poem. There's a lot of anger in it, and frustration because of the impossibility of communicating.

Atwood: But there again, that doesn't rule out the opposite pole. I'll read some love poems in the reading tonight to show it can be done. I'm not a pessimist. People sometimes read my poems and think, Oh, this is a pessimist.

Brans: Anyone who thinks that should read "There Is Only One of Everything." I love that poem, and it is a love poem—wonderful. But it's not only a love poem, it's also a poem about observing the world, and the particularities of the world, I guess. What effect has being Canadian had on your writing?

Atwood: There's a funny poem in Canada called "Recipe for a Canadian Novel" in which it's recommended that one take two beavers, add one Mountie and some snow, and stir. I'm not in favor of anybody consciously trying to be the great anything, but every writer writes out of his or her own backyard. I give you William Faulkner as an example. There's a genre of writing we call "Southern Ontario Gothic," which is something like Southern Gothic. The South has often had problems of making itself felt as something other than a region—it so often just gets called "regional," doesn't it?—whereas, in fact, Southern writers are doing what all writers do. They're writing out of what they know.

There's a story you'll appreciate. When I first met our mutual friend Charles Matthews, who, as you know, is from Mississippi, I said, "Oh, I so much admire William Faulkner. He was so inventive, and he made up all these funny and grotesque things." And Charles said, "He didn't make anything up. He just wrote it all down." That just proves my point. That's what writers do, and Canadian writers are no different from other writers in that respect. They write about what they know. Some of what they know is Canadian. When they travel, or when they think in other terms, then the terms become larger. But the base, the way of thinking, remains Canadian, just as for the Southern writer the way of thinking remains Southern. So to me it's not a question which is particular to Canada; it's a question that's about all writing and all writers.

Brans: And how to transcend region somehow?

Atwood: I don't think you transcend region, anymore than a plant transcends earth. I think that you come out of something, and you can then branch out in all kinds of different directions, but that doesn't mean cutting yourself off from your roots and from your earth. To me an effective writer is one who can make what he or she is writing about understandable and moving to someone who has never been there. All good writing has that kind of transcendence. It doesn't mean becoming something called "international." There is no such thing.

Brans: So you don't think then that there are national literary qualities, even though you wrote a book about Canadian literature?

Atwood: In any transaction involving a book there's the writer, there's the book, and there's the reader. The writer can write the book and make it as good a book as he or she can, and it can be a pretty good book. That doesn't mean the reader is going to understand it, unless the reader has receiving apparatus that's equal to the product. //

I write for people who like to read books. They don't have to be Canadian readers. They don't have to be American readers. They don't have to be Indian readers, although some of them are. I'm translated into fourteen languages by now, and I'm sure that some of the people reading those books don't get all the references in them, because they're not familiar with the setting. I don't get all the references in William Faulkner either. That doesn't mean I don't enjoy the books, or can't understand them. You can pick up a lot of things from context, even though you may not understand that it was that family in Oxford, Mississippi, that was being talked about.

Brans: But as an educated reader you still would have this human rapport with the book.

Atwood: An educated reader has a rapport with all books, depending on taste to a certain extent, but an educated reader would never not read a book because it wasn't by somebody from his home town, right? or because the person was a different color, or because the person was a woman or a man. I've had women say to me that they just don't read books by men anymore. I think that's shocking. //

Brans: Do you have any problems in portraying a character of the opposite sex in your writing?

Atwood: The same problem I would have portraying an English person, or somebody that was just enough different from me that I'd have to do research. So, with men, it depends on what kind of man you're doing, of course; but just to give you an example, writing *Life Before Man* I showed the manuscript to a man (I showed the manuscript of *Bodily Harm* to a West Indian, and that was helpful, too) because I wanted to just have a read on the details—the accuracy of the details—and he caught me in one major mistake, which a man would never have made. He said you cannot shave a beard off with an electric razor. You have to use a straight razor. An electric razor will just get all clogged up if you're trying to shave long hairs with it. Little things like that. I think men have often portrayed women characters, and sometimes they slipped up on those kinds of details. Unless they go do the research on how you put on panty hose, they aren't going to know.

Brans: Well, I'm glad to have you defend him.

Atwood: There again, people, even women, expect men to be better than they are, and better than women. Now, notice what you did. You came after me for Nate, who's actually the nicest person in the book. Now, Lesje is a wimp. Nobody ever attacks Lesje for being unrealistic and wimpish, and so on, because they expect girls to be like that. Hardly ever at all has anybody ever said that. Nobody ever comes after me for Elizabeth being a bitch.

Brans: Well, I would have come after you for that.

Atwood: Next? It's always Nate. And I think the truth is that people expect men to be supermen. Even women—even feminists—take points off them when they aren't. They don't take equal points off the women for having failings, because women are expected to be imperfect.

Brans: Well, I thought of Elizabeth as having a bad childhood, and of Lesje as being young, and so I was willing—you're right. That was prejudiced of me.

Atwood: Women are supposed to be imperfect, but they are also expected to be supermoms, so you can't win, either way.

Brans: What did you have in mind about the dinosaurs in *Life Before Man*? Do you think we've lost something by becoming overly civilized?

Atwood: I don't like to close my symbolisms.

Brans: But you were suggesting something about a sort of purity of action and motive in the dinosaurs?

Atwood: No, they're Lesje's escape fantasy, among other things, but I don't like to explain and pin down things that I've put in my books. They have multiple meanings. One of the meanings is that all kids love dinosaurs, and I was no exception.

Brans: You have such diversity. All of the novels are very different from each other, and then, of course, I love your poetry, which is quite different from the fiction. Do you consciously put on different hats? Do you set out, say, to write a comedy of manners (and I think those terms are too constricting)? Are you consciously doing a particular kind of thing with, let's say, *The Edible Woman* or *Lady Oracle*?

Atwood: Yes, both of those, definitely.

Brans: Were you working for a genre, or did you start with an image that lent itself to that sort of treatment?

Atwood: I start out with an image, and the book develops around it. Yes, I always start with images, and the tone of the book comes later. //

Brans: You're so caught up with the transformation/metamorphosis/rebirth idea. Does that have anything to do with your having studied with Northrop Frye? Did he shape your thinking...

Atwood: No, I think it has to do with the fact that my father was a biologist. I had the kind of reading childhood that Norie Frye would advocate. But he hadn't advocated it while I was having it. In other words, I read very early *Grimm's Fairy Tales*. Greek mythology. I was familiar with the Bible, and so on and so forth. Norie Frye didn't enter my life until the third year of university, when I had already been writing for four or five years. // My interest in metamorphosis may have come from *Grimm's Fairy Tales*. People are always having rebirths there. The culture is permeated with rebirth symbolism. It's Christian, among other things. And it's an idea that is very much around. If I were in India, they would say, Do you believe in metempsychosis, do you believe in the transmigration of souls? But it seems to have been a concept in one form or another that has been run through the sausage machine by many different human cultures.

Brans: But it's clearly so central to you.

Atwood: It's central to me, but it's also central to lots of other people. It's central to any novel. Usually in a novel the central character changes. That's one of the things that happens in novels—the person learns something or they become something more, or they become something less, but they always change. They're not the same at the end as they were at the beginning. If you did write a novel in which they were exactly the same, you would probably find it either terribly experimental or terribly boring or possibly both.

Brans: It seems to me all your novels are affirmative, in a sense. // I was struggling very hard with *Bodily Harm*, because it did seem to me, with the political satire...

Atwood: You made it through to the last page, though.

Brans: But in the last page I thought I found this rather guarded affirmation, because she's "paying attention," that was a phrase that you used, which to my mind is a very affirmative statement. And then, something like she's flying. And her luck is holding her up. So it seemed to me that of all your books this would, on the surface, be the least affirmative, and yet...

Atwood: I think it's actually the most affirmative, because you can only measure affirmation in terms of what it's set against. Having hope for the human race in India is a really different thing from having hope for the human race in Texas. In Texas you don't have to deal with massive poverty and people dying in the street and starvation and beggary and so forth. It's easy to be optimistic here.

Brans: I was thinking too of her personal trauma, because the loss of the breast seems to be...

Atwood: That happens to a quarter of all women over the age of forty. That's what the statistic is right now, so people better begin to deal with it. But part of what the novel does is set our way of thinking, which is an affluent way of thinking. We can afford to worry about our personal health and our fitness and our personal romances, and what we're eating, and whether we're fashionable, and whether we look good, and personal change and growth and all of those things we read about in women's magazines—that's in the forefront of our lives. //

Brans: Why are Americans often so hateful in your books?

Atwood: I don't like American foreign policy, in many instances. But neither do a lot of Americans. Nor do I confuse individual people with decisions made by governments. I think it's wrong to do so.

Brans: But, for example, in *Surfacing*, when the Americans come in they're so clearly the enemy. Or the CIA in *Bodily Harm*...

Atwood: All that stuff is realistic. It's not made up and it's not my attitude. I'm just writing it down. People sit around in bars and discuss who the CIA is this month.

Brans: Are you serious?

Atwood: Absolutely.

Brans: I didn't read *Surfacing* at all on that level. I thought the Americans were a symbol.

Atwood: No, no. No, no, no, no. // I was just writing down people's conversations. That's how people, at least some people, talk about the Americans. But you notice that the guy who talks about them that way the most is also the most spurious person in the book. And the people he thinks are Americans actually turn out to be Canadians. //

Brans: Do you have a specific political position?

Atwood: Politics, for me, is everything that involves who gets to do what to whom. That's politics. It's not just elections and what people say they are—little labels they put on themselves. And it certainly isn't self-righteous Puritanism of the left, which you get a lot of—or self-righteous puritanism of the right I hasten to add. Politics really has to do with how people order their societies, to whom power is ascribed, who is considered to have power. A lot of power is ascription. People have power because we think they have power, and that's all politics is. And politics also has to do with what kind of conversations you have with people, and what you feel free to say to someone, what you don't feel free to say. Whether you feel free during a staff meeting to get up and challenge what the chairman has just said. All of those things. //

Brans: You don't belong to a political party?

Atwood: Not any political party. I belong to Amnesty International, which concerns itself with torture and political imprisonment. I belong to the Canadian Civil Liberties Union.

Brans: But in your books you're not attitudinizing at all? You're simply showing the world as you see it and sense it and feel it?

Atwood: Let me just think about that. I don't think people are morally neutral, OK? But that does not have anything to do with labels. That is, if you call somebody a democrat, if they say they're in favor of democracy, you then have to find out what they're actually in favor of by asking them a number of specific questions. Only then do you find out what's under that. If somebody says they're socialist, same thing. You have to ask different questions to find out what they really mean. The same with the feminist. And what you're really trying to put your finger on is, how will this person behave in this situation or that situation? Is this going to be somebody who's going to vote for burning witches, is it going to be somebody who's going to vote for fair trials, or is it going to be somebody who's going to vote for shooting people?

Brans: And those are not the things you learn by looking at a label.

Atwood: You don't learn those by looking at a label. People use labels for their own purposes—either to put on other people so they can line them up against the wall and shoot them, or to put on themselves to make themselves feel good. So that's why I took you through the mulberry bushes when you asked me about feminism. It's a label.

Brans: And again about politics.

Atwood: That's right. I think when you say "political writer" you usually mean either somebody who writes about doings in the White House or somebody who has a particular ax to grind in that they think everybody should vote for so-and-so, or that the world should be such and such a place, and that this is the way to get it. I don't have any surefire recipes like that. I am, of course, somebody who would vote, as I did recently in the Toronto election, in favor of an East/West nuclear arms freeze. That to me isn't even politics. It's survival.

Brans: You've been writing for so long. Apparently there's a very great need for you to write.

Atwood: It's very enjoyable for me to write. It's a pleasure. I bet you've never heard a writer say that before.

Brans: Writers say various things, but for a lot of them I think it is a torment, but a necessary torment.

Atwood: Don't ever believe that. If they didn't enjoy it on some level they wouldn't be doing it.

Brans: What do you think you accomplish for other people with your writing?

Atwood: It's not my business. That's their business. They are the receivers. They are in charge of their own equipment.

Brans: So you simply do it out of a love for it.

Atwood: Partly. I don't rule out communication, and reading a book is, according to the neurophysiologists, almost the equivalent of having the experience, on a synaptical level, what happens in your head. In fact, you could think of a human being as an enormous computer that you can run programs through. But if you think of a book as an experience, as almost the equivalent of having the experience, you're going to feel some sense of responsibility as to what kinds of experiences you're going to put people through. You're not going to put them through a lot of blood and gore for nothing; at least I'm not. I don't write pretty books, I know that. They aren't pretty. //

Brans: Always, in your books, there's this sense of making do. You have a phrase that runs throughout your poetry and your novels. Something like, it's your life and you're stuck with it. You have to make do.

Atwood: That's a negative line. But there's another way of putting it, which is this: some people, by "freedom," mean freedom to do whatever they want to, without any limitation whatsoever. That isn't the pack of cards we're dealt. We are dealt a limited pack. So I would see freedom more as the power to use what you're given in the best way you can. It doesn't mean that you're given everything. You aren't. Nobody is.

Tightrope-Walking over Niagara Falls
Geoff Hancock

Geoff Hancock's interview was conducted December 12 and 13, 1986, at Margaret Atwood's home in Toronto and originally appeared in his collection *Canadian Writers at Work* (Oxford University Press, 1987). Copyright 1987 by Geoff Hancock.

Hancock: Interviews can take many forms. They can act as an adjunct to literary criticism, or they can act as literary biography. An interview can get inside a writer's work. Do you think I might learn something about your work which isn't readily apparent from an interview?

Atwood: Interviews are an art form in themselves. As such, they're fictional and arranged. The illusion that what you're getting is the straight truth from the writer and accurate in every detail is false. The fact is that most writers can't remember the answers to some of the questions they get asked during interviews, so they make up the answers. A lot of the questions are about things they don't usually think about, or if they do think about them, they don't think about them at the time of writing.

Any memory you have of what you did at the moment of writing is just that, a memory. Like all memories, it's usually a revision, not the unadulterated experience itself.

Also, writers quite frequently conceal things. They either don't want them known, or they think of them as trade secrets they don't want to give away, or they are hooked on some sort of critical theory and they wish to make it appear that their work fits inside the perimeter of that theory. Let's just state at the beginning that interviews as the truth, the whole truth, and nothing but the truth are suspect. They're fictions. //

Hancock: With Robert Weaver, you've recently collaborated on a short-story collection, *The Oxford Book of Canadian Short Stories in English*. Do you still see yourself as part of what you once called "our tough and somber literary tradition"? The anthology covers a century of writing. Or, and here's the flip side of the question, do you see a number of writers working in a variety of different directions not connected to a tradition? //

Atwood: You were thinking about *Survival*, I guess. That was an attempt to say, quite simply, that Canadian literature is not the same as American or British literature. That is now known in the world at large. It wasn't known then, in 1972, not even in Canada at the time. If you read the reaction to *Survival*, some people asked, "Why is she writing a 300-page book about something that doesn't exist, namely, Canadian literature?"

You must believe it exists, because you publish *Canadian Fiction Magazine*. There must be some reason for calling it that, and for putting stories by Canadians in this magazine. If Canadian writing were the same as British or American writing, why put it in a separate magazine? You can say, there's this difference and that difference, and it's changed and gone off in various directions. But you are probably not going to say, "There's no such thing as Canadian literature." That was the attitude of a lot of people only sixteen years ago. The mail I got from ordinary people was, "Gee whiz, I never knew. My high-school teacher told me there was only Stephen Leacock and that was it." This situation—the need to struggle to assert the mere fact of our existence—is no longer with us. //

Hancock: To change subjects here, the imagination of Canadians takes us North.

Atwood: For Canadians, North is a constant. It's one of those ideas that are reinterpreted generation after generation, and by region after region. The idea of North is probably quite different for Quebeckers. But "North" is still the thing that's being considered. When the Americans send icebreakers through the Northwest Passage, why do Canadians get so stirred up about it? Not many people go there. It's not as though it happens where they are physically. It happens in their minds. It's a violation of their mental space.

Hancock: Though Canadian literature has made great steps forward, in some of your stories you've satirized the Canadian literary community.

Atwood: Literary communities are always comic, when they're not tragic; that is, when writers aren't being tortured, shot, and imprisoned. If you take "comic" as that which is divergent from what "normal," "average" people think you ought to be doing with your life, then you, Geoff Hancock, are a comic character. Here you are, running this magazine, devoting your life to this thing which is never going to make any money. It's quixotic of you to do it. You are the Don Quixote of the Canadian literary scene, and so is anybody who runs a literary magazine or a small press in this country. If the society in which you live thinks you should be making millions of dollars playing the stock market or being a doctor and playing golf, which is considered average and normal, then all us artists are defined as whacko. We ourselves may not think that. We may think that we—in general—are the sanest thing around—which I happen to believe. But from the point of view of society—and comedies always take place in that context—we are the "funny people," the eccentrics, the ones who are not in step. And we do have our eccentricities.

Hancock: You like to work in a variety of areas. Do you try to understand the processes of each piece of writing, whether it's a poem, a cartoon, a short story, an essay, a novel, a screenplay, or a theater piece?

Atwood: This word "process" is very fashionable. All it really means, as far as I can tell, is "how do you do it?" You have to understand something about the form before you can do it at all. We might include puppet plays, which was one of the things I started out with. Puppet plays for children's birthday parties. Every one of those art forms has a certain set of brackets around it. You can say, "This is what happens within this form," and, "These are some of the things that don't happen within it." Some of the most interesting things happen when you expand the brackets. For instance, when we do puppet plays, we don't usually show the live people who run the puppets. What would happen if we mixed up live people with puppets? What would we get then? We would get the Mermaid Theatre, one of the most intriguing puppet theaters around. The brackets were moved over to include live people. We've moved the borders, we've changed the rules.

It's the same with any form. You have to understand what the form is doing, how it works, before you say, "Now we're going to make it different, we're going to do this thing which is unusual, we're going to turn it upside down, we're going to move it so it includes something which isn't supposed to be there, we're going to surprise the reader."

For instance, in the novel, for a while it was the fashion not to show the author at work. Before that, it was the fashion to show the author. Now it's the fashion to show the author again. It was a new thing for the 1960s and 1970s. It was standard for 1850s novelists to say, "Now, Dear Reader, let me tell you what I think about these goings-on. Dorothea didn't know this was happening. But I, the author, am going to let you, the Reader, in on the secret." If you go back before then, you have the author talking about himself, saying why he decided to write the story in this way and not some other way. Letting the reader in behind the scenes. All of those things are ways of moving beyond the conventions to include things not considered includable. The kind of material thought to be suitable for novels is constantly changing.

This is one of the things that happened to Canada. For a long time, Canadian material was not thought to be suited to "great literature." You could not make a "real novel" out of Canadian material. You had to go to the States or England to make a "real novel." Canadian novels *per se* were considered second-rate pastiche, or imitation or embarrassing. // Similarly with women's material. What-you-do-in-the-kitchen-when-the-boys-aren't-there. That kind of stuff was considered not suitable for great writing. It was always dismissed or not used. Then Margaret Laurence, Alice Munro, Margaret Drabble, Marian Engel, and others started using this stuff, and making it work. Lo and behold, it *was* usable, as it had been all along, except that nobody had noticed. //

Hancock: How do you keep track of where you are in a long-hand manuscript?

Atwood: I usually start at the beginning and barrel straight through. It's like CBC "Coast to Coast." I start in Newfoundland, and then roller-coaster across the country according to the time change. If I'm working on a novel, I'll write maybe twenty pages in longhand. I start transcribing that longhand into typing, while at the same time on the back end of the novel I write more. I'm always catching up to myself in the typing while continuing on in the writing. That reminds me of what I just wrote the day before and allows me to keep track. But some of the stories I'll write in one sitting. When I'm feeling good I can write twenty pages longhand in a sitting, and transcribe ten on the typewriter. But, of course, there's a lot of revision.

Hancock: Is this a constant method of composition?

Atwood: I don't always start at the beginning and go through to the end. Sometimes I'm going along and I'll come to a scene which is out of sync. I know it comes near the end, but I'll write it down anyway. It becomes quite immediate and I want to get it down before I forget about it. I will have little patches here and there. It's like coloring in a map. It's a form of exploration. You're going along a river. This is "explored territory" and this is "unexplored territory." But from what you know, there's a pagoda which you should be coming up to, though you don't know what's been here and there. You know you'll be coming to some things you already know about. But you don't always know how to get there. //

Hancock: Are you a severe critic of your work-in-progress?

Atwood: Let us put it this way. People have often asked me which of my editors is "the real editor." Is it my Canadian editor, my American editor, or my English one? The fact is, it's not any of them. By the time they get the work, it's been through six drafts usually. // Although I write quite quickly in the first instance, I revise slowly.

Hancock: Do you find your works "link" together? Is there a larger narrative framework?

Atwood: Do you mean does this novel and that novel have something to do with one another? Well, they all have women in them. In *Life Before Man* a male tells one-third of the story. Some of the stories are told from the point of view of men. "Uglypuss" is a case in point: most of that story is told from the man's point of view. The woman comes in at the end. But by and large my novels center on women. None of them are about all-male groups. None of them are about miners in the mines, seamen on the sea, convicts in the jail, the boys in the backroom, the locker room at the football game. Never a story have I set in those locations! How come? Well, gee, I don't know! Maybe it's because

I am a woman and therefore find it easier to write as one. Few male writers write all their books from the female point of view. That doesn't mean they hate women.

Hancock: You also like paired characters: mothers and daughters, nieces and aunts, such as Elizabeth and Muriel in *Life Before Man*, the Handmaid and her sinister aunts, Joan of *Lady Oracle* and aunts Lou and Deirdre. Could you comment on this?

Atwood: Most novelists work in pairs, triplets, quartets, and quintets. It's hard to have a novel with no characters in it except the protagonist. But I am *interested* in the many forms of interaction possible among women—just as I am in those possible between women and men. I'm interested in male-male interaction but can have no first-hand experience of how men relate to one another when women aren't present. For that you have to ask men.

Hancock: Can a fiction be ideal?

Atwood: Do you mean perfect? Oriental carpet makers weave a flaw into the design on purpose, because nothing on this earth can be perfect. // I'm thinking of the uncertainty principle in physics. Even the physical universe is not "perfect," that is, wholly symmetrical, closed, finished. There's something in the nature of things that's against closure. Here's the latest from my nephew— he's the mathematical physicist. They now think the universe is made of little strings, in thirty-two different colors. I said to him, "If the little pieces of string are so small, how do they know what colors they are?" He said, "It's just a manner of speaking."

Hancock: A "string" is supposed to be a quintillion quintillion times smaller than the smallest part of an atom, if I remember correctly. The concept was thought up by a Russian physicist. Along with it goes what he calls the TOE Theory, the theory of everything.

Atwood: Even better, there's supposed to be seven dimensions, four more than we usually think of. Let's not even ask about perfection!

Hancock: Which aspect of fiction writing do you find most interesting or challenging?

Atwood: It's all pretty difficult. The most challenging is to do something that surprises me, the writer, and therefore, I hope, will surprise you, the reader.

Hancock: Do you like to deal with the large format of a social mythology through fiction?

Atwood: I think I used to like that idea. I don't like ideas as a rule—not as a priori determinants of fictional modes. // I started out in philosophy and English. Then I switched.

If you're an academic, you have to concern yourself more with ideas. Ideas make the material a lot more teachable. People find it easier to sit in a classroom and abstract things or turn them into ideas, or consider them from the point of view of ideas. There's not a lot you can say from total immersion in the text. About all you can say are emotional things, like "Wow, it really grabbed me!" Or other reactions that come out in that banal way: "I hated it," "I loved it," "It didn't do anything for me!" Whereas if you deal in "ideas" you can analyze the structure, the prose, the style, or this and that. But as soon as you do that, you're analyzing, making an abstraction from the actual thing.

Academics have to do that at one level or another. They are in the business of teaching people. One of the things that happens when you teach people is that you say, "Let's look at it this way. Let's look at it structurally. Or mythically. Let's look at the prose, the punctuation, the texture." But if you are not an academic, you don't have to spend a minute of your time thinking about those things. If you are a practicing writer, and that only, your engagement is with the blank page and only with the blank page. You never have to toddle off to school. You never have to divide yourself in that way, the blank page at home at night, the daytime at school, where you point out how Marianne Moore's poems have little white spaces in them. You don't have to think about that unless you want to. //

Hancock: Do you prefer people to just experience your work?

Atwood: No, I don't have any of those preferences. It's not a value judgment. You were asking how I went about it, and what my experience was. When I'm not teaching, I don't have to think of my own work in terms of ideas or large social things or any of those concepts. I get right down in the mud, which is what engagement with the page is. It's mud.

Hancock: What makes fiction dramatic for you?

Atwood: Fiction has to surprise me. If a character is going along doing only what such a person would do, I get very bored. I want to know more. Or to have them come to a point where they're not what I thought they were. Or that they're not what they thought they were. It's probably a form of childish curiosity that keeps me going as a fiction writer. I probably want to open everybody's bureau drawers and see what they keep in there. I'm nosy.

Hancock: Whose fiction do you admire?

Atwood: Lots of people's! It's the question at readings that always stops me cold. I feel as soon as I start picking those lists, people are going to be hurt because I didn't include them—but it may just be because I haven't thought of them at the time. If you are wondering what I read recently that zapped me out the most, I can tell you three books. One was J. M. Coetzee's *Foe*. That was zappo! The other was Primo Levi's *The Periodic Table*. Another was Ireni Spanidou's *God's Snake*.

Hancock: Do you learn anything from books you admire?

Atwood: You learn something from everything. But *what* is the question. You often don't know for twenty or thirty years what you've learned. It may appear suddenly a year or two or five years later that you learned something back then that was important to you. I read for pleasure, and that is the moment at which I learn the most. Subliminal learning.

Hancock: Could you say something about the writer's "voice"? Is there a distinctive Canadian voice? Could you say something about your own voice?

Atwood: I hope there is more than just one distinctive Canadian voice. It would be so boring otherwise. I came across a funny thing I wrote some years ago. The Writers' Union of Canada thought it would improve its fortunes by having all its members write a piece of pornography! Andreas Schroeder was going to put these together into an edited book. This was the genesis of Marian Engel's novel *Bear*, by the way. It started out as a piece of porn about a woman fornicating with a bear. The Union gave up the idea because they felt from the submissions that serious writers weren't any good at writing pornography. But I think they were looking for the wrong thing. They should have been looking for the kind of parody serious writers tend to produce when they try their hand at this. They would have got more usable material. I wrote a piece called "Regional Romances, or, Across Canada by Pornograph." It's five different pieces, starting with the Maritimes, then Quebec, Ontario, the Prairies, and B.C. Each one is written in quite a different voice, but quite recognizable. You would know the general area of literature that was parodied. There is not one Canadian voice. There are various voices. But none of them sound particularly British, and as a whole, they don't sound very American either.

It all depends on where you stand in relation to the forest. If you stand very close, you can see the molecules inside the tree. Move back, you see a green thing in the distance. Where are we standing here? Are we right close to the individual author? In which case, it's the author's voice, not the Canadian voice. Do we stand back a little bit and see a region? Do we say there's a Quebec voice, an Ontario voice? Do we put Alice Munro's stories, Matt Cohen's *The Disinherited*, Robertson Davies's novels, Graeme Gibson, James Reaney, and Marian Engel all together in a corral and say, "Southern Ontario Gothic"? This I've done. I've taught such a course twice, once in Alabama, and once in New York. Very teachable. There they are, and yes, they have something in common.

Hancock: Would you include yourself in this group?

Atwood: No. I'm not from southern Ontario. My roots are the Maritimes and northern Quebec, not Ontario small town. But these writers are different from the West and from B.C. and the Maritimes.

In the West, Edna Alford, Sandra Birdsell, John Newlove, Sinclair Ross, Margaret Laurence are part of a group you might call "Western realists." Then someone like Gloria Sawai flies in from left field and writes "The Day I Sat With Jesus on the Sundeck and a Wind Came Up and Blew My Kimono Open and He Saw My Breasts." That's an interesting story because the texture of it is like those other people's. The woman talks in the vernacular, very detailed about laundry and household goods. But then in comes Jesus Christ. Within the compass of Western realism, this is a variation on it. But it's somebody playing with the convention; it's not a different animal.

And in B.C., there is more than just one group of writers. The Canadian voice contains all these different things. But if you stand back from it all, you can ask, "Are these the same things that are happening in the United States or England or Australia? Are Quebec stories and poems like the ones from France?" Not from what I've read.

English fiction is all about social class. In English life you can't get away from it. Canadians have a great advantage in England because nobody can tell who they are just from talking to them.

Standing quite far back, you can say, "Yes, there is a Canadian voice." Standing further up, you would say no: only voices.

Hancock: And your own narrative voice?

Atwood: I would hope it's different in various stories. It's not that I manipulate it. That would imply something a great deal more conscious than what I do. I can't talk a lot about how I write, because I don't think about how I write when I'm writing. That's why interviews are suspect. I could make something up for you, but it would be made up.

Hancock: What do you think your strengths are as a writer?

Atwood: I used to say, in the usual Canadian way, "Well, aw shucks, I don't know." We're trained to be modest. But now that I'm middle-aged I'm going to allow myself to say, "Well, maybe I'm good." Not all the time but enough times, I can get the words to stretch and do something together that they don't do alone. Expand the possibilities of the language.

Hancock: And your weaknesses?

Atwood: Weaknesses? We can't afford to think about those kinds of things. Most writers are tightrope-walking over Niagara Falls all the time. Look down and you've had it. If I thought too much about weakness I'd block. //

Hancock: Do you ever discuss works-in-progress?

Atwood: Hardly ever. I discussed bits of *The Handmaid's Tale* with Graeme. He thought I was going bonkers, I think. That's the problem with discussing works-in-progress. They always sound somewhat crazier than they may turn out to be. He kept saying. "You're going to get in trouble for this one." But he egged me on, despite that.

Hancock: Do you see your work as successful in terms of its intention?

Atwood: If I didn't think it was somewhat successful—and let us keep in mind my remarks about perfection—I wouldn't be publishing it. Success is different from perfection.

Hancock: You don't think afterwards, say, at a reading, that you should have taken something out through another draft?

Atwood: The book I would write this year is not ever the same as something I would have written twenty years ago. I wouldn't be writing that book now, whatever it is. I've changed and so has the world. My interests and perceptions have changed. What was of interest to me then would not be of interest to me now. My intentions don't remain constant, so how can a book be expected to live up to my intentions in 1986 when I wrote it in 1964?

Hancock: Do you find with each book you learn some new aspects of fiction? How to use backgrounds, foregrounds, language?

Atwood: No. I don't think you ever know how to write a book. You never know ahead of time. You start every time at zero. It doesn't count for anything that you were able to pull it off before. It means nothing. A former success doesn't mean that you're not going to make the most colossal failure the next time.

Hancock: Does part of the problem perhaps come with the dubiousness of imposing form on the material? One of the great things about the novel is that it ultimately has a form.

Atwood: It can't help but be a "form" because it is smaller than its container, which is the universe. Which is itself a form.

Hancock: Do you like form? Or are you suspicious of form?

Atwood: I don't see why it can't be both at once. That's how I feel about many people, liking and suspicious at once. Let us say that part of the joy is learning to do something you didn't know how to do before. But once you know that and keep repeating it, the joy goes out of it.

Hancock: What is the novel to you?

Atwood: I'm very suspicious of anything beginning with a capital letter, like Man. Or Woman. Or the Novel. I seem to think from the ground up, rather than from the top down. // "Man" for me is the sum total of all men. Therefore, I have a lot of problems with making general statements about them. As for Woman, capital W, we got stuck with that for centuries. Eternal woman. But really, "Woman" is the sum total of women. It doesn't exist apart from that, except as an abstracted idea.

Hancock: When you sit down to write a long fiction, which eventually reaches three or four hundred pages in manuscript, do you stop to think about a series of characters in a number of situations that have to be shaped somehow?

Atwood: "Material" has to be shaped because eventually somebody going to have to read it. Everything has a shape. An amoeba has a shape, though it's rather malleable. There is no such thing as a thing with no shape. It may be a more contained or less contained shape, or an awkward shape, or a graceful shape. It may be sprawling or rectilinear, but there's a shape of some kind which can be described.

Hancock: I bring this up, of course, because the novel, or long fiction, or long narrative, as recently as the '60s went through a phase where it was considered dead and defunct as a form. Then it got revitalized.

Atwood: But did that ever really happen? Wasn't it just what a few people were saying? They said the same thing about God. Prove it. They claimed all this dead novel stuff, and all the while people were writing and reading novels, as usual.

Hancock: *Life Before Man* struck me as particularly interesting for its narrative strategy. You had three principal characters, with specific dates as an organizing device. Did you get that right the first time?

Atwood: I got part of it right the first time. Some books are a "good read." Part of that book was a "good write." I didn't have to go back to square one as I did with several others. I wanted a triangular structure. From the point of view of A, B and C were wrong. From the point of view of B, C and A were wrong. From the point of view of C, A and B were wrong. I wanted a nice little triangle. That part was not difficult to do.

But *Lady Oracle* was originally written in the second person. It was written as a letter to Arthur. I would have been in the rather stupid position of having the narrator tell Arthur things he already knew. It does end up being a story told to somebody else, but you don't figure out who that person is until the end. It isn't Arthur; it's the guy she beans with the bottle.

I took a couple of runs at *Surfacing* in 1964 or 1965. It was the same time I was writing *The Edible Woman*. I've got several beginnings of what eventually turned into *Surfacing*. It was quite different. It was in the third person. The characters were different, though there were four of them. The woman was older. The other woman was her sister. The first complete write-through was quite bad. I had to go back and rearrange things so that there was more going on. My problem is that I get so fascinated by description and details I forget about anything happening; I have several unfinished novels with that problem. They have wonderful descriptions of things, but nothing actually occurs for a long time.

Once I tried to write a novel from the point of view of eight different characters. That was dandy and I had nice descriptions. But after 250 pages, no events had occurred. If I had followed out my scheme, the novel would have been about 1,500 pages long. It wouldn't have worked.

The Handmaid's Tale is organized partly by the repeated "Night" sections. There are periods of action, punctuated by periods of reflection.

Hancock: Does there have to be event in a novel?

Atwood: Yes, if you want people to actually read it. You can do various "theoretical" works and experiments which will be of interest to a very few people interested in dead ends and what doesn't work. The Andy Warhol movie about sleep is more interesting as an idea than it is as something you'd want to sit through for twelve hours.

Hancock: To deal with events, do you have to look carefully at your characters, their motivations, their psychological makeup?

Atwood: Characters don't just sit in a chair. Everybody has to get up to pee once in a while. Unless, of course, you want to write a novel from the point of view of someone who has had a total lobotomy. Or has no brain and is immobile. Or is in a catatonic trance. In those cases, if you have anything in the novel at all, it has to be unconscious inner event. But it's still event. Something is still happening.

Hancock: Do you try for what T. S. Eliot called "the objective correlative"? To try to reproduce in the reader the same emotional state as the characters?

Atwood: That's evocation, rather than representation. Certainly, that's what any successful piece of writing does. It evokes from the reader. It's not a question even of self-expression, of the writer expressing his or her emotions. Who really cares? You can say the writer felt this, the writer felt that. But unless you can evoke that emotion from the reader, it's merely a statement. //

Hancock: Does a novelist have a social conscience?

Atwood: I never met one without. Even Robbe-Grillet, who was somebody who tried for pure, objective, value-free depiction, is making a statement. You can't show a character doing anything without expecting the reader to have some view about that, because readers live in a society and make moral judgments. "John took an ax and he chopped off Mary's head." For you, the reader, is that good or bad? You are going to react one way or another. The way you react to it is going to depend upon what you already know about Mary, about John. You cannot put those words on paper without in some way engaging the reader's moral sense—supposing the reader has one, and I've never met a reader yet who has no moral sense at all.

Hancock: Does art have to be moral?

Atwood: It is, whether the artist tries to be or not. Even Oscar Wilde was making a moral statement when he said, "Morality is boring, and what I'm after is the beautiful." That in itself is a statement about morality. I'm afraid that engagement is unavoidable. How you handle or approach it is something else again. You can take the Oscar Wilde stance. Or you say, "What I'm after is pure form." By saying that, you imply the moral dimension is not important to your art. Or you can say, "The social conscience is innate; therefore, I will be out on the table about it, and these are the bad guys; let's all spit on the bad guys." However, the closer you get to that view, the closer you get to propaganda. That doesn't mean that art with some moral sense is inevitably propaganda.

Hancock: That argument between form and morality created a tremendous debate in American literature.

Atwood: I know, but I found it so unnecessary. Apostles of the obvious. Even fabulist fictions are moral. They are among the most moral of things. What's more moral than a fairy tale? Science fiction is dripping with message. But if something is only that, then we feel we're being preached to and we resent it. //

Hancock: I just read "Walking on Water" the other night, in *Chatelaine*.

Atwood: That's one of the "Emma" stories.

Hancock: Could you tell me a bit about those stories?

Atwood: Emma is a character who doesn't think a lot. She does things, but she doesn't think about them in great detail. She's not an internal character. Sometimes one gets tired of writing the various ratiocinations of the characters and wants to show a character in action, as it were.

The Emma stories are very heavy on event, light on Emma's inner world. I have known women like this. Usually, we think of female characters as fearful and timorous. But I have known women who really would do anything. Walk up cliffs, and other foolhardy things. It was interesting to write about something like that. Such people interest me, particularly when they are women, because it goes against their socialization. I don't know if I could write a novel or a whole book of stories in that way.

Hancock: Would that be because of market demands?

Atwood: Nothing I do has anything to do with market demands, except in the TV script department. That's my substitute for teaching at university. Teaching university has a lot to do with market demands! But I've always felt my writing was somewhat eccentric. It has been strange that I have acquired the audience I have. Or the audiences, whoever they may be. Literary writers don't usually get those audiences. But I'm not in the position, for instance, of going to magazines or publishers and asking them what I should write fiction about. I've never done that. I've never had to.

Hancock: The story collections seem carefully structured. For example, *Bluebeard's Egg* is nicely framed with the two parent stories. Among many things, these are stories of the natural world framing the urban world of the other stories. Was it planned that way?

Atwood: I wrote all the stories before I arranged them. It's not a question of having to write this or that to make it nice. I usually spread them all out on the floor and see how they look best to me. It seemed evident those stories should be like that. It's like those psychological tests they give you, with different shapes and colors which they ask you to arrange into a pattern according to shape, color, and size.

Hancock: Would you find the main drama for your characters is in their anxieties?

Atwood: The Emma character isn't very anxious. But she gets into situations that would make us anxious. In one story, she almost drowns. In another story, her boyfriend almost drowns. I don't know why they are always almost drowning. Why can't they burn up?

Hancock: I was going to ask you a drowning question. Drowning occurs in *Surfacing*, "This Is a Photograph of Me," "Walking on Water," the other Emma story, "Death of a Young Son by Drowning," "Procedures from Underground," *Lady Oracle*. It seems a powerful image for you.

Atwood: I grew up by a lake. People drowned in it. I know some people who have drowned, or nearly drowned. Canada is full of water. There's just a lot of drowning going on. Now, if you have your choice about how people die in natural accidents in Canada, it's most likely to be by drowning. Look at the statistics. But you don't have to look at them. Look at your own life. How many people do you know who have burnt up in a fire, compared with those who have died in plane crashes, compared with those who have drowned or almost drowned? Is it not so?

Hancock: The women in both *Dancing Girls* and *Bluebeard's Egg* are rich in anxieties.

Atwood: Show me a character totally without anxieties and I will show you a boring book.

Hancock: This in itself raises questions about what is the nature of fiction.

Atwood: What is good fiction? Well, first it has to hold the attention of the reader; not all readers, but what we can call the suitable reader. Once upon a time, a long time ago, I took a course in the eighteenth-century novel of sensibility. I read all kinds of things of the period. One of them was *Sir Charles Grandison*, by Richardson, who had previously written *Pamela* and *Clarissa*. *Sir Charles* starts out at a cracking pace. The heroine is almost abducted from a stagecoach. Unfortunately, to the reader's great dismay, she gets rescued by Sir Charles. For the rest of this 600-page novel Sir Charles is perfect. The heroine notices this and that instance of his politeness, his gentleness, his generosity, his perfection, his chivalrousness, but that's about it. I think I've met only one other person who has finished it. I finished it only because I was not going to let this defeat me; I was going to jolly well get through to the end to see if anything of any interest happened whatsoever.

People ask me, "Why do your characters have these problems?" If the characters have no problems, what's the book going to be about? The problem has to be an internal one, or a problem with another character or an external problem like the Great White Shark, or the end of the world, or the people from Mars, or vampires. Something has to be there to disturb the stasis. Think of a play in which the characters do nothing at all, ever, throughout the whole play. The question then becomes: granted that something has to happen in a novel, why do certain kinds of things happen in my novels, while other things happen in other people's novels? That's the question, not why does *anything* happen.

Hancock: From a content point of view, something has to happen. The "and then, and then," and how and why.

Atwood: The "and then, and then" is basic. But if you don't do that well enough, the how and the why aren't going to interest anybody because there will be absolutely no reason to keep reading the thing.

Hancock: Do you concern yourself with getting the right scenes in the right order and then the right words in the right order?

Atwood: Probably the two things happen at once. I seem to write in quite different ways. Some stories are beginning-to-end straight write-throughs. Others are built up bit by bit. You can tell by looking at "Significant Moments in the Life of My Mother" that the writing of it was episodic. Sometimes you wake up in the middle of the night with a wonderful phrase or sentence or paragraph. You write it down, but you're not sure where it's going to fit. You find out later, or not, as the case may be. My life is filled with pieces of paper with things written on them that I've never used.

Hancock: Do you block out the action after you've got all those notes?

Atwood: Take, for example. *The Edible Woman.* I wrote it on University of British Columbia exam booklets. There was going to be one booklet per chapter. The booklets were white. I wrote that novel in four months, I find with horror in looking back. Then I revised it. Every day I would ask myself, What is going to happen today to these people? In the place where you plot out your exam question, on the left-hand side, I'd make a list, a few notes, on what she does today. Then I would write the chapter.

But the point to remember is that nothing works, necessarily, dependably, infallibly. No regime, no scheme, no incantation. If we knew what worked, we could sell it as an unbeatable program for writing masterpieces. Writing is very improvisational. It's like trying to fix a broken sewing machine with safety pins and rubber bands. A lot of tinkering.

Hancock: Your short stories are all different. You're not writing the same story over and over.

Atwood: *The New York Times Book Review* called them "wilfully unfashionable" or "wilfully eccentric." But I'm not too sure what is fashionable in the short story these days, nor do I much care.

Hancock: The American story writers move in schools, like fish. Right now, it's minimalist fiction, or "dirty realism," as in the works of Raymond Carver and Ann Beattie and Tobias Wolff.

Atwood: But as soon as that gets defined, it's already on the fade. To call this the "new fiction" is a marketing strategy. But Canada doesn't work this way. Everyone is equally weird.

Hancock: In rereading the stories, I was amazed to find a lot of writing about writing. "Giving Birth" for example, has a strong passage about the problem of communicating through language. That's a central concern with *Murder in the Dark*.

Atwood: So it was in *Surfacing*, and to some extent, *The Edible Woman* as well.

Hancock: Is that all interest in theory, or postmodernist concerns?

Atwood: None of the above. As I've said, I'm not very theoretical in my approach to what I do. As a theorist, I'm a good amateur plumber. You do what you have to do to keep your sink from overflowing. I tried for the longest time to find out what *deconstructionism* was. Nobody was able to explain it to me clearly. The best answer I got was from a writer, who said, "Honey, it's bad news for you and me."

Hancock: That's because the text is often deconstructed back to the author.

Atwood: What it also means is that the text is of no importance. What is of interest is what the critic makes of the text. Alas, alack, pretty soon we'll be getting to pure critical readings with no text at all.

I don't have to do that, because I don't have to sell my bod on the academic market. I'm not going to get tenure depending on whether or not I'm in the swim. I think I'd just embarrass everybody by asking those kinds of questions.

Let me put it this way. One of my early jobs was taking those recondite, verbose market-research interviews written by psychologists and translating them into language that the average person interviewed could understand. So it was breaking down "psychologese" into simpler units that could be understood by somebody not a professional in the field. That's impossible to do with certain kinds of things. You can get a rendition of advanced physics, but it is just a rendition.

With literary criticism, I really feel that it ought to be graspable. It should not be full of too many of those kinds of words which only the initiated can understand. It's fun for the initiated to have a language which means something to them and to them alone. It means you can one-up people, and it's a closed circle; you can be declared in or out depending on whether you are using the current language. These things do have a habit of rolling over about every five years.

Hancock: That criticism aside, with all its inherent truths, your work is starting to be read that way.

Atwood: You can read any text any way. You can read it standing on your head. You can use it for toilet paper. It's not a statement about the text. It's a statement about the user.

Hancock: To come back to *Surfacing*, or "Giving Birth," or *Murder in the Dark*, your own prose draws attention to more than just the story, with a character and a particular situation. The prose itself says there's a problem of communicating through language. It implies a distrust of words, that there's a distrust of language, that language is a distortion.

Atwood: Language is a distortion.

Hancock: Do you mean we can't trust language to get through to "truth"?

Atwood: That's true. Although I've used language to express that, it's true. I think most writers share this distrust of language—just as painters are always wishing there were more colors, more dimensions. But language is one of the few tools we do have. So we have to use it. We even have to trust it, though it's untrustworthy.

Hancock: That's an interesting paradox.

Atwood: The question is, How do we know "reality"? How do you encounter the piece of granite? How do you know it directly? Is there such a thing as knowing it directly without language? Small babies know the world without language. How do they know it? Cats know the world without what we would call language. How are they experiencing the world? Language is a very odd thing. We take it very much for granted. But it's one of the most peculiar items that exists. People start to feel that there's some kind of inherent meaning in a particular word. Like "apple." People start to think there's something of *an apple* in the word "apple." But if so, why is it called something else in fifty-seven other languages?

Hancock: As *The Feminist Dictionary* points out, language is now being reevaluated, to find out how language has been maligned and changed through usage. For example, the word "gossip" was originally the dialogue between mother and a midwife. And "trivia" is derived from Trivia, Goddess of the Crossroads, where women traditionally exchanged news. But "gossip" and "trivia" are now seen as negative terms, where they were once positive.

Atwood: Not only is language slippery, but it's limited. The vocabulary we have is limited. There are a lot of things we don't have words for.

Hancock: Perhaps there is something "universal" beneath language. Gabriel Garcia Marquez's *One Hundred Years of Solitude* had an equal impact on Michel Tremblay in Quebec and Jack Hodgins in B.C. (not to mention other writers around the world), though neither read it in Spanish.

Atwood: How did it do among the Inuit? Or the Chinese? It's true you can translate things, sort-of, so that they can kind-of be read. But efforts to translate *haiku* have always frustrated me. I know perfectly well that the English translation of the Japanese may give the literal words. Yet the piece is totally lacking in the resonance you get from a knowledge of the tradition, a knowledge of the culture. "Plum blossoms floating down the stream." What does that mean to you? Not a great deal. It lacks a rich cultural compost. Every piece of writing exists in its surround. It comes out of that surround. It has meaning in the surround. You can take it out of there and look at it. An Assyrian sculpture, a figure of a winged bull with the head of a man, is interesting to look at. But it has nowhere near the meaning for us that it had for whoever made it. We don't know who that person is. We don't know his story. We don't know what magical powers he may have thought the figure possessed. It still has some meaning for us. But it's a different meaning for us. //

Hancock: We don't even know how to "read" a Chinese restaurant in Toronto. The dragons on the wall, the Fo dogs which represent Yin and Yang, the tree figures that represent health, wealth, and longevity. There's something tricky about language.

Atwood: There's something tricky about "reality," let alone language. Insofar as language relates to a cultural experience of reality, to what extent is that transmissible? To what extent can you translate that into another language and have it understood? I'm now translated into over twenty languages, only two of which I can read, more or less. I have no idea what those other versions are saying, to the people who read them.

Hancock: *Murder in the Dark* doesn't have a "plot," but it does have a "character" in the narrative voice in the four parts. Did you make a decision not to plot the book?

Atwood: I was just having fun. Sorry to be so idiotic about this. I know "serious" writers aren't supposed to say things like that.

I started writing these little mini-fictions and little pieces of prose that were not connected to a "plot." They were connected in the way that verses in a lyric poem were connected, or like sections in a long narrative poem. It's not a question of A to B to C to D to E. It's a question of these units existing by themselves, but having a certain vibration with the ones they are placed with.

Hancock: Did that create any technical problems?

Atwood: I wasn't doing them on purpose. I started writing them—fooling around. Then it occurred to me, at some point near the end, that this was probably a book.

Hancock: Michael Benedikt, who edited an anthology of prose poems some years ago, claims the prose poem never really settled down in the English language. That it was something exclusively French, Spanish, or Italian. Generally speaking, we don't see that many prose poems in English in Canada.

Atwood: It's unfortunate. I found they were excellent for readings. Some of them have enough of a plot that you don't have the problem you have with a poetry reading. You can't read very much poetry without people's eyes glazing over. The level of concentration required is so great you can't do it for an hour. I can't listen to a poetry reading for an hour no matter how good it is. I just can't. My attention gets burned out in the first half-hour. Some of the prose poems are funny enough or have another line that isn't lyrical, so they don't require the absolute kind of distilled concentration that an hour of lyric poetry requires.

Hancock: With *Murder in the Dark*, you come back to those concerns that the writer is a liar, that memory is unreliable, that fiction is a distortion, the unspecified narrator. Would I be stretching a point to say there is a connection between this book and *The Journals of Susanna Moodie*?

Atwood: Susanna Moodie was a specific person for me. I thought you were going to say *Surfacing*, in which the narrator lies and her memory is unreliable. Susanna Moodie doesn't lie. Nor is her memory particularly unreliable. She has two different sides to her personality. The narrator of the first eight chapters of *Surfacing* is much more an unreliable narrator.

Hancock: Are you interested in characters, their names, their psychology, their types?

Atwood: I'm very interested in their names. By that I mean their names don't always readily spring to mind. I have to go looking for their names. I would like not to have to call them anything. But they usually have to have names. Then the question is, if they are going to have names, the names have to be appropriate. Therefore I spend a lot of time reading up on the meanings of names, in books like *Name Your Baby*.

Hancock: What does your name mean?

Atwood: "Pearl." And "of the woods." It's an English name. Quite old. Probably fourteenth century or earlier. From *atter wode*. //

Hancock: When the stories of your characters are unfolding, do you look for that moment when their whole world changes?

Atwood: In a novel you hope there's more than one of those moments. In a short story there may only be one such moment. And it may not be their whole life changing. It may be one thing they've thought which they can no longer think. It may not be their entire life, it may be just an area. I don't have any thoughts about what has to happen in a story beyond the fact that something has to happen.

Hancock: Do you have to know more about a character than you can actually tell?

Atwood: I have to know more than I actually tell. Lots more. I get bogged down in detail. I try to tell too much. I try to tell everything about the person. I try to tell too many things about their underclothing and their breakfast foods. I often have to cut some of that out.

Hancock: When the something that is going to happen happens, what is it? Something as basic as an antagonist? Or a social situation?

Atwood: It depends on the story. There are hundreds of possibilities, and many ways of arranging them. That's what I was playing with in, for instance, "Happy Endings." You could start at any point in the story. You could start at the end if you wanted to, then go back and show how that end was arrived at. //

Hancock: Many of your stories, both long and short, are built around shifting identities, the various personas the characters create. You often organize your books around a split point of view. First and third persons, contradictions within the characters, fractured identities. Is that how you see characters?

Atwood: It would depend upon the character. But probably I do them that way because I get bored with writing in the first person, so I switch to the third. I get bored with writing in the present tense, so I switch to the past. I get bored with having just a single narrator, so I have three instead of one. A lot of this is trying to keep oneself amused, isn't it? I don't like to feel I'm doing the same thing over and over. I would die of boredom if I felt I were doing that. I like to try things that are hard for me. That's despite laziness. //

Hancock: Someone said that the center of your work is the power of language to transform our perception of how the world works.

Atwood: I'll buy that, I'll endorse that one! I've got to endorse something in this interview. Whoever said that, it's true.

Hancock: Are you interested in boundary lines? Is there a point where poetry and prose merge? Become something different? Prose looks a certain way, as do poetry and drama. Perhaps there's a point where they run together?

Atwood: Probably there is.

Hancock: I mention this because someplace you wrote that in fiction you were "a curious bemused disheartened observer of society," but you felt differently when you wrote poetry.

Atwood: Probably I do. But I'm not very good at analyzing what I feel like when I do those things. Probably different parts of the brain are involved. If you could hook up somebody's brain while they are in the throes of composing a poem, and hook up the same brain while that person was writing a novel, I'd expect you'd find brain activity in different areas. I think poetry is written more on the right side of the brain, that is, the left-handed side. That side of the brain is sadder than the other side, according to researchers.

Hancock: I'd like to discuss layers and levels in your work. I'll let the explicators get into the depth of *The Handmaid's Tale*.

Atwood: They haven't got around to it yet. The book is still on the level of popular reaction. The explicators haven't had time to get in there and explicate it a lot.

Hancock: Are you glad?

Atwood: None of it has much of an impact on me, to tell the truth. If I were to obsessively read everything everybody wrote on me, I'd go nuts. You couldn't keep up with it and remain sane as a writer.

Hancock: Why do you suppose people want to write about you and your work? There's at least five books now, countless scholarly essays, graduate theses, and a clipping file I've seen is about two feet thick.

Atwood: You got me. Better to ask them. Why do people collect stamps? There is indeed an impressive amount of work. But I don't put them up to it. This is something they do on their own hook. So either they find it pleasurable, or they find it of interest. But it's not up to me to say why they do it.

Hancock: Some people might see you and your work as a nodal point, a focal point of all our interests and concerns.

Atwood: It has certainly been seen as that. But it's not something I did on purpose. Or put them up to doing. It's just one of those things. Maybe it's because of my horoscope. Jupiter in the tenth house—very lucky for a career.

Hancock: Do you follow astrology closely?

Atwood: I know how to do it. I can also read palms. I was taught all this by a Dutch art historian whose specialty was Hieronymus Bosch. She had to know these things because they are built into medieval works of art. A ring on a certain finger means something. When Hieronymus Bosch paints the Last Judgment with the stars in the sky in a particular pattern, the pattern means something. So there we were in Edmonton, during a winter when the temperature didn't go above zero F in a whole month; she lived downstairs, and we did this to pass the time.

Hancock: Do you want to talk about *The Handmaid's Tale*?

Atwood: When I first started thinking about it, I thought it was such a whacko idea. I wrote it with some trepidation. It could have been the worst failure you could possibly imagine. I was afraid people would say it was stupid, silly. There was also the risk it would be thought feminist propaganda of the most outrageous kind, which was not really what I intended. I was more interested in totalitarian systems, an interest I've had for a long time. I used to read Second World War stuff in the cellar when I was twelve or thirteen, for instance.

Hancock: Did the idea that the book is about now, written as if it's the future, told in the past tense, complete with epilogue, create a problem? Do you think you might go in a further direction, like Russell Hoban's *Riddley Walker*, and create a new language for the future?

Atwood: I didn't think that language would be that different twenty years from now. I would never have written *Riddley Walker* because I don't believe after the big bang, supposing we have one, that there will be anybody walking around. I wouldn't have written a post-atomic-war book. So I didn't change the language much, because in the nature of things it wouldn't have changed much, except for the slogans, greetings, etc. Anyway, the character telling the story was brought up in *our* time, in *our* language.

Hancock: Could you tell me about the tape recording as a device in *The Handmaid's Tale*?

Atwood: I had to do it that way. The paper and pencil supply would have been quite limited. It also allowed for the discontinuous, episodic nature of the narrative.

Hancock: Could you tell me about your use of scenes as narrative units? Characters, suspense, tone of voice, thematic concerns are all compressed into short units. The gap is just as important as the text.

Atwood: You're dealing with a character whose ability to move in the society was limited. By the nature of her situation, she was very circumscribed. She couldn't communicate well with people. It was too dangerous. She was boxed in. How do you tell a narrative from the point of view of that person? The more limited and boxed in you are the more important details become. If you are in jail in solitary, the advent of a rat can be pretty important to you. Details, episodes separate themselves from the flow of time in which they're embedded—a flow which tends to be monotonous—and become significant, luminous.

Hancock: The epilogue was interesting. It was back to splitting the point of view.

Atwood: I did that for several reasons. For instance, the character herself was so circumscribed that there were a number of things about the society she could not know. If she started telling us, the readers, about it, we would have thought, Balderdash, how could she know all this? The newspapers are censored, TV is censored, she can't talk to anyone, how can she know all this? So there were things the reader had to know that she couldn't tell us. Especially things that took place afterwards. Also, I'm an optimist. I like to show that the Third Reich, the Fourth Reich, the Fifth Reich did not last forever.

In fact, Orwell is much more optimistic than people give him credit for. He did the same thing. He has a text at the end of *1984*. Most people think the book ends when Winston comes to love Big Brother. But it doesn't. It ends with a note on Newspeak, which is written in the past tense, in standard English—which means that, at the time of writing the note, Newspeak is a thing of the past.

Hancock: *The Handmaid's Tale* is going to be turned into a screenplay.

Atwood: Harold Pinter is writing it, which is very interesting. If anybody can do it, he can. One of his specialties is scenes in which people don't say very much, but convey meaning anyway.

Hancock: Do you embed things in the fiction? I've noticed all these elements of folk tales, Gothic tales, fairy tales.

Atwood: I sometimes embed private jokes. Or little sketches of people I know; they know I've done it, they get a kick out of it. Sometimes, like Alfred Hitchcock, I make cameo appearances. I put myself into *The Edible Woman*—I'm the female graduate student dressed in black, the one who appears at the party and talks about Death.

Hancock: Do you do that after you've got the story-line under control, and the characters are off to meet their destiny, wherever that may be?

Atwood: It's more an impulse towards whimsy. It's like the Gothic cathedrals, where the carvers put imps under the skirts of the angels. Those are my bits of "imperfection," I suppose.

Hancock: Are characters in a natural environment more religious or spiritual? Is that where you find the gods, or the goddesses, or the God?

Atwood: Not usually in church, you'll notice. I can't say the established religions have a terribly good track record. Most of them have quite a history of doing people in—not to mention their attitude towards women.

Hancock: Do you want to say anything about the religious and mystical side of Nature?

Atwood: I don't know if there is one, any more than there is a mystical side to anything. The mysticism is in the eye of the mystic—not necessarily in the stone or the tree or the egg. Or let's say it has to be a two-way street. If we had a sacred habit of mind, all kinds of things would be "sacred." Most are not at present. We would be able to see *into* things rather than merely to see things. We would see the universe as alive. But you're more likely to find such moments in my poetry than my prose.

Hancock: Where does your interest in prehistory come from?

Atwood: As kids, we were fascinated with the idea of things that existed before there were any people. We used to build little plasticine panoramas of dinosaurs. As for aboriginal people, and early inhabitants and lost caves, I think that was the fantasy life of children before there was television. //

Hancock: And your interest in museums?

Atwood: I used to attend the Saturday morning classes at the Royal Ontario Museum. Museums are collections of memories. Each one is like a giant brain. I used to go there with a little girl whose father was an archaeologist and worked there, so we used to wander all over the place by ourselves, after hours.

Hancock: You like to work with closed spaces in your stories.

Atwood: Some stories do, some don't. It's more likely to be the inner space of the character that's enclosed, not the actual space. *Surfacing* takes place mostly outdoors.

Hancock: Are you comfortable with your style?

Atwood: I've never been comfortable with my "style"—by which I mean that I'm never sure I have exactly the right words in exactly the right order. But I don't think I have just one style. //

People sometimes assume that because I have a larger audience than is usual for a literary writer, I must be writing non-literary books. You do get that form of snobbery from this or that mandarin of letters. But the truth is that I am a literary writer who has acquired, Lord knows how, a larger than usual audience for such things.

Hancock: Would you risk losing that audience?

Atwood: Since I didn't go about acquiring it on purpose, and since I don't write down to the reader, and since I never expected

I would acquire it, it doesn't really concern me. If I lose it, I lose it. Probably it would depress me if I wrote a book that was universally loathed. But you take that chance with any book, don't you?

Hancock: One final question: do you have an optimistic sense of resolution? Is there hope in art? In the bigger sense of comedy as life affirmation?

Atwood: Hope for what? Let's put it this way. When I finish a book I really like, no matter what the subject matter, or when I see a play or film, like Kurosawa's *Ran*, which is swimming in blood and totally pessimistic, but so well done, I feel very good. I *do* feel hope. It's the *well-doneness* that has that effect on me. Not the conclusion—not what is said, *per se*. For instance, the end of *King Lear* is devastating, as a statement about the world. But seeing it done well can still exhilarate you.

If you are tone-deaf, you are not going to get much out of Beethoven. If you are color-blind, you won't get much of a charge out of Monet. But if you have those capabilities, and you see something done very, very well, something that is true to itself, you can feel for two or three minutes that the clouds have parted and you've had a vision, of something of what music or art or writing can do, at its best. A revelation of the full range of our human response to the world—that is, what it means to be human, on earth. That seems to be what "hope" is about in relation to art. Nothing so simple as "happy endings."

It's about other things as well, of course, and it's much more complex than I can begin to analyze. But what you're really waiting for, when you read, when you listen, when you look, when you write, is that moment when you feel, "Hot damn, that is so well done!" An approach to perfection, if you like. Hope comes from the fact that people create, that they find it worthwhile to create. Not just from the nature of what is created.

Waltzing Again

Earl G. Ingersoll

Earl G. Ingersoll's interview was conducted by mail in November 1989 and originally appeared in *The Ontario Review* 32 (Spring-Summer 1990). Copyright © 1990 by *The Ontario Review*. Reprinted by permission.

Ingersoll: Since as you know I've been working on a collection of your interviews, could we begin by talking about interviews? You have been interviewed very frequently. How do you feel about being interviewed?

Atwood: I don't mind "being interviewed" any more than I mind Viennese waltzing—that is, my response will depend on the agility and grace and attitude and intelligence of the other person. Some do it well, some clumsily, some step on your toes by accident, and some aim for them. I've had interviews that were pleasant and stimulating experiences for me, and I've had others that were hell. And of course you do get tired of being misquoted, quoted out of context, and misunderstood. You yourself may be striving for accuracy (which is always complicated), whereas journalists are striving mainly for hot copy, the more one-dimensional the better. Not all of them of course, but enough.

I think the "Get the Guest" or "David and Goliath" interview tends to become less likely as you age; the interviewer less frequently expects you to prove you're a real writer, or a real woman, or any of the other things they expect you to prove. And you run into a generation of interviewers who studied you in high school and want to help you hobble across the street, rather than wishing to smack you down for being a presumptuous young upstart.

Let's not pretend however that an interview will necessarily result in any absolute and blinding revelations. Interviews too are an art form; that is to say, they indulge in the science of illusion.

Ingersoll: You've said that when you began writing you imagined you'd have to starve in an attic without an audience sufficiently large to support your writing. Is there a Margaret Atwood who would have preferred the obscurity of a Herman

Melville to whom you refer so frequently, or do you draw upon your readers' responses to your work? How much do you feel involved in a kind of dialogue with your readers?

Atwood: The alternative, for me, to selling enough books or writing enough scripts and travel articles to keep me independent and to buy my time as a writer would be teaching in a university, or some other job. I've done that, and I've been poor, and I prefer things the way they are. For instance, this way I can say what I want to, because nobody can fire me. Not very many people in our society have that privilege.

I did not expect a large readership when I began writing, but that doesn't mean I'm not pleased to have one. It doesn't mean either that I write for a "mass audience." It means I'm one of the few literary writers who get lucky in their lifetimes.

My readers' responses to my work interest me, but I don't "draw upon" them. The response comes after the book is published; by the time I get responses, I'm thinking about something new. Dialogue with the readers? Not exactly. Dickens could have a dialogue with his readers that affected the books when he was publishing his novels in serial form, but we've lost that possibility. Though it does of course cheer me when someone likes, appreciates, or shows me that he or she has read my books intelligently.

Ingersoll: Are you worried by self-consciousness as you write? Or is it an asset?

Atwood: Self-consciousness? Do you mean consciousness of my self? That's what you have to give up when writing—in exchange for consciousness of the work. That's why most of what writers say about how they write—the process—is either imperfect memory or fabrication. If you're paying proper attention to what you're doing, you are so absorbed in it that you shouldn't be able to tell anyone afterwards exactly how you did it. In sports they have instant replay. We don't have that for writers.

Ingersoll: *The Edible Woman, Lady Oracle,* and now *Cat's Eye* seem in large part *jeux d'esprit.* You give your readers the impression that you are having a good time writing—it's hard work, but also good fun. How important is "play" to you in writing? Do you have a sense of how much the reader will enjoy what you write, as you're writing it?

Atwood: I don't think *Cat's Eye* is a *jeu d'esprit*. (Oxford Shorter: "a witty or humorous trifle.") In fact, I don't think my other "comic" novels are *jeux d'esprit*, either. I suspect that sort of definition is something people fall back on because they can't take women's concerns or life patterns seriously; so they see the wit in those books, and that's all they see. Writing is *play* in the same way that playing the piano is "play," or putting on a theatrical "play" is play. Just because something's fun doesn't mean it isn't serious. For instance, some get a kick out of war. Others enjoy falling in love. Yet others get a bang out of a really good funeral. Does that mean war, love, and death are trifles.

Ingersoll: *Cat's Eye* strikes me as unusual in one especially dramatic way: it builds upon the most detailed and perceptive exploration of a young girlhood that I can recall having read. Once we've read that section of the novel, we readers might think, we've had fiction which explores this stage of young boyhood, but why haven't writers, even writers who are women, dealt with this stage of a woman's development before? How did you get interested in this area of girlhood, from roughly eight to twelve?

Atwood: I think the answer to this one is fairly simple: writers haven't dealt with girls age eight to twelve because this area of life was not regarded as serious "literary" material. You do get girls this age in *juvenile* fiction—all those English boarding-school books. And there have been some—I'm thinking of *Frost in May*. But it's part of that "Man's love is of man's life a thing apart, / 'Tis woman's whole existence" tendency—that is, the tendency to think that the only relationships of importance to women are their dealings with men (parents, boyfriends, husbands, God) or babies. What could be of importance in what young girls do with and to one another? Well, lots, it seems, judging from the mail....I guess that's where "dialogue with the readers" comes in. Cordelia really got around, and she had a profound influence on how the little girls who got run over by her were able to respond to other women when they grew up.

I sometimes get interested in stories because I notice a sort of blank—why hasn't anyone written about this? *Can* it be written about? Do I dare to write it? *Cat's Eye* was risky business, in a way—wouldn't I be trashed for writing about little girls, how trivial? Or wouldn't I be trashed for saying they weren't all sugar and spice?

Or I might think about a story form, and see how it could be approached from a different angle—*Cinderella* from the point of view of the ugly sister, for instance. But also I wanted a literary home for all those vanished *things* from my own childhood—the marbles, the Eaton's catalogues, the Watchbird Watching You, the smells, sounds, colors. The textures. Part of fiction writing I think is a celebration of the physical world we know—and when you're writing about the past, it's a physical world that's vanished. So the impulse is partly elegiac. And partly it's an attempt to stop or bring back time.

Ingersoll: The reviewer in *Time* said that "Elaine's emotional life is effectively over at puberty." Does that seem accurate to you now as a reader of your own work?

Atwood: That ain't the book I wrote, and it ain't the one I read when I go back to it; as I'm doing now, since I'm writing the screenplay. I don't think Elaine's emotional life is over at puberty any more than any of our lives are over then. Childhood is very intense, because children can't imagine a future. They can't imagine pain being over. Which is why children are nearer to the absolute states of Heaven and Hell than adults are. Purgatory seems to me a more adult concept.

There are loose ends left from Elaine's life at that time, especially her unresolved relationship with Cordelia. These things have been baggage for her for a long time. But that's quite different from saying she stopped dead at twelve.

Ingersoll: At the end of *Cat's Eye* Elaine has lost both her parents and her brother, and said goodby finally to her ex- and to Cordelia. She has a husband and daughters she loves, but she seems very alone. What do you make of her aloneness now as a reader of your own novel?

Atwood: Writers can never really read their own books, just as film directors can never really see their own movies—or not in the way that a fresh viewer can. Because THEY KNOW WHAT HAPPENS NEXT.

Elaine "seems" alone at the end of the book because she's on an airplane. Also: because the story has been about a certain part of her life, and that part—that story—has reached a conclusion. She will of course land, get out of the plane, and carry on with the next part of her life, i.e., her ongoing time-line with some other characters about whom we have not been told very much, because the story was not about them.

Why do authors kill off certain characters? Usually for aesthetic, that is, structural reasons. If Elaine's parents had still been around, we would have to have scenes with them, and that wasn't appropriate for this particular story. *Cat's Eye* is partly about being haunted. Why did Dickens kill off Little Nell? Because he was making a statement about the nature of humanity or the cruelty of fate? I don't think so. He just had to polish her off because that was where the story was going.

Ingersoll: Related to that question, a reviewer in *New Statesman* has written: "The novel is extremely bleak about humanity. Through most of the novel you feel distance, dissection: a cat's eye. It ends on a note of gaiety, forgiveness and hope: but I don't believe it." When you were writing the novel did you have the sense of painting a "bleak" picture of "humanity"?

Atwood: One reason I don't like interviews, when I don't like them, is that people tend to come up with these weird quotes from reviewers, assume the quote is true, and then ask you why you did it that way. There are a lot of "when did you stop beating your wife" questions in interviews.

For instance, what is this "gaiety, forgiveness and hope" stuff? I'm thinking of doing a calendar in which each day would contain a quote by a reviewer of which the next day's quote would be a total contradiction by another reviewer. I'll buy the forgiveness, sort of; but gaiety? Eh? Where? The jolly old women on the plane are something she doesn't have. You find yourself looking under the sofa for some other book by the same name that might have strayed into the reviewer's hands by mistake. Or maybe they got one with some of the pages left out.

Nor, judging from the mail I received, did readers "feel distance, dissection." Total identification is more like it. Maybe the readers were identifying with the character's attempt to achieve distance, etc. She certainly attempts it, but she doesn't get it. As for "bleak," that's a word that tends to be used by people who've never been outside Western Europe or North America, and the middle class in either location. They think bleak is not having a two-car garage. If they think I'm bleak, they have no idea of what real bleak is like. Try Kierkegaard. Try Tadeusz Konwicki. Try Russell Banks, for that matter.

Or maybe...yes, maybe...I'm bleak *for a woman*. Is that the key? Are we getting somewhere now?

There Are No Texts without Life
Beryl Langer

In August 1987 Margaret Atwood was writer-in-residence at Macquarie University in Australia. Beryl Langer interviewed her in Sydney during this stay. The interview first appeared in *Australian-Canadian Studies* in 1988. Reprinted with permission.

Langer: The first question I'd like to ask relates to apparent changes in the situation of Australian and Canadian writers. It seems to have become increasingly possible to be a "Canadian writer" or an "Australian writer" in a way that it wasn't thirty years ago.

Atwood: Well, people did it, even though it was supposed not to be possible. What you mean is that it is now possible to be an internationally successful, accepted, and non-ludicrous "Canadian" or "Australian" writer.

Langer: That's right. Now does this mean that we have an increase in something called "cultural nationalism," or, Is it rather that we now have a global culture, where it doesn't really matter whether you're an Australian or a Canadian?

Atwood: It matters. There is no such thing as an international piece of art. Art grows from the ground up, not from the top down. There are pieces of art that can translate from one culture to another, but it is only a translation. You cannot live in a 747 jet all the time; you have to live somewhere more real. Possibly what we're talking about is English language culture, in the States, England, Australia, Africa, New Zealand, the West Indies, people from India who write in English. I don't think it's that it doesn't matter where you come from, because all writers write out of their own ground. They may expand the ground. You may have an Australian traveling in the United States and writing about that, but it will probably still be an Australian traveling in the United States. It's easier to switch gender as an author than it is to switch culture, strangely enough, although gender is prior to culture. It would be easier for you to write as an Australian man than it would be for you to write as an English man, and if you had to write as a southern-American man all you would produce is cliché. You would not have the nuance—of language, of feeling, of cultural experience—available to you at all. It just wouldn't be there. You'd come up with Colonel Sanders, something like that. And similarly, if I were attempting to write as an Australian woman, I simply wouldn't have the details available to men, even of language. What is the washroom called here? *Dunny*? How many years would I have to spend here for me to be able to learn those things which you would have automatically at your disposal? I don't think there is any international art—although there are international artifacts like Coca-Cola bottles. But their significance is different, depending on where you find them. Let me illustrate. What does a Coca-Cola bottle mean to you?

Langer: America.

Atwood: Right! To them it means something they drink. To us it means Coca-Cola-nization. Different. Same artifact, different meaning.

Langer: What do you see as our chances of resisting Coca-Cola-nization?

Atwood: Better for you than for us, although you are less aware. The thing you may have to resist, more than we, is Toshiba-fication. You're going to be under more pressure from Japan in future years. Your governments, or some of them, seem hell-bent on selling you out just as fast as they can.

Langer: To almost anybody who's prepared to pay!

Atwood: To almost anybody who's prepared to pay, and they (Japan) have the most money right now. We have a similar tradition. I think it runs in colonies, because the people who originally came there did not come there thinking of the place as a homeland that they had to protect, but as something to be exploited so that they could make a lot of money and go back and buy castles in Scotland which is what many people who came to Canada did. Unfortunately, both countries, although they have become more nationally aware in recent years, have yet to develop a ruling class which is devoted to their existence and essence. You still get among the upper echelons a certain contempt for the country that they are supposed to represent, a feeling that the real game is elsewhere, that they want to play with the big boys, and the big boys are not Australians. They want to play with people with lots more money, and be taken seriously by those people. It's a great disservice to the country. Unfortunately, if you start talking the other way, you sound like some sort of throwback jingo, but surely there has to be a dialogue which will include respect for oneself without sounding like some sort of we-are-better-than-anybody redneck.

Langer: As ex-British colonies, there are obviously a lot of similarities between Australia and Canada. What do you see as the important differences?

Atwood: Canada is *colder*! It's bigger in population, although the operative English-speaking population of Canada is about the same size as that of Australia. Canada is one-third French, and there are another three million people who don't speak either language. Canada is more ethnically diverse. Australia is an island continent, and Canada is not. It's got the United States directly south of it, and the border between Canada and the United States is the longest undefended border in the world. We are much more subject to American influence than you are because we cannot cut it off. You can pick and choose which American things you will let in and broadcast, but they come pouring across our border whether we like it or not. We're probably under a lot more political pressure from them. We are also closer to England than you are, so we have been, traditionally, toad-in-the-middle between those two, and then France of course has been another player. We're alike in that we're both small countries who have been traditionally non-aggressive, as we are both quite outward-turning. We tune into the world a lot. You notice when you go to the States, in particular, that you start feeling very cut off from world news. Probably because the States has been traditionally somewhat isolationist and self-centered. Even when it wasn't a world power, it was like that. If Canada and Australia had to wait for world news to concern Canadians and Australians, they would have to wait a long time, whereas in the States they mostly only deal with things that concern them.

Langer: So you have a paradox, in that the ostensible provinces are actually less provincial?

Atwood: The provinces are in fact less provincial, to my way of thinking. Ninety-eight per cent of the films shown in the United States are made there. All of the books sold in the United States by American authors are published there, because it is illegal to publish as an American author outside the States and import the books. Did you know that? There's a law against it. They import books from other countries, but not much, and most of the foreign writers read in the United States are published there, partly because American book stores are reluctant to buy foreign-published books. They don't want to be bothered with the hassle.

Langer: What's the American response to your work, insofar as one can generalize?

Atwood: The American response to *The Handmaid's Tale* is that it has now sold about 850,000 copies in paperback, and that was in June, so I imagine in North America it sold a million, if you include Canada. That's quite an amazing response, but in fact my books have been in print steadily ever since publication. They don't go out of print, they just keep going into other editions. This one that sold the most initially, but the others have been selling, all that time.

Langer: Even though your books tend to be fairly critical of the United States?

Atwood: A lot of people in the United States are critical of the United States! I've never met anybody that admits to having voted for Ronald Reagan, for instance. There are a lot of people in the United States who are perfectly wonderful people. That's not the problem. The problem is the foreign policy and the governmental structure, as with all countries. There are people in every country who are wonderful people. It's a question of the government, and what the government does. There's no point hating all the people in the United States. It's stupid to do that, particularly since some of them totally agree with everything you think.

Langer: Do you experience Australia as a visibly more sexist society than Canada? That's certainly the cliché.

Atwood: It is a society which has traditionally fostered a straight-from-the-shoulder "I'm tough, I don't fool around. I don't bother with manners" approach, and that produces its female equivalent as well. For instance, it was Carmen Callil, from Australia, who marched into the English old-boy publishing establishment and shook it up, with Virago, and one of the reasons she was able to do it was that she didn't play by the old-boy rules. Another person from the antipodes, not Australia but New Zealand, who is doing that is Liz Calder. People from the colonies are able to go in there and because they don't have English middle-class women's assumptions—that you have to be nice and polite at all times and play by the rules—they are able to do new things. On the other hand, a lot of those clichés are true. When you watch advertising here you can certainly see a lot of them coming into play. I looked at an Australian Airlines ad, for example, which said "We're Making it Together." Every single one of those people making it together was a man. No women making it together!

Langer: Do you think that your own career might have been rather more difficult in Australia?

Atwood: In Australia? I would have got out, because I'm of that generation. Things here are now changing very quickly. I've noticed an amazing change since 1978, when I first came. I met with some feminists, about ten of them, who were very, very mousy, and feeling very on the outs and very unrepresentative. They felt that people were just laughing at them. When I was back in '82, they were much more visible, and now I notice serious stuff in newspapers. It seems to have gained enough public awareness that it isn't just "Ho, ho, ho. Look at those crazy women being funny." It has certainly gained a lot more grass-roots acceptance, and it probably connects up with that rather tough, confident, Australian woman thing. I met with the *Portfolio* magazine people, and they were not timid, mousy, oppressed women. So now may be the time when that breakthrough is going to be made. As the men become more civilized there's more room in their lives for more expansive relationships with women, but on the man-in-the-street, working-man level, I think it's still pretty much the same as it was. It's mateship, and anybody who's nice to women is a poof, and this kind of thing. I read *How to be Normal in Australia,* and the book certainly is endorsing all those myths. What you are seeing is the growth of a more cultured middle class, and therefore more women of achievement coming out of that middle class, and the men in that class being more accepting of that. And despite all the nasty things people say about the middle class, that's where a lot of the initial movement happens, in any society.

Langer: Your work is usually talked about in terms of the fact that you're a "woman writer" or a "Canadian writer," but do you think it contains a broader political critique?

Atwood: Totally. Of course. Yes. Except when you say "broader political critique" you also have to be specific, because the way class operates in one country is different from another. I don't think there are any classless societies, except possibly stone-age man. In that case it wasn't class. It was seniority, age, and gender, but not whole groups of people banding together and getting more than other groups. I don't think there is any country that doesn't have a class structure, but the class structure is organized along different lines everywhere, and the signs and symptoms of it are different. It's totally erroneous, for instance, to say that the United States has no class structure. The ways of moving in it are different from the ways of moving in the English class structure, and there is a lot less class loyalty among the "working class." They want to get out and move up if they can.

Langer: Would you see Canada as more like the United States in that regard?

Atwood: Yes. In England birth still counts for something, although not everything anymore. In Canada and the States, upward mobility is achieved by money and is faster than it is in England. In England it takes maybe two or three generations to make that transition—from despised grocer to acceptable person related to minor aristocracy. In Canada you can do that in one generation—the children of the first-generation immigrants can do it. But since the structure itself is so much more invisible, and looser, you can have a very nice time, thank you very much, anyway. Whereas in England if you are born working class, have a working-class accent, it takes a lot of effort to get out of that, and a lot of people are just stuck in it, particularly now with Thatcherism and unemployment. That's where they are and that's where they're going to stay.

Langer: You've written some fairly devastating satirical comments on middle-class radicals which in a way contrast with what you've said about the middle class being where the movement is. What do you see as the problem with middle-class radicalism?

Atwood: Well, many of the professional radicals have traditionally been middle-class radicals. That's where they come from, because they're the ones with enough education to be able to deal with theory. There haven't been any successful revolutions without a bunch of middle-class radicals involved. Whatever you say about the spontaneous uprisings of the people, the people very rarely spontaneously uprise. The American Revolution had a large middle-class component, so did the French, so did the Russian. On the other hand, middle-class radicals can have theories, but that won't get them anywhere unless they can tie into working-class resentment and inequality. So yes, I think middle-class radicals are silly, or look silly, in situations in which most people are fairly content with their lot and they are not about to agitate.

Langer: Even if perhaps they ought to?

Atwood: Well, what for? If they are getting decent wages, and their little houses and cars and whatnot, what else do they want? In most cases, not bloody much! And in a society like Canada—which doesn't have that inescapable working-class thing, there isn't very much that you could mobilize them to rebel against or for, because what more could they get from it?

Langer: How do you see your association with *This Magazine*, which has a "left nationalist" orientation?

Atwood: It's not card-carrying anything. The reason I support it is that it will publish stuff that nobody else will publish. The Canadian press is quite niminy-piminy. They're not even the *Washington Post*. They're pretty center of the road, middle line, timid, and they just won't break certain stories, or take on certain people, partly because they are those people, by and large. *This Magazine* will, and does. There are a lot of very smart people working for it, and if one believes in freedom of the press then one has to support alternative publications that will do stuff the other ones won't do. They're not weirdo Marxist-Leninist kooks. As I say, they are not card-carrying anything, they aren't ideologues of that toe-the-party-line-no-matter-what, ilk.

Canada has a viable left; the States does not. The remnants of it were snuffed out by McCarthyism and there hasn't really been a viable Left since that—hippie flower children notwithstanding, who were not anything you could call a viable Left, really. What the U. S. tends to throw up are things like the Weathermen, and the Symbionese Liberation Army, which nobody in their right mind is going to endorse because they are too weird. Canada, on the other hand, has a third party. It is the New Democratic Party. It is now top in the polls for the first time in history, as far as I can figure out. There is an alternative, which may be why our voting rate is eighty to ninety per cent and theirs is only fifty per cent in a good year. A lot of people in the States don't vote. They don't vote for anybody because they don't feel they have any choice. Republicans and Democrats are fairly indistinguishable to them.

Langer: In an interview you did in the '70s with Graeme Gibson you talked about the importance of a third way, as opposed to either becoming a victim or becoming a killer, which were the two alternatives posed. Does the New Democratic Party fit into that?

Atwood: Well, that would mean that the Conservatives were killers and the Liberals were victims, whereas it is much more likely that both of them are fairly close and the New Democrats are a little bit different. Canada is a country in which you have to "seize the extreme center" to succeed politically, and if the New Democrats were too far left people wouldn't vote for them. As I say, why rebel, if mostly you've got what you want? Now, there is a growing class of poor people in Canada, as there is in every industrialized country, and the gap between the rich and the poor is widening again, and, as in the States, the middle class is under some pressure, although not as much as there, because we don't run to extremes quite the way they do. We have a lot more social welfare in Canada. We have medicare systems they don't have, except for very poor people. People who get screwed in the States right now are middle-class people who get sick, because they can't get the "poor people" aid and then their money gets all used up until they are bankrupt, then they can get the "poor people" aid. If enough of that goes on they'll get mad enough to change the system. They're not mad enough yet, but if it happens enough then they will become so. But you don't have a radical left or theories that you want to put into practice unless you're motivated and things have to get unpleasant enough that you see some point to it before you will put the energy in.

People tend to think that how they're living is how eternity is going to be, that things will always be like that. In fact, a very small shift in, for instance, gross national product, or mean temperature, or a stock market collapse in Japan, or in the Middle East—there are all kinds of things that aren't under your control whatsoever—can have drastic effects on the way you're able to conduct your daily life. What you have for breakfast, where you live, and whether you have a car or not. All those things can be altered by events not under your control, and if that happens to enough people, panic sets in, and they say, Now is the time for a strong leader and maybe a military dictatorship to "get things back into shape." And that's when you have the danger of totalitarianism coming in. It's only when things are fairly pleasant for enough people that we can afford all this tolerance and kindness and alternative political thinking and liberation for women.

Langer: So you see liberation for women as a precarious achievement?

Atwood: I see it as precarious and based on general prosperity, because you know who goes first in a crunch. You know that when all the men came back from the war the women got kicked out of their jobs to make room for them. Under pressure, you can't depend on human nature to remain the way you think it ought to be. Under pressure people do strange things. They hang people as witches, they riot, they toss out their democratic institutions and put in bad people that you and I don't like.

Langer: So the Republic of Gilead is possibly something that we have to look forward to?

Atwood: Well, it's not out of the question. Possibly they won't bring in the clothing as I have described it, but some of the other things are things that a number of people with political power in the United States have said that they would like to do. When Hitler said those things, people thought at first it was just rhetoric, but I don't think you should ever suppose that what people say they want to do is just rhetoric. If the fundamentalist establishment in the States says that women's place is in the home and that homosexuals deserve death, I don't think that you should ignore that. There are various pressures, forces that will, possibly, come into play, not definitely, but possibly. I expect that AIDS panic has already been used to put in mandatory testing. When people get scared enough they'll agree to all kinds of things they wouldn't agree to before.

Langer: Do you see writers and intellectuals in general as having some special responsibility?

Atwood: Let's say that a very high proportion of them get shot and imprisoned around the world, so governments obviously think that they're in the front line. Why do governments think that? I have no idea. Maybe its because they run off at the mouth in their writerish way. But you can't tell writers that they have to have responsibility. As soon as you do that, as soon as you start dictating to them what they should write about, then you're just like the governments that are telling them what they should write about.

Langer: Tom Wolff made a point in *The Painted Word* about the relation between painting and art theory, and his sense that the relation between the two was somehow reversing, that painting was coming to be determined by theory rather than theory building on painting. Do you see the current directions of literary theory possibly posing a similar problem for writers?

Atwood: No, no, and I don't even see that painting theory poses that kind of problem for painters, because most of it is so impenetrable and stupid that nobody would really pay any attention to it, if they had any brains or talent.

Not all literary criticism is like that; in fact, it has a valid place, but writers who determine their writing because of it are simply lacking other ideas. They're timid and they want to get a badge. They want to have someone saying they're doing "the right thing," so they try to write something that fits that fashion, but that's true mostly of writers who have some connection with academia. There are a lot of writers who don't, and who would you rather read?

Langer: So I take it you're not overly sympathetic to the theories about the death of the author, and to post-structuralist criticism and so on?

Atwood: I think it amuses them. If they enjoy doing it, that's their business. I'm not dead. Neither is any other living author I know of. A lot of it just seems to me a way of saying what everybody knows already. Any author worth their salt knows that what you give the reader is only what is on the page. We all know that. That's what you say in every creative writing class. So what? It doesn't mean you're dead. I think it's also a way of giving critics as much importance as they themselves would like to have. But if they become too impenetrable nobody will read them anyway. Nobody except the military reads documents about anti-personnel weapons—the English itself has been rendered so meaningless— why would you do it for pleasure?

Langer: The other stream of criticism I'd like you to comment on is in feminist critical theory—*l'écriture féminine* and the notion of "writing the difference."

Atwood: I don't know much about it. Writers don't need to know that stuff. Critics need to know it. It's their business. They play games with one another and give papers and go to conferences. That's what they do. But writers don't need to know any of that at all. Any more than children with crayons need to know about painting theory. They draw anyway. Who cares what these other people think about what they draw? They still do it. And in fact if you tell them too much about what they're doing it tends to turn them off and they go and play some other game where people leave them alone. // As one critic, speaking "of the death of the author" said to me—this was real and he wasn't making a joke—"You've written enough to keep us busy for a long time. You don't need to write any more."

Langer: That must have made you feel good!

Atwood: Well, I thought it was quite cheerful. He certainly had a feeling about what my purpose in life was. It was to provide fodder for him. Whoever else I write for, it isn't just for that, and I think once you start writing just for that your work becomes very sterile very quickly.

Langer: Who do you see yourself as writing for?

Atwood: The ideal reader who lives in the sky. But the ideal reader, not the ideal critic.

Langer: Do you think that women writers face problems that are different from male writers', or is writing itself such a problematic activity that it doesn't make much difference?

Atwood: Of course women face problems that are different from the ones faced by male writers because women are different from men. It embarrasses me to say anything so crashingly obvious, but it's true. Women are different from men! We don't know exactly how, apart from the very obvious biological difference. It's interesting to speculate on how much of our behavior is determined by socialization and how much by biology. We don't know. Nobody knows. That's why it's interesting. But, even apart from those kinds of questions, the way women are treated in society is different and therefore their life experience is different. And therefore the material available to the writer is different and the problems are different, and the way women are viewed critically is different. Their level of acceptance is different and their readership is different. All of those things are different. The way a man reads a woman's text is different from the way a woman reads a woman's text. It has to be. The way a woman reads a man's text is different from the way a man reads a man's text. So of course the problems are different.

You have to be better to get level of acceptance A. You have to be better as a mediocre writer to get level of acceptance B. In fact, one of the funnier things that emerged from this whole debate in Canada was that one of the spokespeople for "Life is Bad to Female Writers"' was saying: "We don't have enough mediocre female writers." I said: "Wait a minute!" That's when things get lost sight of, that's when things get really strange. Surely the point ought to be that everybody ought to be trying to be as good as they can, and yes, it's true that Shakespeare rested on the backs of a whole bunch of mediocre Elizabethan playwrights so I suppose the more people playing chess the better the game will get. But, nevertheless, it sounds awfully funny to be caught saying we need more mediocre female writers. One of the social differences is that male writers tend to run in packs, more than female writers have traditionally done. Particularly poets. Men edit the magazines not because someone is keeping the women out, but because the women don't do it. They've got other things to do in their lives, and they don't traditionally push to be the editor of a poetry magazine and they don't traditionally start them, although I now know some who have and in those magazines the ratio of women to men is much more fifty-fifty.

Langer: So patronage networks do operate? // You think that's still the same, even after fifteen years of feminist intervention?

Atwood: No, it's not the *same*. It's a lot more open. But it's still *there*, and you can't disregard that kind of factor. Now, people like me who are "big" girls are not seen as part of the girls' team. They're seen more like the homeroom teacher. You put some of her in because it's a sort of senior writer... But as I say, you have to be better to get there. And then the girls' team calls you a token woman.

Langer: That's what I was going to ask. Does that kind of success, and being a public personage, set up problems in relation to other women?

Atwood: Some problems, yes. People like myself and Alice Munro vastly object to being called token women, because the implication is that they needed one, and they just took any old jellybean out of the bag. The first women who get attacked are the visible ones.

Langer: The last chapter, or epilogue, in *The Handmaid's Tale* seems to me to be a fairly devastating comment on the academic enterprise, and the way it defuses the impact of accounts of human suffering.

Atwood: It's just human nature! You cannot be present in the life experience of someone who lived 250 years ago the way that person was. You can try a bit harder than my academic did, but it is a very hard thing to do. This was brought home to me just this weekend. We were in Tasmania and we went to the Port Arthur penal colony, and that thing is now a tourist attraction. You know, *the* tourist attraction of Tasmania is the Port Arthur Penal Colony, and I thought, These guys must be rolling in their graves. We are coming and strolling around and saying, "Oh wow, look at this. Isn't that amazing, and look what they did here, and isn't that astonishing? And gosh, I never knew that." And it was their lives. It's not our lives. We are after the fact.

Langer: So if it was happening now, it would be a political out-rage and an atrocity, but if it happened in the past it's acceptable.

Atwood: It *is* happening now. Somewhere else. Worse. But we think, in our comforting way, Well, that was 150 years ago. We don't really have to worry about that in our lives now.

Langer: But nonetheless it is there.

Atwood: It's there. It *was* there for them, it is there now elsewhere in the world, but for us it's a tourist attraction. Do you see what I mean? A good historian will try to put you there, try to make you be present at that time. My man is a somewhat different kind of historian. He is the kind who is working on the textual level. He is commenting on the text that he has put together and named.

Langer: So the relation of the text to life, you think, is an important thing to keep hold of?

Atwood: There are no texts without life. Of course, language has ambiguities to it. We all know that. It's part of one of its pleasures, and of course there are subjective readings of texts and what you bring to a text is you and your training and your associations. Of course. But that does not mean that the text has no meaning in itself.

Opening a Door onto a Completely Unknown Space

Mary Morris

Mary Morris's interview was conducted in March 1986 in Princeton, New Jersey, and originally appeared in the *Paris Review* 117 (Winter 1990). Copyright © 1990 by Mary Morris. Reprinted by permission.

Morris: Has the theme of survival always been intrinsic to your work?

Atwood: I grew up in the north woods of Canada. You had to know certain things about survival. Wilderness survival courses weren't very formalized when I was growing up, but I was taught certain things about what to do if I got lost in the woods. Things were immediate in that way, and therefore quite simple. It was part of my life from the beginning.

Morris: When did you make the leap from considering survival to be a physical battle to considering it to be an intellectual or political struggle?

Atwood: When I started thinking about Canada as a country it became quite evident to me that survival was a national obsession. When I came to the States in the '60s I felt that nobody knew where Canada was. Their brother may have gone there to fish or something. When I was at Harvard I was invited as a "foreign student" to a woman's house for an evening for which I was asked to wear "native costume." Unfortunately, I'd left my native costume at home and had no snowshoes. So there I was, without native costume, with this poor woman and all this food, sitting around waiting for the really exotic foreign students in their native costumes to turn up—which they never did because, as everybody knew, foreign students didn't go out at night.

Morris: You've written about the theme of foreignness a good deal.

Atwood: Foreignness is all around. Only in the heart of the heart of the country, namely the heart of the United States, can you avoid such a thing. In the center of an empire, you can think of your experience as universal. Outside the empire, or on the fringes of the empire, you cannot.

Morris: In your afterword to *The Journals of Susanna Moodie* you write that if the mental illness of the United States is megalomania, that of Canada is paranoid schizophrenia. Could you say something more about that?

Atwood: The United States is big and powerful; Canada is divided and threatened. Maybe I shouldn't have said "illness." Maybe I should have said "state of mind." Men often ask me, "Why are your female characters so paranoid?" It's not paranoia. It's recognition of their situation. Equivalently, the United States' feeling that it is big and powerful is not a delusion. It is big and powerful. Possibly, its wish to be even bigger and more powerful is the mentally ill part. Every Canadian has a complicated relationship with the United States, whereas Americans think of Canada as the place where the weather comes from. "Complication" is a matter of how you perceive yourself in an unequal power relationship.

Morris: How do you view Canada and its literature within this political relationship?

Atwood: Canada is not an occupied country. It's a dominated country. Things are more clear-cut in an occupied country—the heroes and the villains are obvious. One of the complicating things, of course, is that the United States will eagerly swallow anything. It's very welcoming; in that way Canadian writers often find that they have a better time in the United States than they do in Canada, because living in Canada is to some extent like living in a small town. They will rally around you when you break your leg, but on the other hand, if you get too big for your britches, well, they perceive it as exactly that. Alice Munro's book, which is titled *The Beggar Maid* in the United States, is called *Who Do You Think You Are* in Canada…as in, "Who do you think you are, behaving like that—the Prime Minister?" The U.S. loves success, the American dream that anybody can be President of the United States or get into *People* magazine. But with Canada, it's much more likely to be: "You know, people might not like it if you did that." There are a lot more snipers in the bushes.

Morris: Where have you been treated better as a writer, would you say?

Atwood: I suffer more vicious attacks, more personal attacks, in Canada, because that's where I'm from. Families have their most desperate fights among themselves, as we know. However, if you look at per capita sales figures, people recognizing me in the street, of course it's more in Canada. If I sold as many books per capita in the United States as in Canada, I'd be a billionaire.

Morris: Is it more difficult for women to get published than men?

Atwood: I'm afraid the question is simply too broad. Do we mean, for instance, in North America, or in Ireland, or in Afghanistan? There are categories other than gender. Age, class, and color, for instance. Region. National origin. Previous publication. Sexual orientation. I suppose we could rephrase the question and ask, Is it more difficult for a first novelist who is female than for her male counterpart, of the same age, class, color, national origin, or location, and comparable talent, whatever that may be? Judging from the experience of Latin American female writers—of which there are many, though few are known in translation—the answer would be, yes. Women in many countries find it difficult to get published at all—consider the Middle East, for instance. Or black women in South Africa. In fact, they find it difficult to write. Or difficult to become educated. The barriers to women writing are often put in place at a very early age and in very basic ways.

But if we're just talking about, say, North America, obviously commercial publishers want to publish things they can sell. Whether such publishers will publish a given book—whether by a man, woman or turtle—depends a lot on what they think its reception will be. I don't think there's an overt policy against books by women, or an overt quota. Much depends on the book, and on the intuition of the publisher. It's true, however, that the majority of books that do appear are still written by men and reviewed by men. Then there's the subject of reviewing. That's where you're most likely to see gender bias, bias of all kinds.

Morris: Is it difficult to write from the point of view of a male?

Atwood: Most of the "speakers" or narrative points of view in my books are those of women, but I have sometimes used the point of view of a character who is male. Notice I try to avoid saying "the male point of view." I don't believe in the male point of view, any more than I believe in the female point of view. There are a good many of both, though it's true that there are some thoughts and attitudes that are unlikely to be held by men, on the one hand, or by women, on the other. So when I do use a male character, it's because the story is about something or someone that can't be otherwise conveyed, or that would be altered if it were to be conveyed through a female character. For instance, I recently published a story in *Granta* called "Isis In Darkness." It's about the relationship—the tenuous relationship, over the years—between a woman poet and a man who has, I guess, a sort of literary crush on her and how the woman affects the man's life. If I'd told it through the woman herself…well, you can't tell such stories about romantic infatuation from the point of view of the object of the infatuation without losing the flavor of the emotion. They would just become "who is that creep hanging around outside the balcony" stories.

Morris: Can you tell the gender of a writer from reading the text alone?

Atwood: Sometimes, certainly, but not always. There's a famous case in England of an Anglican vicar who said he couldn't get anything published. So he wrote under the name of an East Asian woman, and got a novel accepted by Virago. There's a certain amount of opinion around that says, for instance, that women can't or shouldn't write from a male point of view, and so forth. Men are very sniffy about how they're portrayed by women, but the truth is that most of the really vicious, unpleasant male characters in fiction or theater have been written by men. The ethnic joke principle seems to be at work: it's OK to say a man has smelly feet, no ethics, and bad table manners if the writer is a man, but if it's a woman saying exactly the same thing, then she somehow hates men. The male *amour propre* is wounded. And if she writes nice male characters, they're seen as "weak" by other men—though if a man puts a man in the kitchen, that's realism. And on and on.

We have fallen very much into the habit of judging books by their covers. "Authenticity" has become a concern. I tend to side with creative freedom. Everyone should write as she or he feels impelled. Then let's judge the results, not the picture of the author on the back flap.

Your question also assumes that "women" are a fixed quantity and that some men are "better" at portraying this quantity than others are. I, however, deny that the quantity is fixed. There is no single, simple, static "women's point of view." Let's just say that good writing of any kind by anyone is surprising, intricate, strong, sinuous. Men who write stereotyped women or treat them like stuffed furniture or sex aids are portraying something— about their inner lives, perhaps—and that's interesting to know about, up to a point. But it should not be mistaken for life outside the author's head.

Morris: How do the activities of writing poetry and writing prose differ for you?

Atwood: My theory is that they involve two different areas of the brain, with some overlap. When I am writing fiction, I believe I am much better organized, more methodical; one has to be when writing a novel. Writing poetry is a state of free float.

Morris: I have the feeling that you work out problems in your poetry, but that you hold onto the metaphors and dramatize them in your novels.

Atwood: The genesis of a poem for me is usually a cluster of words. The only good metaphor I can think of is a scientific one: dipping a thread into a supersaturated solution to induce crystal formation. I don't think I solve problems in my poetry; I think I uncover the problems. Then the novel seems a process of working them out. I don't think of it that way at the time; that is, when I'm writing poetry, I don't know I'm going to be led down the path to the next novel. Only after I've finished the novel can I say, Well, this poem was the key. This poem opened the door.

When I'm writing a novel, what comes first is an image, scene or voice. Something fairly small. Sometimes that seed is contained in a poem I've already written. The structure or design gets worked out in the course of the writing. I couldn't write the other way round, with structure first. It would be too much like paint-by-numbers. As for lines of descent—that is, poem leading to novel—I could point to a number of examples. In my second collection of poems, *The Animals in That Country*, there's a poem called "Progressive Insanities of a Pioneer." That led into the whole collection called *The Journals of Susanna Moodie*, and that in turn led into *Surfacing*. Or, another line of descent: the poems in parts of *True Stories* have obvious affiliations with the novel *Bodily Harm*. It's almost as if the poems open something, like opening a room or a box, or a pathway.

And then the novel can go in and see what else is in there. I'm not sure this is unique. I expect that many other ambidextrous writers have had the same experience.

Morris: Do writers perceive differently than others? Is there anything unique about the writer's eye?

Atwood: It's all bound up with what sorts of things we have words for. Eskimos, the Inuit, have fifty-two words for snow. Each of those words describes a different kind of snow. In Finnish, they have no "he" or "she" words. If you're writing a novel in Finnish, you have to make gender very obvious early on, either by naming the character or by describing a sex-specific activity. But I can't really answer this question because I don't know how "others" observe the world. But judging from the letters I receive, many others recognize at least part of themselves in what I write, though the part recognized varies from person to person, of course. The unique thing about writers is that they write. Therefore, they are pickier about words, at least on paper. But everyone "writes" in a way; that is, each person has a "story"—a personal narrative—which is constantly being replayed, revised, taken apart, and put together again. The significant points in this narrative change as a person ages—what may have been tragedy at twenty is seen as comedy or nostalgia at forty. All children "write." (And paint and sing.) The real question is, Why do so many people give it up? Intimidation, I suppose. Fear of not being good. Lack of time.

Morris: Why is there so much violence in your work? *Bodily Harm*, in particular.

Atwood: Sometimes people are surprised that a woman would write such things. *Bodily Harm*, for instance, was perceived as some kind of incursion into a world that is supposed to be male. Certainly violence is more a part of my work that it is of Jane

Austen's, or George Eliot's. They didn't do it in those days. Charles Dickens wrote about Bill Sikes bludgeoning Nancy to death, getting blood all over everything, but if a woman had written that, nobody would have published it. Actually, I grew up violence-free, and among people who were extremely civilized in their behavior. When I went out into the wider world, I found violence more shocking than would somebody who was used to it. Also, during the Second World War, although there was no violence in my immediate vicinity, the *angst*—you know, the anxiety about the war—was ever-present. Canada went into the war in 1939, about two months before I was born. The per capita death rate was high.

Morris: Yet you write as if you've lived through violence.

Atwood: But I write as if I've lived through a lot of things I haven't lived. I've never lived with cancer. I've never been fat. I have different sensibilities. In my critical work I'm an eighteenth-century rationalist of some kind. In my poetry I'm not at all. There's no way of knowing in advance what will get into your work. One collects all the shiny objects that catch the fancy—a great array of them; some of them you think are utterly useless. I have a large collection of curios of that kind, and every once in a while I need one of them. They're in my head, but who knows where! It's such a jumble in there. It's hard to find anything.

Morris: Is sex easy to write about?

Atwood: If by "sex" you mean just the sex act—"the earth moved" stuff—well, I don't think I write those scenes much. They can so quickly become comic or pretentious or overly metaphoric—"Her breasts were like apples," that sort of thing. But "sex" is not just which part of whose body was where. It's the relationship between the participants, the furniture in the room or the leaves on the tree, what gets said before and after, the emotions—act of love, act of lust, act of hate. Act of indifference, act of violence, act of despair, act of manipulation, act of hope? Those things have to be part of it.

Striptease has become less interesting since they did away with the costumes. It's become Newtonian. The movement of bodies through space, period. It can get boring.

Morris: Has motherhood made you feel differently about yourself?

Atwood: There was a period in my early career which was determined by the images of women writers I was exposed to— women writers as genius suicides, like Virginia Woolf. Or genius recluses like Emily Dickinson and Christina Rossetti. Or doomed people of some sort, like the Brontës, who both died young. You could fall back on Harriet Beecher Stowe or Mrs. Gaskell; they both led reasonable lives. But then George Eliot didn't have any children; neither did Jane Austen. Looking back over these women writers, it seemed difficult as a writer and a woman to have children and a domestic relationship. For a while I thought I had to choose between the two things I wanted: children and to be a writer. I took a chance.

Morris: In much of your work, love and power seem to be intricately connected—love as a power struggle in *Power Politics*. Do you see any other way between men and women?

Atwood: Love relationships between men and women do involve power structures, because men in this society have different kinds of, and more, power than women do. The problem for a woman in a relationship is how to maintain her integrity, her own personal power while also in a relationship with a man. Being in love with somebody is an experience that breaks down ego barriers. The positive part of that is a feeling of "cosmic consciousness," and the negative pole is a feeling of loss of self. You're losing who you are; you're surrendering—the fortress has fallen. But is it possible to have an equal exchange in a society in which things aren't entirely equal? *Power Politics* is fourteen years old. People tend to put it in the present tense. Each of my books is different—presenting different situations, characters, and involvements. My most domestic novel is *Life Before Man*. In it, there's an equilateral triangle. There are two women and one man, and viewed from any one point in the triangle, the other two are not behaving properly. But you can go around the triangle and look at it from all sides. To be asked what I think as a person is a different thing. I have a very good relationship with a man, and I've had it for some time. The novel is not merely a vehicle for self-expression, or for the rendition of one's own personal life. I'm quite conservative in that way: I do see the novel as a vehicle for looking at society—an interface between language and what we choose to call reality, although even that is a very malleable substance. When I create characters in novels, those characters aren't necessarily expressing something that is merely personal. I draw observations from a wide range of things.

Morris: How do you work? Can you describe how you write your first draft?

Atwood: I write in longhand, and preferably on paper with margins and thick lines with wide space between the lines. I prefer to write with pens that glide very easily over the paper because my handwriting is fast. Actually, I don't churn out finished copy quickly. Even though I have this fast handwriting, I have to scribble over it and scratch things out. Then I transcribe the manuscript, which is almost illegible, onto the typewriter.

Morris: Do you have a time, a day, or a place for writing? Does it matter where you are?

Atwood: I try to write between ten in the morning and four in the afternoon, when my child comes home from school. Sometimes in the evenings, if I'm really zipping along on a novel.

Morris: Do you write a novel from page one through to the end?

Atwood: No. Scenes present themselves. Sometimes it proceeds in a linear fashion, but sometimes it's all over the place. I wrote two parts of *Surfacing* five years before I wrote the rest of the novel; the scene in which the mother's soul appears as a bird, and the first drive to the lake. They are the two anchors for that novel.

Morris: What is the most difficult aspect of writing?

Atwood: That would be book promotion—that is, doing interviews. The easiest is the writing itself. By "easiest" I don't mean something that is lacking in hard moments or frustration; I suppose I mean "most rewarding."

Halfway between book promotion and writing is revision; halfway between book promotion and revision is correcting the galleys. I don't like that much at all.

Morris: Do you work closely with editors?

Atwood: I used to be an editor, so I do a lot of self-editing. I rewrite a lot before I show things to people. I like to have a manuscript in more or less its final shape before anyone sees it. That doesn't mean I can spell. There's that, and the fiddly things like punctuation—everyone has different ideas about that. So I work with an editor to improve that aspect of the text, of course. Ellen Seligman of McClelland and Stewart was devoted and wonderful when we worked on *Cat's Eye*. Things like, "You have 'soggy' twice on the same page." Meticulous. And I've had great fun doing some stories by phone with certain magazine editors— Bob Gottlieb of *The New Yorker* and Bill Buford of *Granta*, for instance. These sessions always take place when you're in Switzerland or about to get into the bath, and they have to have it done right away. Bargaining goes on, horse-trading. "You can have the dash, if I get the semicolon." That sort of thing. But an editor doesn't just edit. She or he sees the book through the whole publishing process. I have close and longstanding relationships with, for instance, Bill Toye of Oxford, Canada; Nan Talese, who's been my U.S. editor since 1976, and Liz Calder of Bloomsbury in the U.K. One of the things you want from an editor is simply the feeling that he or she understands your work. Money is no substitute for that.

Morris: I've noticed that money is a very important factor in your thinking. Have you always seen things in such sharp economic terms?

Atwood: When you're poor, you do. I went through a period of being quite poor, of having to really watch it in order to buy myself time to write, and indeed in order to eat. My poverty wasn't the same as real poverty, in that I had some sense of direction. I didn't feel trapped. Actually, since my family lived in the woods, it was rather difficult to tell whether we were rich or poor, because none of those things applied. It didn't matter. We had what we needed—we grew a lot of our own vegetables and things. So I grew up outside of that. I wasn't in a social structure in which it mattered at all. Then I was out on my own quite early. I was brought up to believe that I should support myself. I had a bank account quite early on and learned how to use it. I was taught to be financially independent, and I always have been. Money is important for women, because you'd be amazed how it alters your thinking to be financially dependent on someone. Indeed, anyone.

Morris: Have you ever thought of writing a novel in which a woman had an extremely important job?

Atwood: Yes, I have thought of doing that. But I've shied away for the same reason that George Eliot never wrote a novel about a successful English nineteenth-century woman writer, although she was one. It's still so atypical as to be a social exception. Besides, I'm not a business person. I'm a self-employed person. I don't have to deal in a power structure in the same way. I don't have to claw my way up through the corporate world. There is a successful woman in one of my books. She's the young, female judge that Rennie interviews in *Bodily Harm*. She's just so perfect. She has modern paintings, a wonderful husband, children; she loves her work—remember her? Rennie interviews her and can't stand it. A woman interviewer—of the "lifestyles" variety—once got very peeved with me because she felt I wasn't telling her the real dirt. She wanted the inner guck. I finally said to her, "If you had your choice, what would you like me to say to you?" She said, "Well, that you're leaving Graeme right now, and that I've got the scoop on it, and that I can come home and watch you pack."

Morris: How do you come by your titles?

Atwood: I like "come by," because that's about the way it is. I "come by" them, much as you "come by" some unexpected object in a junk store or lying beside the road. Sometimes the title arrives almost at the beginning of the writing of the book: *The Edible Woman* and *Lady Oracle* are cases in point. Sometimes you've been looking very hard in other directions, and the right title will just leap at you from the side. *Bodily Harm* came while I was doing some unrelated reading of a legal nature. Several books have gone through a number of working titles: for *Surfacing* there were two serious previous titles and about twenty possibilities—some of them variations on the final one. *Cat's Eye*—I think that came early on, and was very necessary in view of the central physical object in the book. *The Handmaid's Tale* was called "Offred" when I first began it. It changed by page 110. I know this because I kept a sort of working diary—not notes, but a running total of pages written—to encourage myself. I've read and continue to read the Bible a lot—partly as a result of being in all those hotel rooms, partly a long-standing habit—so the final title really did come from Genesis 30. I think too that it was one of those words that puzzled me as a child. "Hand-maid." Like "foot-man." It's a very odd word.

Morris: Is the Bible a literary inspiration to you? I know that you've spoken of having "the gift" in almost religious terms.

Atwood: That's not an analogy I'm particularly comfortable with because it is religious. But "the gift" is real. Along with it goes a sense of vocation and dedication. You get the call.

Morris: At the end of *Lady Oracle*, Joan says, "I'm not going to write Costume Gothics anymore. Maybe I'll write science fiction. Maybe I'll write about the future." In a sense you have done this in *Handmaid's Tale*. There is an evolution in your work toward a larger focus on the world.

Atwood: I think the focus has become wider, but surely that happens with every writer. What you do first is learn your craft. That can take years. In order to do that, you have to pick subjects that are small enough for you to handle. You learn how to do a good job with that. Of course, in the larger sense, every novel is—at the beginning—the same opening of a door onto a completely unknown space. I mean, it's just as terrifying every time. But nevertheless, having made the journey a few times, you have little guideposts, little signposts in the back of your mind. One of the most salutary things is writing a novel that fails, doesn't work, or that you can't finish, because what you learn from these failures is often as important as what you learn from doing something that succeeds. The prospect of having it happen again isn't so terrifying because you know you got through it.

Morris: Can you look over your past work with pleasure; would you change it if you had the chance?

Atwood: I don't look over my past work very much. I would not change it anymore than I would airbrush a photo of myself. When I do look at my work, I sometimes don't recognize it immediately, or I'm indulgent, as one is towards the work of the young. Or I wonder what I could possibly have been thinking about, and then I remember. I suppose when I'm eighty I'll have a good old pig-out on my past productions, but right now I'm too preoccupied with what's on my plate. What a lot of food metaphors!

Morris: Have Canadian critics been hard on you lately?

Atwood: My Canadian critics haven't been any harder on me than they usually are. If anything, maybe a bit easier; I think they're getting used to having me around. Growing a few wrinkles helps. Then they can think you're a sort of eminent fixture. I still get a few young folks who want to make their reputations by shooting me down. Any writer who's been around for a while gets a certain amount of that. I was very intolerant as a youthful person. It's almost necessary, that intolerance; young people need it in order to establish credentials for themselves.

Morris: You seem to know a great deal about visual art. Does this come from research or firsthand experience?

Atwood: All writers, I suspect—and probably all people—have parallel lives, what they would have been if they hadn't turned into what they are. I have several of these, and one is certainly a life as a painter. When I was ten I thought I would be one, by the time I was twelve I had changed that to dress designer, and then reality took over and I confined myself to doodles in the margins of my textbooks. At university I made pocket money by designing and printing silk screen posters, and by designing theater programs; I continued to draw and paint in a truncated sort of way, and still occasionally design—for instance, the Canadian covers of my poetry books. It's one of those things I'm keeping in reserve for when I retire. Maybe I can be a sort of awful Sunday painter, like Winston Churchill. Several of my friends are painters, so I've witnessed the difficulty of the life. The openings with the bad wine and drying-up cheese, the reviews with the perky headlines that don't quite get it, and so forth.

Morris: Is there anything that sticks in your mind as having been your greatest reward as a writer?

Atwood: The first poem I ever got published was a real high. Isn't it funny? I mean, all the other things that have happened since then were a thrill, but that was the biggest.

Morris: I mean something more personal, though.

Atwood: All right, yes. I was in Copenhagen, and just walking along, you know, window-shopping in a crowded mall. Denmark has a historical relationship with Greenland where a lot of Inuit live. Along the street came some Inuit dancers done up in traditional Greenland dress. They had their faces painted, and they had furry costumes on, impersonating beasts and monsters, spirits of some kind. They were spirit dancers, growling and making odd noises to the crowd. They had clawed hands and face-distorters in their mouths—pieces of wood that made their cheeks stick out in a funny way. One of these furry spirit-monsters came over to me, took his face-distorter out of his mouth, and said, "Are you Margaret Atwood?" I said yes. He said, "I like your work." And then he put his face-distorter back in his mouth and went growling off into the crowd.

The Beaver's Tale
Bruce Meyer and Brian O'Riordan

The following conversation originally appeared as "Figure It Out: Margaret Atwood" in Meyer and O'Riordan's collection, *Lives and Works*, published in Windsor, Ontario, by Black Moss Press in 1992. Reprinted with permission.

Interviewers: Is there one myth or particular misreading about your writing that you wish could be corrected?

Atwood: Myths tend to explode themselves. The horrible secret is, I don't read a lot of critical writing about my work. There is so much, I would be driven mad if I did. If you had asked me that question in, say, 1973 or 1974, it would have been a lot easier to answer because there was a lot less written. At that time, people were very struck by the fact that a female writer was writing books that had tough things in them. But this is no longer true: many women writers have gone into those territories. For a while, I was getting, "Her stuff is very bleak, dark, and negative." Then people figured out it was funny, and they said, "Gee, she's really funny." As with any writer, people look up the previous criticism and then write something to contradict it, because that's the only way they can make an impact. They say, "The others had it all wrong. I am now going to reveal the real truth." They must overturn, you see, the previously held view.

Interviewers: They never knock you off stride, though?

Atwood: Well, there's nothing anybody could possibly say that hasn't already been said. But some things are going to be recycled because there are only so many versions of a person you can come up with. I've had Medusa. I've had the Virgin Mary. You wouldn't believe the stuff that started coming out when I had a baby.

Interviewers: Margaret the Mother?

Atwood: Yes. Suddenly, they wanted to see me as warm and motherly. I was still the same person, but they used a different iconography. I've been accused of hating women. I've been accused of hating men. I've been accused of not hating either of them enough. Getting too soft on everybody. I've been accused of being ideological; of not being ideological enough. You can make it up with filing cards: write down everything you can think of, and then write down the opposite of everything you've written. And there you have it. You could do a fun calendar to promote some worthy cause, using excerpts from critics who mutually contradict one another.

Interviewers: Like a kaleidoscope image where they keep turning it around to get different patterns of the same picture?

Atwood: Maybe it's good, because it means there's enough in your work to support many different analyses. How much can you write about something one-dimensional? The real drawback is that at a certain point you, as a person, and your work, get condensed into something else; you become like the word *socialism*, or *fascism*—everybody is now supposed to know what that reference means. You become one of those "idea chips" that people move around.

Interviewers: You recently gave the Clarendon Lectures at Oxford.

Atwood: Yes. That was lots of fun. I enjoyed that.

Interviewers: In the first lecture, published in *Books in Canada*, one of the authors you wrote about was Robert Service. You noted that most serious critics usually dismiss him.

Atwood: His work is the mother lode of Northern imagery.

Interviewers: You went on to say, in that lecture, "To sum up: popular lore, and popular literature, established early that the North was uncanny, awe-inspiring in an almost religious way, hostile to white men, but alluring; that it would lead you on and do you in; that it would drive you crazy and, finally, claim you for its own."

Atwood: That's certainly Service's version of the North. There were four Clarendon Lectures. Three of them were on different groups of images associated with the North. The first one was, basically, the Frozen Explorer group, in which the North is represented by a group of female images which you can trace from Service right through Pratt and Gwendolyn MacEwen. The second lecture was on people who wanted to turn themselves into Indians.

Interviewers: Like Ernest Thompson Seton, Grey Owl, or Frank Prewett?

Atwood: Yes, and how that carried through into other works such as Robert Kroetsch's novel *Gone Indian*, in which the hero is a person who wants to imitate Grey Owl. He doesn't want to imitate an Indian; he wants to imitate a white man who wanted to imitate an Indian, which is a different thing. The third one was on Wendigos. The fourth one was on how the imagery changes when the literature is written by women. The odd thing is that when women write literature in which the protagonists are male, things stay very much the same. When, however, women writers write pieces in which the protagonist is female, things change.

Interviewers: In what way?

Atwood: The Service complex, in which the North is mean and female, changes. When you change the protagonist from a man to a woman, as in Ethel Wilson's *Swamp Angel*, Nature does not have a gender. But when the protagonist is male, as in that classic story, "The Old Woman," by Joyce Marshall, the complex image "mean/north/female" is very close to Service's. Gwendolyn MacEwen has this icy virgin as well. When the protagonist is male (and the problem with explorers is that none of them were female in the Canadian North, and if you made up a poem about one it would obviously be an ironic fantasy— Jane Franklin meets Mrs. Rasmussen), the landscape ends up driving the guy nuts, as is the case in Joyce Marshall's story. Nature, in that instance, is very obviously female. The writer is a woman, but the protagonist is a man. However, when the protagonist is a woman, what are your choices? You could have a mean female Nature if you wanted to, but what relation would she bear to the female protagonist? Would she be a mother? An evil sister? A wicked step-mother? A lesbian lover? Usually, the women writers using female protagonists don't give Nature a gender. In these cases, Nature is more often viewed as a place in which to seek refuge rather than something that will destroy you. In Marian Engel's *Bear*, for instance, the bear is male, but the natural world surrounding it is gender-neutral. It is not Mother Nature.

Interviewers: Pratt's iceberg in "The Titanic" for instance…

Atwood: Is female. Just before he started work on "The Titanic," Pratt was working on a poem about the Franklin Expedition, and the only reason he didn't write that poem was that he couldn't get up there to see the terrain at first-hand.

Interviewers: One of the recurring themes in literature about the North, as you point out in the first lecture, is that of submergence. You mention MacEwen's passages about Franklin's ships *Erebus* and *Terror*, and she has them sink. Klein's "A Portrait of the Poet as a Landscape" is another work of "submergence" that comes to mind.

Atwood: Everyone seems to want to get those dead people under the water.

Interviewers: Why?

Atwood: I don't know. Some of my speculation centers around the fact that the Victorians, in general, were very fascinated by drowned people.

Interviewers: Arthur Henry Hallam of Tennyson's "In Memoriam"?

Atwood: That's the one I mentioned in my lecture, but he's not the only one.

Interviewers: An echo of Milton's "Lycidas," perhaps?

Atwood: Who knows? Could be. Victorian English poetry is keen on drowned people. What we may have been doing as Canadians was borrowing the drowned people, although we have a lot of water and many people do drown in it. There are quite a few drowned people in Ethel Wilson's works, by the way.

Interviewers: Is it because we have a craving, in our literature, for an unattainable pastoral vision? "Lycidas" is, after all, a pastoral poem.

Atwood: It may all go back to Shakespeare.

Interviewers: To *The Tempest*?

Atwood: Yes. Drowning seems a more poetic way of dying than sticking your fork into an electrical outlet. There are a lot of literary associations with drowning.

Interviewers: And the artistic associations in the Canadian context, such as the death of Tom Thompson.

Atwood: Yes, but he was just "falling into" an established mode. He became part of the tradition of the female North claiming those whom she loves, taking you unto herself; the tradition of the drowned artist, the drowned lyrical person. Let's just say that drowning, and to a certain extent freezing, are more literary ways of dying than car crashes.

Interviewers: Except in the case of Albert Camus?

Atwood: Or breaking your neck by falling down the stairs. Many people die that way, but we don't have lyrical poems about them; we don't have any mythology about the goddess of the cellar stairs taking you unto herself. You're just as dead, but there aren't the same associations.

Interviewers: The North has those associations of danger. In an article you wrote for *Saturday Night*, "True North," in 1987, you said that the North "focuses our anxieties." What are those anxieties?

Atwood: Let me just say that in any country, there are a couple of key words that will cause people to lean forward in their chairs and start telling you stories. You can test this out if you go to Australia and say the words "Outback" or "sharks." You'll immediately hear a number of stories about people who encountered sharks and escaped them, people who knew other people who encountered sharks and did not escape them, people who got lost in the Outback, and people who knew other people who got lost in the Outback, even though most Australians live in cities, never encounter a shark, and never get lost in the Outback. Those are very potent words for them. Those are the words that focus their anxieties, even though they are much more likely to die in a car crash.

For us, it's getting lost in the bush, drowning, freezing to death, and bears. Of these four things, "bears" is the most universal fear. Coast to coast. Bears are an imaginative possibility, even though they might not be a real possibility.

We do many more dangerous things every day than getting lost in the bush; and maybe we should refocus our anxieties. If we really were aware of what it might involve to get into a car and drive, we probably wouldn't do it. But the notion of a large, dangerous animal still haunts us.

Interviewers: Isn't there a discrepancy between the way Canadians live their day-to-day lives in Southern cities and the way they imagine themselves through the concept of North?

Atwood: Just as there is a discrepancy between what English people experience in their day-to-day lives and the ideas of castles, the Tower of London and Shakespeare's Stratford-on-Avon. They are not living that life anymore. But it remains part of the imaginative world.

Interviewers: And our discrepancies are things like the Franklin Expedition?

Atwood: Yes. Those symbols still exist, and act as orientation points.

Interviewers: Do readers buy that because literature is a means of escaping to something different?

Atwood: It depends what you're being asked to buy. If you are reading Mordecai Richler's *Solomon Gursky*, and you come across the parody of the Franklin Expedition, it helps to know something about the primary material.

Interviewers: Throughout your work, you've touched on the theme of the tension between the creator and the creation. In "Speeches /or Dr. Frankenstein," in *Lady Oracle*—where you have a writer writing a novel—and in *Cat's Eye*, where Elaine Risley is trying to deal with her own past through her paintings, you touch on this.

Atwood: That's interesting. I don't think about that a lot myself. I'm not a preacher. I'm not a politician. I'm not "developing themes." I'm telling stories. I'm rendering material.

Interviewers: Sometimes, in fact, you rework that material, rework situations, as is the case with Marlene in *Lady Oracle*, who seems to be a precursor of Cordelia in *Cat's Eye*.

Atwood: In *Lady Oracle*, though, that's the sideshow. In *Cat's Eye*, it's the seminal incident. The harassment of Elaine by Cordelia, and the subsequent fallout, is the subject of the book. That book is about nasty relationships among little girls, which have not been treated very much in fiction for adults. In *Lady Oracle* it's done as a comic turn, much as it is in *Anne of Green Gables* with Josie Pye, and much as it is with many of those Enid Blyton schoolgirl novels in which the bad little girls are ultimately deflated and conquered. In *Anne of Green Gables* you have Diana, who is always good, and Josie Pye, who is always bad. In reality, they were probably the same person, sometimes good, sometimes bad. No one is all good or all bad.

But bad little boys are bad in different ways. Little boys have much more stable hierarchies than little girls do. The reason for the leader of the little boys being the leader is very obvious. He's the best at baseball, or he's got the best collection of baseball cards. He's good at something, and you can see what he's good at. The hierarchy does not change unless the reasons for the establishment of the hierarchy change. With girls, there's no obvious reason for the top girl being on top. Because of this, the opportunities for girls to be more manipulative and con-spiratorial and Machiavellian are greater, and conspiracies to overthrow the top girl are much more possible. There is a lot less physicality among little girls. Little boys fight, but don't hold grudges. Girls are more verbal, and more subtle. Little girls have an overt dislike of out-and-out confrontation; they'll whisper and exclude rather than fight. The early mythology of the Women's Movement—that women were born into sisterhood—is no more true than to say that women are born into motherhood. The styles of motherhood are very much learned, as are the styles of relationships among women.

Interviewers: There is of strong sense of inquiry in your approach to your material, whether fiction or non-fiction.

Atwood: Surely that's at the root of all writing. I'm interested in exploring the consequences of situations.

Interviewers: Do you, therefore, write with a view to what the ending will be?

Atwood: No. The ending emerges.

Interviewers: You satirize the whole notion of endings in "Happy Endings," in *Murder in the Dark*.

Atwood: When you read Part A out loud, people burst into spontaneous laughter and cheers. Why is that? It's because everyone knows how they want to live, but they know life isn't like that. They know nobody's life goes that smoothly. Everyone wants to be happy. But it's not so easy.

Interviewers: You wrote in "Writing the Male Character" that as a writer you wanted the "Cloak of Invisibility and the ability to teleport your mind into somebody else's while still retaining your own perceptions and memory."

Atwood: I'd settle for a telephone tap.

Interviewers: And you went on to say "these two fantasies are what novelists act out every time they write." This seems to suggest, as you write in *Cat's Eye*, that you almost have to exist in two places at once in order to write. There's a sense of working out a personal nostalgia for a time and place.

Atwood: *Cat's Eye* is not based on "personal nostalgia;" it's a rendering of a time. According to the mail I received, it's not very "personal" at all, because almost everyone who has written to me has indicated that he or she has gone through some of the experiences I write about in *Cat's Eye*. Some of them send me samples of their marble collection. But real marbles aside, I do realize that the marble is the structural element in the book. The marble is to *Cat's Eye* as the madeleine is to Proust. It's a very nice structural element, because marbles go back at least to ancient Egypt as divination objects. They were used for telling the future.

Interviewers: At the beginning of *Cat's Eye* you quote Stephen Hawking, the English physicist: "Why do we remember the past and not the future?"

Atwood: Hawking was one of the seven or eight of those kinds of guys I was reading at the time. I also have a nephew who sets me straight on matters relating to physics. But Hawking writes so well.

Interviewers: It is unusual to have scientists as characters in novels, as you do in *Life Before Man* and *Cat's Eye*.

Atwood: This is because most novelists don't know enough about science, or it just wouldn't occur to them. Their characters are more likely to be journalists, university professors, somebody within their reach. My scientists are not Gothic scientists. They're not evil, like Dr. Moreau. //

Interviewers: It seems apropos to blend science and fiction because they both seek explanations.

Atwood: Maybe. Then, of course, there's science fiction, which is hard to write well. You can't cheat on the facts or get sloppy, because you'll get called on the floor right away; the scientists will catch you out. You can't write Buck Rogers stuff anymore.

Interviewers: You have dabbled on the fringes of science fiction in *The Handmaid's Tale* and in your short story written after that: "Freeforall."

Atwood: Which is another extrapolation—like *The Handmaid's Tale*—from the present situation in the world.

Interviewers: The situation in the story seems to be reversed from that in the novel. The males are now the handmaids…

Atwood: Figure it out. If AIDS, a sexually transmitted disease, is the big plague, that's how things would be, because you can tell whether a woman is a virgin or not, but you can't tell whether a male is. Lock them up, some would say: it's the only way! If you want uncontaminated marriages, that's what you're going to have to do. You're going to have to lock up the male children before you marry them off.

Interviewers: The story is the flip-side of *The Handmaid's Tale*. Are you saying anything is possible in a totalitarian regime?

Atwood: Any twist in human life is possible if there is somebody with absolute control. We have seen all the elements of this in our own time. I didn't invent anything in either story. Both are based on actuality or possibility. They aren't science fiction of the green-monster variety, they're speculative fiction of the George Orwell variety.

Interviewers: In the "Epilogue" to *The Handmaid's Tale*, besides obviously being able to use it to send up standard academic analysis…

Atwood: What's to send up? It sends itself up.

Interviewers: The "Epilogue" certainly provides a much different conclusion to the work than what is offered by the ending of the film version of *The Handmaid's Tale*.

Atwood: Films are a different medium. Films are short, and they're made with images, not words; they can only handle two or three levels of meaning; they can only handle two or three levels of time; they can't handle metaphor; and everything in them is very literal and visible. If the film makers had kept the "Epilogue," suddenly at the end of the film there would have been a whole new set of characters you'd never seen before. The audience would have said, "What's going on?" The problems they had were the problems of film. The other problem with film is the problem of internal monologue. They were planning on using a voice-over narration, but that disappeared in the process. Film starts. It goes at the pace at which it goes. It's like an airline trip—you're buckled in. But with a book, if there's something you didn't get, you can turn back and re-read it, slow it down. A book is much more malleable in the hands of a reader than a film is in the eyes of a viewer. A viewer can't stop the film or slow it down (unless you're using a VCR). The book, to me, is a much more democratic form, even though film is a larger mass medium. The viewer of a film is more manipulated by it—more controlled by it—than a reader is controlled by a book. In order to read a book, the readers must use their imaginations. They fill in, they help create the scenes and the characters. The characters in a film look like the actors, not like your idea of the characters. Films create very definite images which are powerful but monolithic.

Also, books are a lot easier to produce than films, in that they are cheaper to make. Publishing books is something else again, although still a lot less expensive than films. If you write for film, unless you are very, very stupid, you learn early on that films are not a writer's medium. You're not in control of the process. Scenes get carved up, taken out, end up on the cutting room floor.

Interviewers: You have a fascination with "Middle Kingdoms," in your works, places that stand between extremes, or are in themselves in transition from one extreme to another. Gilead, for example, in *The Handmaid's Tale*. Even the Arctic is a kind of a middle kingdom.

Atwood: A strange land between heaven and hell, as Service has it.

Interviewers: Frye used to point out that Canada was in that situation politically between the U.S.S.R. and the U.S.A. On the subject of politics, during the Free Trade debate you told the apocryphal story, in front of the Commons Committee on International Trade, of how beavers, when frightened, chew off their own balls and offer them to their enemies. You seemed to be saying that this was what Canada was doing by agreeing to free trade with the U.S.

Atwood: That metaphor certainly got a lot of those guys upset.

Interviewers: Did they see themselves as beavers?

Atwood: No. They saw themselves as threatened. They saw their sexual prowess as having been called into question. That sentence got quoted a lot, with great indignation.

Interviewers: You wrote in the poem "Notes Toward a Poem That Can Never Be Written," "in this country you can say what you like because no one will listen to you anyway." Was that the case for you during the Free Trade Debate?

Atwood: Well, the reality is that those of us opposed to the deal did not have four million dollars to throw around during the last two weeks of the campaign.

But these are not things I do as a writer. These are things I do as a citizen. Writers end up saying things like this because most other people would be fired for saying them.

The Ancient Mariner Experience of Writing, and Reading

James McElroy

James McElroy interviewed Margaret Atwood in February 1993 while she was a Regent's Lecturer at the University of California, Davis. The interview appeared in *Writing on the Edge* in Fall 1993. Reprinted with permission.

McElroy: Did you ever take courses in writing?

Atwood: No, not exactly. But I did take (if that's the word) something called English 400. It wasn't a writing course in any known sense of the word. It was just about five people who sat around with a professor/poet and talked about each other's work.

McElroy: Who was the poet?

Atwood: Jay Macpherson.

McElroy: Did you talk exclusively about poetry?

Atwood: No, we discussed everything. But mostly people talked about poetry because we had time to write poetry between essays for final-year English. But the idea that you could grade it, that you could put a value on a certain piece, would have seemed odd. What would you give Keats for "Ode to a Nightingale"? Would it get an A? Or what would you give *A Tale of Two Cities*? A B+ on the grounds that it's too long?

McElroy: Your introduction to *The Edible Woman* mentions that you taught freshman composition for at least a year at one point.

Atwood: Yes. My first teaching job was at the University of British Columbia, where I taught freshman composition to engineering students at eight-thirty in the morning in a Quonset hut—huts named, one presumes after Mr. Quonset. Anyway, when World War II ended the Canadian government granted its soldiers free entrance to universities. As a result of the large enrollment, the authorities used a load of Quonsets as teaching facilities for things that weren't deemed especially important—for one thing, teaching composition to engineers.

McElroy: What approach did you use with your engineers?

Atwood: No approach. I just used Kafka.

McElroy: Kafka?

Atwood: I gave the students short pieces from Kafka, and I got them to write parables.

McElroy: And how did Kafka work out?

Atwood: Oh, it wasn't so bad. We knew we were in it together. They had to take it. I had to teach it.

McElroy: Did you ever do "technical" stuff with them?

Atwood: No. I just wanted them to be able to write a coherent sentence with a subject, a verb, and an object. And that's the level we were at. I mean, the whole point of the course (as I saw it) wasn't so much for them to express their thoughts; rather, I wanted them to have some thoughts to express. The idea was to get them to write something that would hold their reader's attention for a page or more. So, in the end, I decided to start off with parables. After all, it's a form people understand—short, condensed narratives with a message, or, in Kafka's hands, short, condensed narratives with a message in waiting.

McElroy: Have you taught any composition courses since UBC?

Atwood: No, not really. But I did teach creative writing a few times; I've taught it in both structured and open environments.

McElroy: "Structured"? "Open"?

Atwood: In a structured class I would give assignments and students would produce work according to assignment outlines—we would concentrate on technical skills. An open class, on the other hand, was where people brought their work, handed it out, and sat around a table as the conversation went: "I don't know, Mel. This works for me," or, "I don't know, Susan. This just doesn't work for me." It is the approach that I have found least useful even though there are some useful things you can do with it. But usually they are things that you do yourself and the students listen because they don't know how to edit; they sit and watch you edit other people's bad poems.

McElroy: In one of your critical articles ("An End to Audience?") you refer to a U. S. university where the creative writing program left a lot to be desired. Here's the passage: "One was not, it appears, supposed to question the *raison d'être* of such classes. One was not supposed to discourage the students. One was supposed to radiate the air of genteel encouragement appropriate to, say, physiotherapists, or people who teach recreational ceramics. The role of the poet in society…was not to be examined. The goal of the class was to keep its enrolled and fee-paying students from quitting in despair, to give them all passing grades so as not to discourage next year's crop, and, with luck, to teach the students to turn out poems publishable in the kinds of little magazines favored by the instructor. None of this was said. It was all implicit." Would it be reasonable to view this as an indictment of creative writing programs?

Atwood: No, it wouldn't. It would be reasonable, however, to view it as an indictment of that specific program because it created a situation in which people were sucked in and kept on; the program left the people who taught it with a bunch of students who shouldn't have been there because they didn't want to be. I mean, they didn't want to be writers. Instead, they viewed the course as part of a basket-weaving phase (circa 1969) in which all you had to do was be in the course if you wanted to pass. For the one or two people who were really serious about it, maybe it was nice. But the others were just passing time. They were churning out third-rate poems because that's what was expected of them. There was no idea that writing had to be something you couldn't avoid; instead, it was regarded as something you turned out to meet a course requirement.

McElroy: I take it, then, that you are not a devotee of the "open" approach?

Atwood: Actually, I wouldn't come down on either side. I think it's like anything else—it depends on the teacher, and also on what your criteria are for the students and how motivated they are. I mean, it's like saying something positive or negative about dental school. There are, however, some criteria for dental school. For example, if you drill a hole in somebody's face, you fail. In writing, however, the criteria are less clear. People often make a blithe assumption that we ought to make things easier for people so they'll feel good. Well, I don't think writing is about "feeling good." And I don't think encouragement means anything if you're encouraging everybody as if they're equals. "That's nice, dear"—Is that what you'd want as criticism? Not if you're serious.

I was just in Clarence Major's class. I told his students that writing should be an Ancient Mariner experience for both the writer and the reader. In other words, you're going about your business and something grabs you and says, "There was a ship." You say, "But, but I have to go to a wedding." And then they say, "No, this is more important. There was a ship." It has to be like that—otherwise, it's just connecting the dots. You know, it's paint by numbers. It's just doodling.

McElroy: But don't we all, in some sense, have to "paint by numbers"?

Atwood: I suppose so, if by that you mean practice. But we also have to go beyond that.

McElroy: Has the Ancient Mariner experience now taken over your life?

Atwood: No. It hasn't. It's just taken over the part of me that writes.

McElroy: Could you take a month off and never put pen to paper?

Atwood: Yes, I've done that. The truth is that I'm happy to sit and paint. However, the desire to paint is often pushed aside because of an Ancient Mariner experience of some kind. For example, quite often when I say, "I'm going to sit down and paint," something else says, "Just a minute, this is more important."

McElroy: So how do you go about your business?

Atwood: A day in the life? Well, I'm inherently lazy, but I'm also inherently puritanical. So it's frequently a contest between a laziness which says, "Goof off," and a puritanism which says, "You must put in five hours of work." It's like swimming. There's that moment where you think: Do I really want to do this today? The water's too cold. And the other part of you that says: "It will be good for you. You'll enjoy it once you're in. Get in there."

McElroy: Has it gotten any easier?

Atwood: No, it never gets easier. You have to work at it. For example, when I was younger I spent the day having anxiety attacks, sharpening pencils, getting up, sitting down, filling coffee cups, going to lunch, phoning friends—all the things you do to avoid writing. Then, once I had a young family, I couldn't write until two in the morning anymore, so I quickly cut the anxiety attacks down to about five minutes of screaming paranoia and moved my writing to an earlier and less frantic point in the day.

By now I've grown used to earlier starts. If I'm good, I get to go out for lunch.

McElroy: Where do you work most of the time?

Atwood: At home. It's a large house where I have two offices, one for me, and one for my assistant, who does all the "other" things. She does the bookkeeping. She files the contracts. She does the banking. She answers the telephone. When you've got almost thirty books in twenty-five countries to keep track of, it's a lot. I just couldn't do it by myself.

McElroy: You have asked students why they want to write, asked them if the desire for revenge (or envy) played a part in their desire to be writers. So how, for the record, would you answer your own question?

Atwood: Well, both can enter into it.

McElroy: You've felt…

Atwood: I've felt both.

McElroy: And revenge? What does "revenge" look like?

Atwood: Charles Dickens and the blacking factory where he was forced to work as a child. He never got the blacking factory out of his head. I think every writer has some form of the blacking factory. However, the blacking factory can be a motivation. I suppose if we were being psychoanalytic we'd say that writers make an effort to "work it all out."

McElroy: And the "envy" part. Is there a specific author you envy? Is there a poem or a book about which you've said, "God, I wish I had written that; wish I could write like that."

Atwood: I suppose, in a sense, all the books I admire. But, then, that's not real envy, is it? For example, Toni Morrison's *Beloved*. I couldn't have written that book because I wouldn't have had the material for it. But that has more to do with admiration. Perhaps "envy," much like "revenge," is an inadequate term for something that runs much deeper.

McElroy: Somewhere in your review of *Midnight Birds* [short fiction by black American women writers], you write, "If you were to ask a white American male writer who he's writing for, you would probably get a somewhat abstract answer, unless he's a member of an ethnic minority. But the writers in *Midnight Birds* know exactly who they're writing for. They're writing for other black American women, and they believe in the power of their words. They see themselves as giving a voice to the voiceless." My question is, then, who do you write for?

Atwood: I think that's changed over the years. My ideal reader has aged somewhat. I don't ascribe gender to this reader, although a lot of people do. I assume that the responses to some of the things I put on the page will be different according to who's reading it, but you really can't concern yourself a whole bunch with that or you start to get paranoid. What you have to do is to make your writing the best it can be, and then you just have to have faith. You just have to throw your writing away and assume that whoever picks it up will be the right person. I'm therefore not sure who exactly I write for. All I am sure of is that people have always told stories and passed them on. At the same time, though, I'm quite sure that writing—who, what, why—is more than just a sociological exercise. It's not, "This is moral behavior that you are witnessing here and nobody ever does anything wrong." It's not "Everybody in this book must be politically correct." And it's certainly not all those worthy things we so often expect from our society. Because if that's all it ever came to, we would certainly never have inherited Shakespeare's tragedies. I mean, what does the spectacle of Iago do for us? What good does it do?

McElroy: Would you like to name the "good" in question?

Atwood: No, I'm not a theorist of that kind. Whenever you try to pin something down, the thing itself evades you; once you start to formulate a definition of what writing should be, someone comes along and contradicts you. After all, art has to do partly with the violation of conventions. Which means, I suppose, that there have to be conventions to violate: a convention is violated, new conventions are set up, masterpieces are produced, and then conventions are violated all over again.

McElroy: And what about women poets? You mentioned, for example, that Canada had a strong tradition of...

Atwood: Canada had—has had—a British tradition. I mean, Canada was, until quite recently, just not visible in a literary sense. For decades you could have sailed through life without giving Canada (or its women writers) a second thought, even if you lived in it. That was not true for me, however, because I was interested in becoming a writer: I sought out writers who had published because I wanted to know how to do it. As a result, I soon realized that a number of women had published in the '50s, and that some of the best poets of the generation preceding mine were women—among them, P. K. Page, Margaret Avison, and Jay Macpherson. The fact that women had published in Canada meant that I had something to work with: the idea that women were publishable.

McElroy: And what about women in the United States?

Atwood: Well, there weren't a lot then. You know, there really weren't. I guess we all stumbled on Sylvia Plath in the '60s. At least she's the one I remember.

McElroy: And Rich?

Atwood: Well, Adrienne Rich's earlier work was quite unlike her later poems. In fact, if you go back and look at it, you'll see that her first pieces were rather disguised, quite formalistic. She didn't hit her stride until much later on. But, yes, I loved *Diving into the Wreck* when it came out. However, you asked about influence. And I was too old for Rich to be a real influence.

McElroy: And Harvard? What influence did your studies at Harvard have you?

Atwood: When I first went to Harvard, I discovered that the university kept its modern verse in the Lamont (i.e., NO WOMEN ALLOWED) Library. And this left me, for the most part, to browse through Widener stacks where some eccentric had compiled a Canadian section—underneath Witchcraft and Demonology.

McElroy: Thus, your line that Canadian literature is "insecure"?

Atwood: In part. But later experience taught me that Canada's *insecureness* was a very colonial affair: people who couldn't get a job at Oxford came to Canada and got a position in a Canadian university, and British academics who came to Canada felt it was their duty, if not right, to civilize the natives; once Canada had been told its literature was barbaric, it became clear that Canadian literature would have to become *British* if it ever wanted to be taken seriously. And then came the U.S. threat—a wave of American academics who offered us much the same advice that the Brits had: "This isn't a real culture. You're barbarians and now we're going to civilize you." So, you see, we had to carve out a space for *ourselves* amidst the same people who said real literature was Faulkner—the same academics who insisted English Literature (capital "L") was the measure of all things.

McElroy: What would you like to do that you haven't? What about drama?

Atwood: Well, it's not that drama doesn't interest me. But as a form it's quite specialized. It's difficult to write well without a certain amount of devotion and vocation—without an Ancient Mariner experience.

McElroy: And speaking of Ancient Mariner experiences, what about your current novel?

Atwood: It's almost finished.

McElroy: And the title is?

Atwood: Not telling.

McElroy: "Not Telling"?

Atwood: No. That's not the title. The fact is that I'm superstitious. And until the final dot is in place, I'm not telling a soul.

Struggling with Your Angel

Beth Richards

The following interview was conducted on 5 April 1989 at Trinity University in San Antonio. It originally appeared in the Winter 1994 issue of *Prairie Schooner*. Reprinted with permission.

Richards: I saw an interview, Bookmark, the program…

Atwood: With Erica Jong and Jay Parini and Lewis Lapham.

Richards: Yes. And you mentioned that you had had readers respond to *Cat's Eye* and that women in particular had remembered these experiences.

Atwood: They all know Cordelia. About ninety-five percent will tell you that they knew Cordelia, and a very small percentage will say that they were Cordelia or that they had Cordelia-like episodes in their lives. Mostly they remember other people being Cordelia towards them, and the times when they were Cordelia tend to fade in their memories.

Richards: That's logical. Yes, I had a Cordelia myself, and so I think this is why I felt some connection with the book…

Atwood: I was actually quite amazed at how many, and I even got letters beginning, "As one who was buried in a snow-bank" and "As one who was almost drowned" and "As one who was…etcetera. Some of them had rather dangerous Cordelias, Cordelia experiences.

Richards: Has it been true for women of all ages?

Atwood: Women of all ages. I think that towards the younger end of things you run into a group of schoolteachers and parents who were more aware and also into a situation in which kids are no longer allowed to run wild the way they used to, because people are too worried about psychopaths in the bushes. Partly the children's play is more contained where people can have more of an eye on it, and partly the parents and teachers are more aware of socialization. "Socialization" wasn't a word in the '40s. Nobody paid any attention to that, you were in school to learn to read and write and that was it, not to be socialized.

Richards: This novel shows the socialization of the time to be very different for girls and boys.

Atwood: It shows the socialization of the time, but nobody called it "socialization."

Richards: That's the term now.

Atwood: Yes, certainly, but not then. Some things are very different, other things are very similar. For instance, many parents tried unisex toys on their kids and found that they just didn't take, either through commercial pressure or because little girls just weren't that interested in trucks, you know. A few of them were. Little girls are more likely to be interested in role-playing boys' games than they are in boys' games involving machinery. So you'll probably find more who played tomboy or played baseball or who played cowboys and Indians or who played war, but you'll find very few whose play was exclusively trucks and little miniature steamrollers.

Richards: Did you have any specific purposes or effects with language that you were looking for in *Cat's Eye*? One thing I noticed is that you're dealing with fashions in language as much as you are fashions in clothing over time.

Atwood: Words change. That's true. But any novelist dealing with time will notice that undoubtedly. I'll tell you a story about *Surfacing* which is about language as well. The person who did the proofreading of the galleys at Simon and Schuster had never proofread a novel before, he'd only done history textbooks so he changed and regularized all of the punctuation. The punctuation in *Surfacing* is run-on, and there are a lot of excluded middles—that is a thought will go from A to C, and B will be left out because of the state of mind of the narrator—and there are a lot of comma splices. I had to go over those proofs with a magnifying glass, putting back all the little commas and all the semicolons. He broke up a lot of sentences and made them into single sentences. //

The problem with *Cat's Eye* was to get a voice which could be both the child's voice—but immediate enough and primitive enough, if you like—to be the child's voice for the child's section, but yet that we would also realize was an adult going back into that time rather than the child being in that time primarily. So that was the problem of language. The appropriateness of a word. The appropriateness of *each* word. The appropriateness of the sentence structure for those sections and making a difference between that voice and the older woman as herself now. You could say that the entire novel takes place over a period of about a week and a half, but there is also a movement back in time and that has to be indicated by the voice. So the "now" voice is more sophisticated, a lot more adult, if you like, considerably more retrospective.

Richards: I find the voice of the girl Elaine very authentic. There's one line that I think is wonderful towards the beginning of the novel: "We're impervious, we scintillate, we are thirteen." I like that line because I think that's how you do feel when you are thirteen.

Atwood: That's a description of how you feel. Those are not the words you would use then. It is an adult voice remembering the feeling and describing it. But at the age of thirteen, you would not think of those words at all. You would be so within the experience that you would not be without it, describing it. And also at the age of thirteen you have nothing else to compare it with, except being twelve or eleven or ten. It's only as an adult that you can get that kind of fix on what you were like.

Richards: Looking back, getting perspective, and then naming it afterwards.

Atwood: And then name it, that's right.

Richards: There are two distinct languages, the "boy" talk and "girl" talk. Elaine feels that they are separate worlds and comes also from that society, the separate doors when they go to school and that kind of thing, and she feels closer, it seems, to the "boy" world.

Atwood: Because it has been friendlier to her. I had a fascinating experience when I was in England. I met a woman who had been the only girl student at a boys' school for about three months. They had been opening up this boys' school to girls, and she was the first one. And she said that when she came out of that experience she could no longer talk with women for a while, because she had learned to talk "boy," she had learned to talk as a boy. I said, "What was the difference?" Much less emotion was described, sentence structures were different, a lot of things were just very different. So there do seem to be, at that age anyway, two distinct languages or two distinct modes of language.

Richards: That's part of Elaine's culture shock, too, when she has to learn…

Atwood: She had to learn "girl." "Girl" was learned for her rather than assimilated. If you grow up with a lot of girls around, then you just absorb that as you absorb your native tongue, but if you come into it…

Richards: Elaine mentions that she feels like she's acting part of the time, that it's not natural.

Atwood: That's what you feel when you go into a culture before you have assimilated that culture. Have you ever learned another language? You must have if you're a graduate student.

Richards: Yes.

Atwood: Have you ever been in a situation where you are actually speaking that language?

Richards: Not very often, no.

Atwood: Part of speaking a language is knowing the words, but the rest of it is knowing the intonation and the body language. If you are a natural linguist you will just absorb this, but if you are, on the other hand, the kind of person who is consciously observant you will find yourself doing the Gallic shrug. It is a form of acting when you're learning something like that. When I speak French, which I do fairly badly, I do use my hands a lot more, because French people do use their hands a lot more. It's part of the talking.

Richards: When you learn a language in a classroom…

Atwood: When you learn a language in a classroom, you don't usually learn the body language. That's the thing that you don't learn. You don't learn the idiom usually unless you have a very good teacher, and what you have to pick up if you want to be a speaker is those extras. Facial expression. I know a man who is very good at languages, and one of the reasons he's good is that his face changes whenever he speaks one. When he speaks German, he looks like a German, when he speaks French, he looks French, and when he speaks Russian, he looks Russian. It's so uncanny. One of my friends is a housewife from London, Ontario…

Richards: William's hometown in *Life Before Man*.

Atwood: It's known to be a very square city. And when she [the friend] is speaking English, that's what she sounds like. But they spent quite a lot of time in France, and when she switches to French, she becomes this scintillating, vivacious, flirtatious Parisian woman. It's a transformation, it's another personality. It's so funny to watch.

Richards: Just from language.

Atwood: It's not *just* language.

Richards: And what goes with it.

Atwood: It's a mode of being. And one of the reasons she likes going there is that she is another person. She can be another person there, and it's a person she quite likes. She can go and bargain with the waiters to make them give you a seat when they don't have any. She can go to the bakery and make them produce the croissant they've been hiding in the back. She's amazing.

Richards: In *Cat's Eye* does Elaine, who is a painter, distrust words?

Atwood: As all painters distrust words. All artists distrust words up to a point. I think the writer's relation with words is like the painter's with paint. There are a limited number of colors.

Richards: Do you feel limited as a writer?

Atwood: Yes and no. It's everyone's struggle with their angel. Do you get the allusion?

Richards: My mind is racing.

Atwood: Do you have a Bible with a concordance?

Richards: No.

Atwood: As a student in literature you need this, because then you could look up "Jacob" or "Angel" and you could go right to the passage. It's appropriate to writers, because it closely describe what they feel they're doing when they write.

Finding the Inner Silence to Listen

Gabrielle Meltzer

Gabrielle Meltzer conducted the following interview during Margaret Atwood's German visit in March 1994. It originally appeared in *Zeitschrift fur Kanada-Studien* in 1995. Reprinted with permission.

Meltzer: First, a question about your novel *The Handmaid's Tale*. You once said, "There is nothing in the book that hasn't already happened. All things described in the book people have already done to each other"–so singular phenomena, that is well-known or known facts, do not make up a work of art, but rather a combination of them? And the next question: Does the process of creativity then resemble the devising of a mosaic?

Atwood: Only up to a point. No, I don't think so. What I said about *The Handmaid's Tale* applied only to the plot and the events, but then there is a whole other part to the book, which is the interior monologue. That has to do with the experiencing of the events rather than the fact itself. It's how the fact feels to a human being. So that part is not like a mosaic.

Meltzer: But then you have to have the feeling first so that you can give your characters that feeling, so that you know how they feel.

Atwood: I think a lot of novel writing comes from the childhood playing of games and the assumption of roles, and if you watch children playing you will hear them say: "You'll be the mother" or "You'll be the maid" or "I will be the leader" and then they change the roles, they take turns playing out these roles, and you can see that they indulge in a lot of imitation and mimicry. What they are doing is they are acting how they think the mother would act or how they think the leader would behave, and then the other people have to act out the other role: how they think the follower would behave, or how they think the bandit would behave or whatever it is. Children do this all the time, they do it unconsciously. So it's really telling a story. You do the same thing: You enter into the story. There is nothing very mysterious about it.

Meltzer: So do you think that artists feel and behave like children during their lifetime or that they don't lose...

Atwood: They don't lose the ability to imagine. And a lot of what people do in their later lives is also role-playing. They act in a way that they think a doctor should act or they act in a way that they think a businessman should act. And part of what you are probably trying to do is to get them to expand their role definition so that they can act with more flexibility; that a businessman does not just put on a suit and sit behind a desk; he also does these other things. What you're trying to do is to give these people permission to expand their roles and play them more imaginatively. But it's not just artists who role-play. Everybody does. They behave in manners that they feel are appropriate and they've learned those manners.

Meltzer: Are artists necessarily mentally schizophrenic? So, for example, when they describe a mouse do they get into the skin of the mouse? Not to speak of getting into the skin of a lion! [cf. Michael Ondaatje's novel *In the Skin of a Lion*]

Atwood: Well, I think schizophrenia is an often overused term that people use rather loosely. Obviously, I don't think that artists are schizophrenic or else they would all be on medication, wouldn't they?

Meltzer: Mentally schizophrenic...

Atwood: No, I prefer to think of it as flexible. In other words, rather than confining themselves to one role they—certain kinds of artists—have the ability to take on more than one role or to imagine what it is like to be another person. But everybody needs this ability. I have a book on negotiations which you might find quite helpful. It's called *Getting to Yes Without Backing Down*. It's published by Penguin and it's by a group of people who work on nothing but negotiations. They're called "The Harvard Negotiating Team," and one of the first things they tell you is, "Try to imagine what it is like to be the other person." In other words, the United States should try to imagine what it is like to be Saddam Hussein. Because if you can see the problem from the point of view of the other person, you have a much better chance of resolving it. And that is the use of your imagination, to be somebody else.

Meltzer: So you think that the origins of creativity are not inheritance or socialization or lack of something else?

Atwood: All children are creative. Some to a greater degree, but they all have this, and it's how they learn. If you watch a child, all children sing, all children experiment with language, all children draw, all children role-play, all children tell stories. It seems to be a part of child development and if you remove this from the child, the child's growth will be stunted. So let us just take it as a given that all children are creative and then ask: What causes some people to continue to be creative and what stops other people? Probably we'll find in everybody's life a little corner where they keep their creativity; maybe it's gardening. //

Meltzer: Regarding *The Handmaid's Tale*, did you have that idea of writing a negative utopia first, and did you then collect the facts systematically? Or were there all these facts which led you to the idea of creating the Gilead system?

Atwood: Neither one. When you have ideas, they come out of a lot of work or experience that you may have done earlier without thinking it was going to lead to that. For instance, at one point in my life, I studied very intensively the American Puritans of the seventeenth century, and in another period of my life I read quite intensively a very large number of utopias and dystopias. But I did that many years before. I first read George Orwell's *1984* when I was fourteen without thinking, "Now I am going to write a negative utopia." What happens I think, with the creative idea is that a lot of work that you may have done before comes together at a certain point, and any scientist will tell you this as well. Archimedes would not have had his eureka experience in the bathtub if he had not been thinking about physical principles. Newton would not have had his intuition about gravity when the apple fell on his head if he hadn't been thinking about it. In other words, you don't have creative ideas about things that you never think about.

Meltzer: But it's not like a flash of lightning. It's a gradual process?

Atwood: No, it could be a flash of lightning, but it's a flash of lightning connected with what you've already been doing. I'm never going to have a brilliant mathematical intuition because I don't deal with mathematics. On the other hand, Einstein wasn't a very good poet. In fact, he probably wasn't a poet at all.

Meltzer: Do you design your plot elaborately before you start to write?

Atwood: No.

Meltzer: Do you see your characters visually?

Atwood: You can tell I can see them visually because I describe them visually. But any novelist will do this; you always hear what people look like.

Meltzer: Do you develop the plot during the process of writing?

Atwood: Yes. If I were a writer of murder mysteries I'd have to know what the plot was before I begin because—as Edgar Allan Poe said—all mysteries are written backwards. You have to know who done it before you begin. Then you can plant the clues as to who the murderer is. You have to know in advance who is the murderer. When you begin a novel you know some things about the characters, but I don't like to know too much because then it gets boring to write it. So I don't write murder mysteries. The end would be too predictable, because I already know it.

Meltzer: When you are writing a novel, do you start from the beginning?

Atwood: No, usually not. Sometimes I do, sometimes I don't. I'll often write a part that then migrates somewhere else in the book. *The Handmaid's Tale* began with the hanging scene, which is now towards the back of the book. If you watch two-year-olds playing in a sand table, it's much the same thing. They arrange something, they dig it out, they rearrange it, they take elements that they have and make something out of it. People mystify creativity. But it's not some very rare esoteric thing that only a few people have.

This is my workbook that I carry around. This is a manuscript. There's another one. There's more of it. Sometimes I start at the back. This is the beginning of an essay that I'm doing. There are some notes to it. You can see how messy it is. Not very orderly. On the other hand, that's how people work.

Meltzer: Are there certain phases during the process of writing? A high concentration phase combined with a total withdrawal from human relationships, from life in general?

Atwood: That's a very romantic thought. Occasionally you find that in the biographies of men. They are able to do this because they have somebody else who is doing the dishes for them and the laundry and preparing the meals. Sometimes I go off by myself and write for short periods of time. I wrote part of *The Robber Bride* while spending a week in a log cabin with no electricity. And I go to other countries to write, but total withdrawal from human relations? No, you can't do that if you have a family.

Meltzer: But sometimes men say that they wrote a book in one stormy night. For instance, Rilke. He said that he wrote a book [*Die Weise van Liebe und Tod des Cornets* Christoph Rilke] in one stormy night, and that's not true because there are three really different versions.

Atwood: Well, he may have written the first draft in one stormy night. Like Rider Haggard said that he wrote *She* in six weeks, etc., etc. Obviously, you have periods when you are working more quickly than in other periods. But so it is with any kind of human endeavor.

Meltzer: Do you sometimes suffer when you're writing?

Atwood: This is another romantic idea. Everybody suffers anyway. It's not just artists who suffer. Artists articulate suffering, but that doesn't mean that other people don't suffer. The reason that people turn to certain kinds of music and poetry is that those kinds of music and poetry articulate what they themselves are feeling. I once had a young writer say to me: "In order to be a writer, do I have to go out and suffer?" And I said, "Don't worry about it. You get the suffering anyway. You don't have to go out looking for it."

Meltzer: Goethe once said, *"Mir gab ein Gott zu sagen, was ich leide."* God gave me the gift to say how I suffer.

Atwood: Yes, but notice that it was the gift of saying, not the gift of suffering.

Meltzer: So you wouldn't say that there are clear-cut phases in the process of writing?

Atwood: The thing about people who do this a lot is that they don't usually think much about how they do it. It's other people who are interested in analyzing creativity, not creative people. So I suppose you could discover this from looking at the journals of some artists. In a way, that applies to all creative artists: first you do this, then you do this, and after that you do this. Obviously, first I write a first draft, then I revise it. In other words, you can't revise it before you've written it. So there are some things that logically follow. Then you think about the cover design, etc. I think one generalization you can make is that in order for a new idea to come you need a certain amount of empty space in your life. Someone who is continuously occupied with many small details is unlikely to have the space for a new idea to come into their life, and often the work ethic interferes with creative ideas because the work ethic says that every minute of our time has to be filled with work that we do. Well, for a creative person, some of the work is doing nothing. It drives other people crazy. But unless you have that moment of listening, unless you're able to listen…You need silence within yourself in order to listen, if you're talking all the time you're not listening. Unless you can listen, you won't hear anything.

Meltzer: Do you think if people have lost their creativity they could go to the desert and live there for some days or weeks because there is silence?

Atwood: It's an old shamanistic technique. Well-known to the prophets. Yes, of course. And it doesn't have to be the desert. The seashore will do or any place where they are not pursuing their ordinary round of chores. That's why people take vacations. They take vacations to have what they call "time to themselves." But what does that mean, time to yourself? It means time when you are not occupied with the small, usual concerns of your world. Some people use that time just to rest. If you want to go and renew your creativity you probably need longer than two weeks. So what you're going to be writing about is executive burn-out. People who feel that their energy has all been used up. //

Meltzer: You once said: "My life is full of unfinished stories. It always has been."

Atwood: That's right. Yeah, but I might lose interest in finishing them.

Meltzer: So there are thousands of ideas. What leads you to one particular idea which you then develop in your writing?

Atwood: It becomes the most interesting.

Meltzer: Do you write a daily diary?

Atwood: No. No, I'm very unsatisfactory in that respect. I know that everybody is constantly telling people to do this. I don't do it and I never have. I might write in a journal once a month and once every two months. That's pretty sporadic. //

Meltzer: The protagonist in *The Edible Woman*, Marian, is roughly the same age as you were at the time. Now the main characters in your last novel, *The Robber Bride*, correspond again to your age. What would be your explanation for that?

Atwood: Well, they do and they don't. Remember they each have a childhood and they each have a young womanhood, so each of them is three different ages. Again, most of the answers to most questions are extremely simple. It's very obvious that somebody who has lived fifty years is better equipped to write about a fifty-year-old than someone who has lived twenty years. To put it in an extremely simple-minded way: old people have once been young, but young people have never been old and therefore they don't know very much about it, although they think they do.

Meltzer: Do you think you could write a novel or a text where the protagonist, the female protagonist, is fifteen years old?

Atwood: Yes, of course, and I have.

Meltzer: I mean now.

Atwood: Yes, of course.

Meltzer: Are artists somewhat like vampires?

Atwood: Well, that's another romantic idea. It was much promoted in the nineteenth century. I don't think so. I mean, you can be very interested in Gothic horror, you can write stories like that, you can make that equation. But I think it's only one way of looking at things. By "vampires" do you mean that they take real life and use it for their own ends? I think that might be true if nobody else ever read what they wrote. But in fact whose ends are they really using it for? If you postulate writing which has no readers, or if you postulate painting that has no viewers, or a musical composition that has no listeners, then you could say that the artist was selfishly taking this material and using it only for his or her gratification, but what the artist really does is take the material, make it into something and then give it back. Vampires are not noted for giving things back.

Meltzer: Do you think that you can teach creative writing?

Atwood: You can do workshops that are helpful to people, but you cannot tell another person how or what to write, especially what. You can't turn a person who is really not very gifted into a person who is a genius. You can take someone who is not a very good writer and turn them into a competent writer. That's about it.

Meltzer: What do you think could be literature's contribution to the economic world? Flexibility, for instance?

Atwood: The economic world makes a lot of money out of literature. Think of all the printers, designers, booksellers, etc., that it actually supports in a very simple-minded way. Paper-making, printing. But apart from that, well, every single human being has a "story of my life." Everyone has his or her own narrative, which he or she is constantly revising. By which I mean that the story you tell about yourself now is quite different from the story you told about yourself ten years ago, though it might contain the same events. Your point of view about those events has shifted and the story that you will tell about yourself ten years from now is going to be different again. // So, everybody is involved in narrative and to that extent, everybody is involved in fiction. People fictionalize themselves. They turn themselves into characters in their own dramas and they turn other people into characters in their own drama, so they fictionalize other people constantly. They project onto other people roles that they carry around inside their heads, probably left over from their childhoods and families, and they see other people in their lives as those roles. Often quite unjustly. By studying real fiction they might gain an insight into how they themselves are fictionalizing and into what is really fiction, that is, what they've made up about other people and what is really there.

Meltzer: So it is to problematize reality as well?

Atwood: No, to deproblematize it. If you look at how fiction writers problematize it, you can see that it's partly an invention. Then you can see to what extent you yourself are inventing, so you can demythologize the way you're connecting your life and divest yourself of dangerous illusions which you have invented yourself. OK? Some psychoanalysts describe what they are doing with their patient as "working on the patient's narrative." They are working on the patient's fiction. It is not that it's safe to become a fiction entirely because we can't do that, we will continue to fictionalize. That's what human beings do. But they can revise the fiction, so that it's a more optimistic fiction and less prone to disaster. In other words, if the scenario that you have written for yourself is a tragedy, you will constantly arrange your life so that the outcomes to your adventures will be tragic, because that is what fits your narrative. Whereas if your fiction is comic, then your episodes will probably have happier outcomes for you because you will not arrange to have these psychic disasters occur.

Meltzer: Is there anything else you want to say about creativity that I didn't ask?

Atwood: I think everybody should go out and get themselves a set of colored pencils and play with them. They will have fun. I think one thing about being an adult is that the role definition that we have made up for adults is that they have to be very serious and boring all the time. So I think that if we expanded the role definition of adults to include more play—and I don't mean just golf—probably people would be happier and would enjoy their stay on earth more than they do.

Meltzer: You are tremendously encouraging...

Atwood: Well, I'm just old. You get that way after a while. Especially men, they think they have to be really serious all the time. Poor things. Think of how difficult it is for them. I think women have more latitude for play, if only in the clothing department.

Meltzer: That's a beginning.

Atwood: People often say women are frivolous for being so interested in clothes, but I think dressing up is a form of play. Clothing yourself in different ways is again a continuation of what children do when they play dress-up. //

To Write Is to Wrestle with an Angel in the Mud

Rudolf Bader

The following interview originally appeared in the March 1995 issue of *Anglistik: Organ des Verbandes Deutscher Anglisten.* Reprinted with permission.

Bader: From the volume *Margaret Atwood: Conversations* we can conclude that you take rather a critical attitude towards literary interviews. So let us agree on one point: First and foremost, a writer's work ought to speak for itself. However, it seems to me there are a number of areas to be explored in such an interview as this, and there are some questions whose answers might be very fruitful for the critical reception of your work in the German academic community as well as for the awareness of Canadian/ international/post-colonial writing in this part of the world.

In *The Handmaid's Tale*, Professor Pieixoto has considerable difficulties in his attempts to discover the truth about the tale. This raises basic questions about scholarly research in general. In this light, what are your opinions and feelings about the fact that German professors of English are studying and teaching your work, probably discovering many "truths"?

Atwood: It's not so much that I'm "critical" about interviews; I simply acknowledge that the interview form is a form, too— sometimes an art form—and one can't expect it to arrive at "the truth," the whole truth, and nothing but the truth. Having worked in Market Research, I'm very aware of how the way questions are posed, and by whom, and in what context, and even in what order, can influence the answers.

A good interview is like a good conversation. It's an exchange. Impressions may be gained from it; things may be learned; but it doesn't necessarily provide the reader with "the truth." Notice that only one who has respect for "the truth" as a concept would bother making such distinctions. But "truth" is like "goodness." No one perfectly attains it, but that doesn't mean we should stop thinking about it, or give up on it altogether.

As for literary criticism, I have nothing against it. It's a human activity, in that human beings like to comment on things that other human beings have done, and they also like to attempt to extract symbolic meanings from their environments. In general, there are two lines of descent for literary criticism: first, exchange of news and gossip around the village well, which has given us newspapers and book reviews, which concentrate especially on the "new" aspects—so-and-so has published a book, and this is what it's about, and this is what we think about it, and its cover, and its jacket photo; and second, priestly prophecy—examinations of birds' entrails, and the like—which has evolved into the exegesis of sacred texts such as the Sibylline Leaves, the Bible, the Koran, and so forth, which developed, in the Protestant tradition especially, into the sermon, and later into academic literary criticism, in which a text considered "sacred" enough for the purposes has its entrails examined to see what it means, and what it may mean for the society, and what the commentator has to say about previous commentaries.

I've done both kinds myself, so I know the hazards. I grew up among scientists, and was made very aware of the fact that what you find is often influenced by what you think you're looking for. Again, what you get is one person's version of "the truth," not necessarily "*the* truth." And the process of analyzing a work— to paraphrase a recent speech of mine—is almost completely opposite to the process of creating it. Literary critics start with an already-written text. They then address questions to this text, "What does it mean?" being both the most basic and the most difficult. Novelists, on the other hand, start with the blank page, to which they similarly address questions. But the questions are different. Instead of asking, first of all, "What does it mean?" they work at the widget level; they ask, "Is this the right word?" "What does it mean?" can only come when there is an "it" to mean something. Novelists have to get some actual words down before they can fiddle with the theology. Or, to put it another way: God started with chaos—dark, without form and void—and so does the novelist. Then God made one detail at a time. So does the novelist. On the seventh day. God took a breath to consider what he'd done. So does the novelist. But the critic starts on Day 7.

In short, the novelist's concerns are more practical than those of the critic, and less concerned with metaphysics. It's only with a completed work that the overall pattern can be investigated.

Bader: You seem to view academics like Antonia Fremont, one of the protagonists in your novel *The Robber Bride* (and others, in your earlier novels), in a particularly ironic light. Even though this might be a touchy question, what is your experience with academics, and what do you think of the value of their work?

Atwood: Was it George Steiner who said that the critic was the postman to the future? I've been an academic myself, so I can't have disapproved of them entirely. I don't think I'm anymore ironic about them than I am about anyone else, although their calling does allow for a bit more irony, since the gap between the great and high-minded concerns they're supposed to be involved with professionally and the minutiae of daily life does tend to be rather wide. "To be or not to be," and the backbiting and power politics and petty jealousies at the departmental meeting, and who left the dirty coffee cup in the staff room sink…well, there's lots of scope. And when we get into the realm of obfuscation, jargon for its own sake, shibboleth fetishism, deliberate mystification, and sloppy logic, then surely social satire is not uncalled for. Not that all academics do these kinds of things. I myself, when an academic, was entirely free of these faults, and always, always washed my own coffee cup…

As for "the value of their work," that does depend on the individual work, doesn't it? Northrop Frye was one of my teachers. Perry Miller was another, Jerome Buckley a third. I learned a great deal from all of them, though not always what they thought they were teaching. Jay Macpherson, at Victoria College, Toronto, was invaluable; also Jack Robson, and Geoffrey Payzant, one of my Philosophy teachers. And many others. So the work of these people was valuable to me.

One theory about the university is that it provides a sort of haven, or protected enclave, in which activities can go on that don't have any obvious commercial application. Academic work therefore affirms that there are human values apart from the making of money. I myself happen to think that's a good thing, but an economist might not. For more on the subject, see

Lewis Hyde's book, *The Gift: Imagination and the Erotic Life of Property*—a book I'm in the habit of recommending to young writers—which notes that there are two methods of human exchange—money exchange and gift exchange—and that different rules apply in each area. Academic work and artistic pursuits exist in the realm of the gift, and have value, or fail to have it, according to those laws.

Bader: You are indeed the best-known Canadian writer, not only in North America but also in Europe. I have attended several of your readings in the past ten years, and you seem to me an extremely talented reader of your own work and indeed an excellent performer. Do you find many differences in your audiences' responses between Europe and Canada, and between academic and general audiences?

Atwood: Audiences vary from country to country, from city to city, and even from night to night. They also vary according to such things as the excellence of the sound system—if it's bad you can't be heard—and how close the reader is to the listeners, and whether elevated on a stage or not. (In general, the closer you are, the more intimate the experience.) Language problems play a part; political perceptions; gender ratios; and cultural expectations—is the audience there to have a good time, or to be educated? Are you supposed to laugh? and so forth. Audiences can also sense whether a reader is ill at ease—your discomfort will make them uncomfortable, too.

With so many factors at work, it would be risky to generalize, but I'll do it anyway. The Swedes are very shy, but interested in social significance. British people don't want to ask the first question; they aren't afraid of the speaker, but of the other British people; they don't want to look foolish in front of them; or that's my theory. (Less true of the Celts.) Southerners in the United States, Texas included, have a rowdy sense of humor. British Columbia is relaxed and open. Los Angeles wants to know if it will be a film—or if it has been one, what you think of it. They aren't alone in this. Germans appreciate it if you speak a little German, but are usually surprised when you do, and want to know how you learned it. New Yorkers are very quick, and ask challenging questions (and lots of them). Nova Scotia is friendly to me because my family's from there. But Toronto is the hardest place for me to read in. I started there, in 1960, in a coffee house, when I was very young— poetry readings used to make me physically ill—and it still makes me nervous. I always feel that my slip must be showing, even if I'm not wearing one.

Bader: To what extent do you feel related to other writers in the post-colonial context?

Atwood: To those of my own generation, and from British ex-colonies, quite strongly, because we had similar educational experiences: a mostly British curriculum, with not much about our own countries. Austin Clarke, who comes from the Barbados, has a book entitled *Growing Up Stupid Under the Union Jack*, which I expect a lot of "colonials" would find relevant. And, as colonial or recently post-colonial writers, we had similar difficulties publishing—in our own countries, and elsewhere—and as a result became involved in parallel kinds of cultural activities. In Canada, in the '60s and early '70s, that meant the starting of new publishing companies, the effort to get Canadian literature taught in Canadian schools, the formation of writers' organizations, and a certain amount of lobbying of our government.

But I expect it's different for younger generations—though they too have to deal with big-country domination of popular culture. It's been different, too, in countries in which the governing class as a group were a different color from the majority of the governed. (The problem if you were a white Canadian was invisibility, not visibility; you were always mistaken for someone else.) The situation of women, too, differs from country to country. And it's very different for people from countries that now have self-rule, but a dictatorial and oppressive self-rule. One thinks of Nigeria— which has produced such great writers, and now seems bent on squashing them.

Not many political leaders have a great deal of respect for writing and other cultural matters, no matter what country they come from. They do seem to be more interested in power and money. But that doesn't seem to be a "post-colonial" problem. Just a universal one.

Bader: You stated on various occasions that *Grimm's Fairy Tales* have been an important influence on your own writing. This is easily understood in relation to your earlier novel *Lady Oracle*, but it is also visible in your most recent novel *The Robber Bride*. For the benefit of our mainly German audience, could you tell us a bit more about your fascination with the so-called "Gothic" aspect and your attitude to the Germanic tradition?

Atwood: I first encountered the Grimm's tales when I was quite young—my parents sent away for them, by mail order, not really knowing what they would be getting. What arrived was complete and unexpurgated, and my parents were somewhat horrified—they hadn't realized there was so much gore—and were worried that the children would be frightened by them. We weren't, though—maybe we'd been broken in by having Beatrix Potter read to us; she's fairly gory, too. So these stories have been important to me because I read them very early. To them I added many volumes of fairy tales—the Andrew Lang collections—and things like the "Arabian Nights"; then the Greek myths. And of course, the Bible stories.

Stories like these are important to writers—or were important to me, as a writer—because they convey an idea of what a "story" is. They give a sense of pattern, of design. They also do not color within the lines of "realism"; they spill over into the areas of dream and the paranormal, which are also an important part of human experience—whatever you think of the physical or psychological realities underlying these phenomena. I read Poe at this time, as well; it was an era in which primary-school librarians thought that anything without sex in it was suitable for children.

Later on, I read Native myths, which was important for me; for a Canadian reader, some of these characters have now attained "known" status, in stories by Native and non-Native alike—think of the use to which Mordecai Richler puts Raven in *Solomon Gursky Was Here*, and how Sheila Watson uses Coyote, in *The Double Hook*—and Thomas King's Coyote in "One Good Story, That One", and Tomson Hiway's Nanabush. And of course the Wendigo, which has turned up in many places.

Writers use references to known stories to give resonance and pattern to their work, and I have found some Grimm's tales (among stories from other sources) useful for that purpose. I think the Grimm's stories are often more available to women writers—

when featuring woman characters—than the Bible or the Greek myths, because they contain a larger number of active female protagonists—possibly because many of the stories were retold by women. (See Marina Warner's recent book on the subject.)

But there's another element, too, which is suggested by Michael Hurley's recent book, *The Borders of Nightmare* (University of Toronto Press). This is a study of a well-known nineteenth-century Canadian writer. Major Richardson—author of *Wacousta. Wacousta* is an intensely Gothic book, and Richardson's other work is even more so. Hurley suggests that Richardson is in fact the ancestral figure to a whole strain—one might even say "school"—of writers, which he and others have called "Southern Ontario Gothic." They would include James Reaney (who adapted *Wacousta* for the stage, among other things); the Marian Engel of *Bear*; Michael Ondaatje, especially in *In the Skin of a Lion*; Graeme Gibson, almost throughout; Jane Urquart, especially in *The Whirlpool*, Gwendolyn MacEwen; Sylvia Fraser; Alice Munro, in some of her recent stories; Robertson Davies, especially the *Deptford Trilogy*; Timothy Findley; Matt Cohen, at times; the younger writer Barbara Gowdy, especially in *We So Seldom Look on Love*, and Susan Swan; and myself. I am sure there are others, but I'm writing from memory. (This list is partly Hurley's, and partly mine.) In his analysis, he talks about the region, and suggests why the literature has shown such leaning towards the Gothic. Part of it has to do with his theory about borders. (Canada is populated mostly along its borders.) In *Grimm's Fairy Tales* there are borders, too, the most noteworthy one being that between forest and non-forest, and here one might consider what happens in forests, in literature, in general. (Canada has a lot of forests.)

So there may just be a certain number of affinities.

Bader: Do you think that Gothic mystery (or horror) adds to the provocative potential of a (postmodernist) novel or short story?

Atwood: All novels are mystery novels; that is, there's something we know by the end that we didn't know at the beginning (or so we fondly hope, when we begin to read; if not, we call the novel "predictable"). This is true even of works based on "known" plots; in this case the unknown thing is a how, or a why, not a what.

Said another way: in a novel—or a narrative of any sort, such as a play—something has to happen. And that something has to involve change and conflict. This is why Milton found Heaven so difficult to write about—it's static, because perfection cannot change—whereas he obviously enjoyed rendering Hell much more. Ditto for Dante.

I'm not sure what you mean by "horror"—not just violent or gruesome events, I take it—atmosphere? Usually the "horror" part of a horror story is in the buildup, not the denouement. One of the most successful psychological horror stories is Henry James's "The Beast In The Jungle," in which the horror is that nothing has happened. I think "horror" only really interests us when it represents a hidden part of the soul—the shadow self. What we have concealed from ourselves. Certainly those pieces that overdo the gore, in a Grand Guignol way, are more likely to end up being funny or kitschy, or merely tedious—just a matter of icky bits. (I myself have not actually put in that many icky bits, when you count them up.)

But lots of people have lots of opinions about the Gothic, by which they seem to mean almost anything that doesn't consist of getting up in the morning, having breakfast, an amorous interlude, etc. Come to think of it, in real life all stories have a Gothic beginning (blood, screams); an unsolved mystery (what am I doing here?) and a Gothic ending (death); and we spend a third of our lives in the Gothic underworld (asleep). Then of course there are the newspapers—most of the stories in them are Gothic. (Wars, murders, lies, brigands, bloodsucking, mysteries, false identities.) These sorts of things appear to be of interest to human beings.

As for the answer to your question: it all depends on how well it's done.

Bader: Whereas your earlier work (poetry and prose fiction) was generally understood as typically Canadian in feeling, atmosphere and thematic approach—not only in terms of the Survival myth—your more recent work, let's say your two novels *Cat's Eye* and *The Robber Bride*, though still set in Canada, seems to deal more generally (universally?) with dramatic and traumatic implications of changes: in human relationships as well as in any individual's *raison d'etre*. In this perspective, *The Handmaid's Tale* would appear as a kind of turning point in your writing career. Would you regard this as an oversimplification, or to what extent could you go along with this view in terms of your own perception (and not in critical or academic terms, which, as you have repeatedly pointed out in interviews, you leave to others)?

Atwood: Well, as you've indicated, this is the kind of thing I can't really say much about. The reason I can't is that I don't know much about it. The reason I don't know much about it is that I don't think much about it. The reason I don't think much about it is that I'm not very interested in it; also, it would make me too self-conscious. I don't get up in the morning and ask myself what point I've reached in my writing career. I think, "What about Chapter Six—should I try to fix it, or just scrap the whole thing?" I don't think about what I do as "my writing career." I think of it as this book I'm writing; more likely, this chapter, this paragraph, this sentence. To write is to wrestle with an angel in the mud. When that's going on, you don't have much perspective on your "writing career"—I do like to try different things. Otherwise I'd get bored.

(But *Wilderness Tips* seems to me—post-wrestling—a very Canadian sort of book. I guess that would kind of shoot down your proposed theory.)

Bader: One of your preoccupations in *Cat's Eye* appears to be with the passage of time and how we humans experience it. Your novel carries echoes of other great novels tackling this dimension, such as Marcel Proust's *À la récherche du temps perdu* and Anthony Powell's *A Dance to the Music of Time*. Did you address the philosophical question of the time dimension consciously in your work, and where did this preoccupation originate in your own perception of the world?

Atwood: It's hard to write about the passage of time when you haven't lived through very much of it. (When I was sixteen. I wrote a short story about a character I thought was tottering on the brink of the grave—she was forty—which I now find embarrassingly funny.) That's why novels by very young writers tend—as a rule—to focus more on the present time-line. The heroine of my first published novel, *The Edible Woman*, hardly has a past at all. You could possibly do a *Bildungsroman* at that stage, but writers mostly don't. They mostly wait until they're a little older.

Time is a fact of life. In some ways, it is *the* fact of life. It might even be considered the true hidden subject of all novels. As the Henry James biographer Leon Edel says, you know it's a novel if it's got a clock in it. In that sense, all novelists are writing about time—because in a novel, something has to happen, and it can't happen except in time, and over time. As for tackling a long stretch of time—*Cat's Eye* covers forty-plus years. *The Robber Bride* covers about fifty, if you count them up—doing that can be useful for a writer, because things look different from different perspectives. What was a tragedy when you were twenty may seem a comedy at forty and by sixty you may have mostly forgotten about it. Or what was long viewed as an insignificant detail may assume colossal proportions, in light of new information. Alice Munro does this beautifully in her most recent book of stories, *Open Secrets*.

I wish time were merely a philosophical problem. I don't think of it as that, however. It can't be "solved." But as one of those can't-live-with-it, can't-live-without-it foundation stones of life, like sunlight. You know you're subject to it every time you look in the mirror. But when people ask me how I react to growing older, I simply tell what is to me, so far, the obvious truth: it's better than the alternative.

Anyway, when you're older, you've got more material.

Bader: Let's talk about your most recent novel, *The Robber Bride*. Which of the three protagonists connected with the devilish, oppressive and elusive Zenia do you like best? Tony, Charis or Roz? Which woman, in your opinion, handles Zenia and the awkward situations connected with her in a manner most satisfactory, ethically most acceptable, and/or most typically Canadian?

Atwood: It's not really the business of writers to "like" their fictional characters in the same you would hope to "like" a roommate. The writer should like creating them, but that's a different thing. (Read John Keats on Shakespeare, in which he says that Shakespeare got as much pleasure out of creating Iago as he did out of creating Imogen; or The Book of Job, re: Leviathan, excellent in his own way; or William Blake on Tygers; or Charles Darwin on beetles. But you would not want to room with Iago, or Leviathan, or a Tyger, or a beetle.) Nor is it the business of the writer to judge the characters in the way you propose: to create people that can be approved of morally, and so forth. One of my teachers once said that the only thing that mattered to her about a work of art was, is it alive, or is it dead? Robert Louis Stevenson tackles this goodness versus energy problem in *The Master of Ballantrae*; then there's *Wuthering Heights*. (Heathcliff would have been a terrible roommate—he would never have helped with the dishes—but he's certainly alive.) Characters may be ethically acceptable and all the rest of it, and we might vote for them as mayor, but they can still be dead as the proverbial doornail.

As for "typically Canadian"—ten provinces, a climate that ranges from the Carolinian to the Arctic, two "official" languages, many other unofficial ones, fifty-two autochthonous ones— typical? Anyway, women whose men are being hoisted by impostors don't worry about being typically Canadian, as a rule. I suppose it might be typical that none of these women commits murder. We do have a fairly low crime rate. But that could be a gender difference…

Bader: You must have gained enormous satisfaction creating a character like Zenia. Have you been criticized for what you did with a female character? Or, to put it even more provocatively: Isn't the Devil a male?

Atwood: There seem to be two questions here. I'll take the last one first: Is the Devil a male? Those versed in their demonology know that the Devil is a spirit, and as such can assume the form of whatever it wants to—man, woman, dog, etc. It depends on what the Devil is up to at the moment and who it's tempting. Satan is depicted as a snake with the torso of a woman in several medieval Temptation scenes (Adam, Eve, tree, Satan-as-snake-woman wound around it). During the times of the witch hunts, the Devil was always assumed to be male, so as to allow room for all that devilish sex that was supposed to be going on; women were supposed to be particularly susceptible to his charms, which was held to account for the high ratio of women witches that were hanged, disemboweled, and burned as opposed to male ones. If you believe that, I'd like to sell you the Brooklyn Bridge!

Of course, it's convenient for the Zenias of this world to have men believe that the Devil is a man. It makes them less subject to suspicion.

Your second question contains a whole host of hidden assumptions For instance, have we now reacted so strongly against witch hunts that it's assumed to be morally wrong to depict a woman behaving badly? Or, from whom is this criticism supposed to have come? Men? Women? People with no sense of humor or literary background? Some sort of theoretical "feminist"? In real life, the feminists are now turning out books with titles like *Lesbian Vampire Stories*, which make poor Zenia look like rather tame stuff.

The idea that women are nicer, "gooder," and better-behaved than men is really a mid-nineteenth-century one. If all women really were like that, they wouldn't have inspired so much literature telling them that that was the way they *ought* to be. Pedestals do place one higher up, but there isn't a lot of room on them to move around. Define women as altogether innocent, and you define them as potential victims—you limit their roles in literature to suffering and running away. Also if women are good by nature, they have no free will. The power to act must include the power to act badly.

It's true that women don't conduct all-women wars, nor do they rape and murder—so far—as much as men do. But Zenia is not a murderer. She is a confidence artist like Felix Krull of Thomas Mann's novel, though more malevolent than him. Her patron, too, is Mercury—god of tricksters and thieves, but also the messenger of the gods, and the guide to the Underworld. Her methods are somewhat different from Felix's, though she too is physically attractive; but their aims are much the same. Zenia has many female ancestors. Think of Delilah, Medea, Moll Flanders, Thackeray's Becky Sharp, Tennyson's Vivien, almost anything by Swinburne, Edith Wharton's Undine Spragg, Daphne Du Maurier's Rebecca, Aldous Huxley's Lucy Tantamount, the Dietrich of *The Blue Angel*—and that host of femmes fatales that haunted the second half of the nineteenth century, not only in literature but in art—the Pre-Raphaelites, art nouveau—and opera (*Tales of Hoffmann*), and ballet (*Swan Lake*). Nor is such a figure entirely a male fantasy. Look into any women's magazine, and you'll see a lot of vampy ads, especially for lingerie and perfume. The idea that such things are just male projections being imposed on women implies that women are zombies and idiots, with no minds of their own. The fact is that such images represent power. It may not be a kind of power you approve of, but it's power all the same.

As for the female reaction, as I've experienced it in person and in letters, there have been many statements from women whose men have been the target of a Zenia (of course, any woman who goes after another one's man is seen by the first as a Zenia). And there's also been a surprising amount of sympathy for Zenia and identification with her. As one Englishwoman put it: "Women are tired of being good all the time."

Bader: How do you feel about your own work in translation? Do you feel that the translator's consciousness stands between you and your work, or doesn't it bother you?

Atwood: There are only two other languages about which I'm at all qualified to have any opinion whatsoever—French, and to a lesser extent, German—and even in these two I'm not competent enough to pronounce on such things as nuance, *jeux de mots*, slang and patois, etc. When it comes to the other languages in which my work has appeared I'm completely at sea. I know, for instance, not a word of Finnish, Japanese, Chinese, or Urdu—though I might be able to make a stab at Icelandic since it's so close to Anglo-Saxon! In these matters, a writer has to rely on the judgment of the publisher; after the fact, you can ask the opinion of any native speakers who may cross your way.

The translations are usually longer than the original, because the English language has a very large vocabulary, since it hasn't been shy about adapting or borrowing words from all sorts of other languages. (French and Latin and the Celtic languages, of course; but consider, too, *kimono, hara-kiri, verandah, pyjamas, igloo, anorak, chinook, wigwam,* and so forth.) That means that one English word may take several words in another language to render its precise meaning. But as we all know, some words just can't be translated; and some cultural concepts don't cross borders very easily, either. I read many books myself that have been translated into English. Sometimes they add footnotes to explain things that would not be self-evident to a Westerner, and I am invariably grateful for this.

I'm also grateful to be able to read these books, and the fact that I can is entirely due to the labors of translators. I know, of course, that I'm not getting the original book, but I'm getting something of the original, and if well-done, something I can understand (to a certain extent) and enjoy—which without translation I wouldn't be able to.

A good translation is not a literal transcription, but a rendering; translation isn't just a skill, but a form of art. //

Not a Cash Crop

John Stone

The following interview took place in Barcelona during Margaret Atwood's Spanish visit. It originally appeared in the November 1995 issue of *Revista Española de Estudios Canadienses*. Reprinted with permission.

Stone: "Political correctness" hasn't really arrived here in Spain yet. Could you comment on the effects of political correctness, on how the Canadian experience has differed from that in the United States, and (perhaps more importantly) how political correctness influences society beyond the university? Does it change the dynamics of a literary scene? (I know there was a "Writing Thru Race" conference organized in Canada a while back, to which only "minority" writers were invited.) Why is class not a factor in PC calculations?

Atwood: "Political correctness" seems to be on the way out, as it is now used as a term of derision to describe someone who is foolishly, puritanically fanatical in his or her notions of what you "should" say or not say. The whole thing began in a well-meaning way as an attempt to counteract the discriminatory effects of racism, sexism, and, yes, classism, and a myriad of other isms that have since appeared on the scene (age-ism—discrimination against old people; height-ism—discrimination against the short, and so forth). In some quarters of society there have been efforts to redress imbalances through, for instance, selective hiring policies. But if you hire one person you can't hire another who might have expected the job. And if you confer power on a person, then that person is a person with power and may exercise it in turn by rewarding allies and excluding non-group members. To quote Kurt Vonnegut, "and so it goes." Let us just say that when the pie is smaller than the number of people wishing to eat it there will be a certain amount of jostling.

And, of course, if you make a word—such as "racist" or "misogynist"—into an effective weapon, some people will be injured. This has happened in Canada. Also there has recently been a backlash, particularly on the part of those who have privilege and wish to keep it, as is usually the case with human beings. But the whole thing was set in motion in the first place by a devotion to the ideas of fairness and equity—which are surely not in themselves bad ideas.

Let us just mention that another form of "political correctness" was long in force in North America, was barely challenged, and can still be a very potent destructive weapon—I mean the political correctness of the conservative Right, which uses words like "communist" and "atheist" as search-and-destroy weapons. This form is so pervasive and so widely accepted that it is hardly ever mentioned in the popular press. It's these folks who have done most of the book-banning.

Stone: "Mestizaje" (a mixing of races, now used to denote a mixing of cultures) is a popular, all-purpose word here at the moment. Spain has received very few immigrants in its modern history so it's hard to say what the reality of "mestizaje" is. Canada has received a great many, especially in the last thirty years.

Atwood: In fact, in the Middle Ages and earlier, Spain had quite a lot of "mixing," via the Moorish regime and the reconquest. And Spain currently contains a certain amount of ethnic and linguistic mixture—witness Catalonia and the Basques. But these "mixtures" have been present for some time. I suppose the region of Spain which is now experiencing the most new mixture is. Catalonia, where there is a migration of Spanish-speakers coming into a Catalan-speaking area—or so I've been told.

In Canada immigration—the flow of populations into territories which they did not "originally" inhabit (I place "originally" in quotation marks, because all human populations anywhere other than Africa are a result of migration by homo sapiens)—is a motif with a very long history. It predates the arrival of the Europeans and was greatly accelerated after their advent. All people alive in Canada today who are not Native people (and the Native peoples themselves now include quite a lot of "mixture") are either historically recent immigrants or the descendants of such immigrants. These immigrants arrived in waves—for example, French during the seventeenth and eighteenth centuries, political refugee Loyalists from the United States immediately after the American Revolution in 1776, Scots after the Highland Clearances, Irish after the Potato Famine, escaped slaves from the United States up to 1860, Eastern Europeans in the early twentieth century, and many Dutch, Germans, and Italians right after the Second World War. The most recent immigrant waves have been from the Caribbean, from Somalia, from Portugal, from India and Pakistan, and from the Far East, Hong Kong in particular. But immigration *per se* is not a novel phenomenon.

Stone: Twenty years ago you wrote a thematic book of criticism on Canadian literature, *Survival*, which couldn't take into account the Canadian writers who are themselves immigrants (few of them had started to publish). Writing by people who came to Canada is now a big part of Canadian literature. Why such abundance? Other countries receive immigrants, but writing often begins with the second generation and concentrates on the immigrant experience. In Canada that would almost be the exception.

Atwood: One of the recurring themes in Canadian literature has been the immigrant experience—the encounter with a new land, a new culture, and new problems. And immigrant literature of this kind was by no means confined to second-generation immigrants, especially when English or French were the first languages of the immigrants. Some of the first books to come out of Canada were of this kind—the Jesuit Relations and the work of Susanna Moodie and Anna Jameson, for example.

But you probably meant work by more recent immigrants. Actually, *Survival*—which was published in 1972—does contain a chapter on this very subject. It is called "Failed Sacrifices: The Reluctant Immigrant." Naturally, *Survival* couldn't talk about writers who hadn't yet written, but immigrant literature written since that time has quite often fallen into similar patterns: What am I doing here, why did I come, why is it so cold, why aren't the people the same as the people I left behind? Or else, what I think of as "the missionary position": These people are barbarians. I am from a better culture. I will civilize them and lead them to the true religion, and so forth. As for why there is so much recent-immigrant literature right now, multi-culturalism and ethnicity are hot numbers in North American universities these days, so books that might once have been passed over by publishers as not being mainstream enough are able to appear. And some of them also find audiences, as the readership right now finds the general area of interest.

A parallel development has been the appearance of a number of fine Native novelists, poets, and playwrights. (See, for instance, the work of Thomas King and Tomson Hiway.) The end of the twentieth century, at least in North America, appears open to a multiplicity of voices.

Stone: At a PEN Club conference here two years ago you spoke about voice appropriation, a controversy in Canada over arts funding. What was meant by "voice appropriation"? I understood that writers setting their work in cultures too far removed from their own—a white writer of juvenile fiction using, say, Micmac legends as the basis for a collection of stories—were to be considered too risky for writers' grants. Where did this idea come from, and what has happened to it?

Atwood: This idea—so I'm told—originated some years ago among certain radical lesbians, who felt that one should not write from a lesbian point of view unless one had lived the life—that one somehow didn't have, not the artistic, but the moral right to do so. And some Native people felt that one shouldn't make money by writing about Native art, etc., unless one were indeed a Native person. A linked view was that non-Native people were likely to get it wrong in any case, and to present a distorted version to the world. In each case the group in question felt that others should not profit by exploiting them as literary resources. This notion spread so that some purists got it into their heads that no one should create a fictional character that was not (in color, ethnicity, age, gender and sexual preference) co-extensive with the author. Some thought that a man—for instance— should not write from a female point of view, which would certainly invalidate *Anna Karenina*, *Ulysses*, and *Madame Bovary*.

Of course, this "pure" theory only really works for, say, personal journals, or lyric poetry of a confessional nature. Anyone writing novels or plays quickly comes up against a wall. I suppose you could have an experimental play in which all five characters were you, but such an idea would only work once. We live in a world in which there are other kinds of people—especially on a continent in which different kinds of people have been bumping up against one another for centuries—and as writers we may have occasion to describe them. This fact of writing has now been generally recognized, and one hears a great deal less about "voice appropriation." But I suspect that many (probably white) writers are still self-censoring, lest they be accused of it.

Stone: A woman told me there are books she could get something out of at fourteen, and those that had to wait for her to do a little growing up, to reach twenty-five. She wasn't talking about difficult styles: she meant the things the writer said. Your books she puts into the second group.

Atwood: I think she is entirely correct. I myself don't believe that anyone under, say, twenty-two, can really understand George Eliot's *Middlemarch*. For the more complex, less judgmental works, you have to have undergone a certain amount of time. You need a few wrinkles. Older people have been younger so you can understand that; but younger people have never been older and are sometimes scornful of such things as resignation and compromise.

When I was fourteen, I was reading witless science-fictions, shockers like *Donovan's Brain*. (Though I was also reading Jane Austen and the Brontës.)

Stone: I've read *Surfacing* twice, and found it an equally spooky book on both occasions. I mean "spooky" in the sense of haunted: there are ghosts everywhere: in the landscape, in the language, in the absence of language, and especially inside the protagonist. And in the end the book haunted me. Was it your intention to write something that would leave the reader feeling haunted? Can the experience of going through a "haunting,"even in fiction, change one's ways of seeing?

Atwood: It was indeed my intention to write a ghost story—a venerable narrative form, and one of which I have always been fond. There are several kinds of ghost stories—ones in which the ghost haunts a place, but has no particular relationship to any given individual who may stumble into that place (you get haunted because you're there, not because of anything you did;

many M. R. James stories are of this type); ones in which the ghost returns to an individual because of a past relationship—love, crime (stories about vengeful ghosts are common); and more modern ones, in which the ghost is really a split-off fragment of the protagonist's psyche. Henry James's "The Jolly Corner" springs to mind. In the very best kind of ghost story, all three elements are present—place, past relationship, and psyche fragment. See, for instance, the ghost of Catherine Earnshaw in *Wuthering Heights*.

I wished to write a ghost story with all three elements, but without writing a genre-limited "ghost story." That is, I wanted the ghosts to be an element in my book but not the whole point of it. I wanted them to be simply there, the way dreams are there—just as a part of what may occur to us as human beings, because we are human and we do have "non-rational" experiences. (There's a ghost in *The Robber Bride*, by the way.) In other words true realism for me—faithfulness to life as it is experienced, rather than explained—includes more than "Realism."

So I am glad you felt haunted—it's a compliment! The landscape in which *Surfacing* is set—the northern shield country of Canada, with its many lakes, its lagoons, its dark forests, its loons with their eerie cries, its drowned people—is *per se* a haunting landscape that may have helped. And, of course, people are different after a "haunting." Less convinced that what is there is merely what can be seen, for one thing.

Stone: The story in *Surfacing* is about looking for a disappeared father, but the ghost story is about (among other things) trying to see the ghosts of both parents. On re-reading, the story about the mother's ghost became more prominent for me than the story about the father's ghost. Did you intend that pull on the reader to be as strong as it is?

Atwood: Yes, I did intend it. I wanted there to be two ghosts (obviously I wanted it, or I wouldn't have put them in), but the mother's is more of a surprise.

Stone: *Surfacing* reminded me of two Canadian films, *Dead Ringers* and *The Adjuster*. In both there's a very explicit sense of personalities that are divided, divided and in a sense haunted by the bits that have split off. The effect in all three cases is art that can make you feel very uneasy (spooked). For a lasting, deep fright, go to Canada. Is there any reason why Canadians should be good at producing terror, especially this lingering terror?

Atwood: I would say that both David Cronenberg and Atom Egoyan are firmly rooted in an already existing tradition, and that it's no accident that both are from Toronto, capital of Southern Ontario—a city well-known for being normal on the outside but strange on the inside. There is a branch of Canadian Literature that is spoken of as "Southern Ontario Gothic."//

Let's just say that inhabitants of borderlands generally—and Canadians in particular—tend to be conscious of their dual (or triple, or multiple) personalities, and of the possibilities of shape-shifting and metamorphosis. It may also have to do with the ratio of human beings to landscape (low), with the dominant element (water), and with the hypnotic effects of snow.

Stone: Another concern in *Surfacing*, and in many of your books, is the way the characters experience themselves through their bodies, through ideas they have about bodies. Has that always been a concern of yours? Is it something that foreign readers would find especially Anglo-Saxon about your work?

Atwood: Ah, the body. I thought Anglo-Saxons were considered prone to ignoring the body. My interest in bodies has usually been analyzed as a female one.

To put it very simply: we all have bodies. Writers write about people; some choose to leave their bodies out of it and to concentrate on their thoughts, but I put the bodies in. Perhaps my interest in them, especially in what people put into them, is quasi-anthropological. I grew up in a fairly isolated way with fairly limited resources in many directions, and as a result I find a lot of the things that people do—but take for granted—quite fascinating.

Stone: I've only been able to find three of your books in Spanish (*The Handmaid's Tale*, *Cat's Eye*, and *The Journals of Susanna Moodie*), and one in Catalan (*Cat's Eye*). Has anything else been translated? Are there any countries where translation of your work has been especially extensive?

Atwood: During the Franco years it was difficult for my books to be translated in Spain, as they were considered too radical. Or, they often appeared first in other Spanish-speaking countries, such as Argentina.

Stone: The biggest Catalan-language publishing house, Edicions 62, has just brought out an *Antologia Bilingae de Poesia Anglesa i Nord-Americana*. In the introduction the editor explains that for "English" poetry the publishers have understood poetry written in England, Scotland, Wales, and Ireland, while "North American" poetry is from the United States. He writes: "Thus Margaret Atwood and Elizabeth Smart, two Canadian 'border' poetesses who have projected their work from the United States and England respectively, could not be included because of the strict application of this criterion."

Have you projected your work from the U.S.?

Atwood: Well, this is merely insulting, when it isn't incomprehensible. I haven't projected my work from the United States. I'm published and reviewed in that country, as in many others, but is that a determinant?

Every writer concerns him- or herself with the widening concentric circles of categories that I expect we all wrote in the fronts of our schoolbooks, as Stephen Dedalus did: the individual, the family (house and street), the neighborhood, the village or town or city, the province, the country, the continent, the world, the solar system, the Milky Way, the universe. (You could add in, these days, skin color, language, gender, and sexual preference.) One may concentrate on one or two areas, but all are implicitly present. In my case the country is Canada and the continent is North America—which I share with the United States and Mexico. Mexico, by the way, is just as annoyed at not being considered part of North America as Canada is. //

Stone: The languages we speak here in Catalonia lead to that agglomeration, encouraging the notion that Canada is vaguely part of the U.S. Have you ever had to explain to a Spanish-speaking audience or journalist that such was not the case? If one country is made invisible in the language of another, is that just bad luck?

Atwood: I'd say it's a case of the tall brother making the short brother look shorter than he really is. When people in Europe look west, often all they can see is the United States. But we don't have those kinds of problems (or not as much!) with Spanish-speakers from Latin American countries.

Canada remains *terra incognita* to a lot of people, which in some ways is an advantage. Let's put it this way: nobody hates us. When U. S. kids travel, they frequently put maple leaves on their packsacks so they will be mistaken for Canadians.

Stone: // Reading *Survival* I find a nationalism that sees political and economic movements as centralizing, cultural movements as decentralizing, recognizing the constant inter-involvement of the two and the need to get some national sense of direction about that inter-involvement. In making statements such as "Canada is an unknown territory for the people who live in it" you add, in so many words, "and it's partly our fault."

Could you comment for us on nationalism in your country, on healthy and not so healthy ways in which you've seen it develop? Is it more a question of resisting those centralizing political and economic forces on all levels (something Cuba has tried), or of creating the right conditions for culture to do its own decentralizing? If the latter, how do you create the right conditions?

Atwood: Canada has, if anything, been too self-critical. It was just rated Number One as a place to live by—I believe—the U.N., and yet it continues to be diffident and self-deprecating. Even Quebec, noted for its nationalism, has based that nationalism partly on a sense of victimization by "Anglos."

As for "Canadian cultural nationalism," it came from a desire simply to have its existence recognized, even within the country itself—not from a desire to proclaim Canada as superior to anything or anybody. As for "creating the right conditions," artists are not a cash crop. Sometimes you structure what you'd think would be "right" conditions, and nothing much appears. But under other, "undesirable" conditions talent bursts forth. Ireland produced Joyce and Yeats and Synge when it wasn't even a country, and certainly without any arts grants.

"Official" arts policies often foster what is merely safe from a bureaucratic point of view. As Gide said, "it is with the best of intentions that bad literature gets written."

Starting with the Back Shelves of the Museum

Rebecca Garron

The following interview was conducted by Rebecca Garron in 1994 just before Margaret Atwood appeared at Literatur Haus in Hamburg to read from her novel *The Robber Bride*. The interview originally appeared in *Clockwatch Review* in 1995. Reprinted with permission.

Garron: One thing I'm particularly curious about, because it's come up in interviews and critical works since you've started writing, is your "political" view towards writing. I'll be more specific: in 1978 Joyce Carol Oates asked you, "Why are Canadian critics"—and I think by extension, writers—"so obsessed with statement and theme at the expense of a thoughtful consideration of technique?" And you answered, "We've tried very hard to demonstrate our own existence and our own right to exist. One can only afford a thoughtful consideration of technique when the question of existence is no longer a question." Now, in 1994, having successfully established your existence, do you believe it's even possible to distinguish between a "content" and "technique" and...

Atwood: Of course, I do.

Garron: For example, have you ever sat down and thought of your own work in terms of "I want to write this sort of story" and then tried to come up with the story to fit the formal pattern, or do you say, "I'm concerned with this issue in Canada, or I'm concerned with friendships among women, and now I'm going to sit down and try to figure out what form best communicates what I'm trying to say"?

Atwood: OK, let's just pretend we're in writing school again. Sometimes I've taught writing students, and it's fun to get them to write the same content, as it were, as if done by different writers. For instance, having a hamburger in the corner hamburger joint as done by Hemingway, or Edith Wharton, or Henry James, or Gertrude Stein, or Charles Dickens. I mean, that separates "technique" from "content" real fast…and also it makes you take a really close look at the techniques of others…how they put sentences together, what angle they come from. One of the best furniture writers in the world is Raymond Chandler; he does very good furniture…and that is the angle you would come from if you were doing the hamburger joint. Whereas Gertrude Stein probably wouldn't consider the furniture at all. It's usually only people from the United States who think that it's odd for a writer to have political interests. Nobody else finds it strange.

I just got the *New Yorker* film issue, and in this issue—after I read the piece on the blacklisting of the Hollywood Ten—now there was a point at which filmmakers are making political films and writers are writing political things and then along came Joe McCarthy at the end of the '40s and early '50s and what you'll read in this piece is the film people talking about the new "political correctness" that was coming in in 1948, in which they were saying, "We can't any longer show an industrialist as bad, we can't make films about labor unions…or we will be accused of being Communists." And in the '50s there was a kind of backing away from political themes. When it came heavily back at the end of the '60s to the point where a lot of people overdid it—they had to write their Vietnam poem whether they felt inspired to write their Vietnam poem or not. And when you write stuff because you think you should, it's usually bad.

I think what we're talking about here is where the impulse to do a thing comes from.

Garron: Right.

Atwood: In other words, if you're doing something because you think you should, whatever it is, it's likely to be bad. If there is no real energy behind it, it becomes billboard, it becomes dutiful. And that goes for anything, including feminism, trade issues, Canadian nationalism, race relations, including any of the things you can mention. The thing may be a good cause, and as citizens we may deeply approve of it, but if as writers we don't feel organically inspired to write about it, we shouldn't.

Garron: This touches upon what I am trying to get at in the content/form distinction: I've often found that among my literary peers many believe in "technique" as if "technique" were divested of any political content or concern. That the decision to write like Hemingway is purely a technical decision and has nothing to do with the necessity of the subject matter.

Atwood: Yes, but for Hemingway it was a political decision. But we can use this word "political" pretty widely. I think if more people did their politics in their lives as citizens they wouldn't have this problem. And the other thing that's happening now on American campuses is, everything is seen as political, and that's wrong, too. But as for young writers, of course, you have to learn to play the piano before you can be Beethoven. And learning the piano is a matter of technique. It may be a deeply inspired decision to learn to play the piano, but the actual learning of it is a lot of slogging, hard, detailed work. Then once you have the instrument at your disposal, then you can explore the ways in which you wish to go with it. But if you don't know where the noun goes...

Garron: It's more or less mastering an advanced form of grammar.

Atwood: Well, you've learned a foreign language. You know that there are ways of putting words together in that language that are different from the way you put them together in English. It's very good for someone who is a writer to learn a foreign language, not so much for the language itself, but because it makes you really think about the language you're writing in. You probably found you were thinking about that language and how it works, and how it doesn't.

Garron: Yes, it leads you, as well, to think about the presumptions upon which certain words are based, or certain techniques are based.

Atwood: Or certain word orders, or certain ways of describing things. Anyway, let us just say that writing is very different from the criticism of writing. It's a very different thing.

Garron: Can you elaborate?

Atwood: The critic starts with the text that is already closed. That's a very different thing from starting with the blank page. And the questions that the critic asks are very different from the questions that the writer asks. A writer is deeply immersed in the actual progress of the text, as it goes across the page and hopefully as it moves the reader into the story. The critic has the luxury of being able to stand back.

Garron: What do you think, then, about recent distinctions between the critic and the writer; that is, a writer, when she takes a subject to write about, is, like the critic, looking at an "historical text," or even her very own work, to "read" and critically evaluate?

Atwood: I think in the '80s people involved in universities—which I'm not, lucky me—went through that phase. You always have to ask, if anything, "cui bono," To whom did it do good, in whose interest was it? They went through a phase in which they were really backing off from the point at which writing and real life intersect. There was a lot of interest in self-referentiality and texts referring only to other texts…so everybody's done that, and now it's boring. You're at liberty to do something else.

Garron: Again, I ask this all primarily because I know that from other interviews and criticism, it has been a little difficult to sort out what your "aesthetic" take on it all is: when you looked at the body of your work, did you say to yourself, I see I'm a writer who's been compelled to write primarily by my concern with Canadian nationalism, or with feminism.

Atwood: No, I started to write when I was sixteen because I loved it. And unless you love it, there's really not any point. If your burning interest is in some other area, then maybe you can be an activist in that area.

Garron: But you can't be an activist in your writing?

Atwood: Well, you can, if you want, but you may not be very good. You can do whatever you want to, but unless you have respect for the form that you're working in, then you are just using that form for some other thing that is much more important to you.

Garron: You had mentioned early on in your career that you started with a somewhat similar "art for art's sake" view.

Atwood: Well, everybody works their way through a whole bunch of influences. I'm no different from anybody else in that respect.

There's a book out in the States now called *First Words*, which contains the first writings of a number of authors of historic importance, some juvenilia—including myself. It's very funny.

It's very uplifting because they wrote awful things when they began…it's very encouraging. You can go and look at that stuff and you'll see that some of what I was writing showed political concerns at that time, political concerns that you wouldn't expect. I wrote a poem on the Hungarian Revolution when I was sixteen.

Garron: So, the issue is not so much a refusal…

Atwood: Let's get one thing really straight. I have no interest in dictating to other people how they should live their lives. "The Spirit bloweth where it listeth." Shakespeare. It's in the Bible. It's a good quote. Some people's leading light may be to explore technique. Somebody else's leading light may be to explore something else. That's up to them. There is no one right way. If there were, I'd package it and sell it on QTV. I write because I'm a writer. That's what I am. I don't see any other necessary reason has to be produced. Usually people who are worried about that are people who have no respect for Mensa or who are feeling insecure about it. Usually such persons come from North America, and usually they get this from a society that does not respect artists, but only respects money. And it's very well to be a successful writer, because then you've got money, and you're a success. But to be a young writer like you is really discouraging. People say, "Why do you do it?" You say, "I'm a writer." And they say, "Oh, how too bad for your parents. How pretentious!"

Now here I'm going to give a piece of advice. And it's the only book I ever recommend to writing students or young writers, and it's not a How-To book about How to Write, It's called *The Gift: Imagination and the Erotic Life of Property* by Lewis Hyde, published by Vintage. It's about gift theory. Why is it important to you? Because it will straighten out in your head forever the relation between art and money. The biggest confusion that young writers in the United States have—they have a double confusion—number one: if I'm so talented why aren't I rich? Number two: if I get rich through my writing…

Garron: I've sold out.

Atwood: I've sold out, yes. This will help straighten all of that out, because this says, there is not one medium of exchange, i.e., the money one, as we were formerly led to believe and whereby we are led to measure everything. There are two. There's the money exchange, and then there's the gift exchange. And Hyde then goes into the occasions upon which we give gifts and what that implies. Money exchanges imply nothing. If I go buy something at a store, I give them the money, they give me the thing I've bought, I may never see them again. A relationship has not been established. But if somebody gives me something, an obligation is incurred. That's why politicians are not allowed to accept large gifts, that's why you have to be very careful if someone in the Mafia presents you with a gift; you have to really wonder about whether or not you want to accept that. That's why kids wishing to make breaks from their families don't go home for Christmas; it involves the gift exchange network. You can put it all very simply by saying, What is the "Ode to a Nightingale" worth, in money terms? Well, nothing. It doesn't exist in that area. Paintings are now sold for huge amounts of money that once you couldn't give away, but really they have no money value. It's just a kind of convention. I just saw a letter of James Joyce's in the window of a store in New York which sells people's letters. $12,000. That's setting a value on authors. But the content of the letter, what he said, does not have the money value. So there's this other area called gift exchange. You give gifts to people when they cross thresholds—when they get born, when they get married, when they die...flowers to the funeral, money to charity in their name...giving gifts used to be much more extensive, but we still do it. And Art, [Hyde] says, is in the area of gift exchange. Not in the area of money, or at least that part of it which makes it Art. He begins with an analysis of Silhouette Romances. He says, Here's how Silhouette Romances were conceived; this is the idea—it was all done through market research—even the covers, even the length of the manuscript. He says, What is it about this description that leads us to believe that none of these books will ever be great works of art? Because they've been conceived entirely as commodities. So, let's consider the artist. We call a person who has a talent, gifted. If such a person is gifted where do they receive their gifts from? And if what they have is a gift, what are the obligations that they have?...What I tell my writing students is: the part of what you do that has to do with the writing of the book belongs in the gift exchange. But then in order to get it to the people who can receive it as a gift, it has to go through the commodity exchange. It has to cross that membrane. Now, there are always helpers in very dangerous gift exchanges, and there are barriers. Doctors don't wear the costumes they wear just to protect [them] from germs. They wear the costumes they do to protect them from the idea of sickness, so they can act as the messenger across this barrier between the sickness and the well, and to protect themselves from getting sick. So, that's what agents are for. They're the people who can cross the membrane. They can deal with both sides of the exchange, not because writers are so stupid that they can't arrange their own contracts, but to keep the writer from having to do that, from having to enter into a bargaining position in relation to the writer's own work.

Garron: Do you really think that's problematic? What would happen to the writer if the writer had to deal with that directly? Is it really a "corrupting" influence, or is that a fallacy...

Atwood: It's dangerous. No, it's not a fallacy. In order to do that you'd have to split yourself off from the part of yourself that writes. And you'd have to become a commercial writer. You'd have to be a dealer in commodities. You'd have to huckster your own wares, as it were.

Garron: You'd have to measure yourself in terms of the "money value"...

Atwood: And talk yourself up, because that's what agents do for writers. They say, "Oh, it's worth more than that. Come on, come on...." But imagine doing that about your own work.

Garron: And you'd have to conceive of your work in very different terms, "harmful" terms?

Atwood: Yes, the agent sits down with the publisher, figures out how they're going to market this, and whether they think it's going to sell. And those are conversations I would much prefer not to be present at. OK. Then the thing gets packaged, then it gets put out to bookstores and then people buy it. Now some of the people who buy it aren't the people it's for: they're the wrong reader. Some of the people who buy it are the right person, who it's for, and those are the people who write you letters. What do those people say? Their letter never says, "This book costs too much," or "Hey, I really got a good deal on this book." They say, "Thank you." You don't say thank you for something you buy. You say thank you for something that's given to you. So that's when the thing comes full circle, goes back across into the area of gift exchange. It has to go through that money thing in order to get there.

Garron: Do you find that there is a problem with a readership who expects certain things or doesn't expect certain things, and you say to yourself or them, "That's a market condition, that's not my problem!"

Atwood: I don't care. The reason I don't care is that you can not second guess who your reader is going to be. You never know...so you might as well just not think about it.

Garron: But do you ever have concerns that there are writers whose works are not being read because of market conditions...

Atwood: I'm sure that's so, and if I were a publisher I'd be interested in it, but I'm not a publisher.

Garron: I was just reading the autobiography of Kenneth Rexroth, who was very concerned with publishing in America in the '40s. He sent out a survey to major universities and publishing companies and said, "Why aren't you publishing so-and-so?" Most publishers' responses were, according to market conditions: we don't make money.

Atwood: That's right.

Garron: But he also said it is possible, as writers, to begin small presses that can stay afloat financially, that can also begin to publish, let's say what my friends down the street say they'd like to see...

Atwood: Yeah, they started City Lights Books. And I've worked for a small publisher, too, and I can tell you what they run on. They run on people's blood. Next question.

All publishing to a certain extent runs on people's blood. I mean, the hours of work those people put in are astonishing. And if it's a really small publisher and if they're really underfinanced then they really underpay their staff. We all know this, and that's where the gift part comes in, because people don't do that unless they love it. There's a high rate of burn-out in those jobs. You could say it's so with any small business. // There's always less money coming in than there are people to be paid. It's always a function of that, and it gets more so because, if you have high volume and you're doing a commercial book, you can give the bookseller special prices on that book, and then their margin is bigger, and then they're more interested in doing it…if they do a yearbook they sell fewer of them and they make less money. There has to be what's called the "cookbook" factor to keep themselves afloat.

Garron: What do you think readers have found most appealing in Atwood's work?

Atwood: If you talk to these people and say, "When did you start reading my work, some of them started in 1965 and others started in 1985, and others started in 1975. For somebody who's been around that long you can't generalize. What you can say, is that if they go in at a certain point of entry, and they like that point, then they go back and read the previous stories.

Garron: Most of my friends started with *The Handmaid's Tale*, and part of that was encouraged by the film, because for better or for worse, the film gets more publicity…

Atwood: Of course. It would be normal for your generation to do that. But I think the point I'm making is that your generation is not the only one. Shocker of the century.

Garron: In one of your early interviews the interviewer had asked you, "Do you see recurring themes in your novels?" and you said, "Well, I just finished my second one so it would be very hard for me to say if there are recurring themes." After twelve novels…

Atwood: Eight.

Garron: Yes, sorry, eight novels plus…

Atwood: Three books of short stories, ten books of poetry, three children's books, a book of essays and a book of history.

Garron: Speaking of the novels in particular, do you find that there are recurring themes now that you can look back on and say, "This has obviously been an obsession for me," or whether there's a particular issue or a particular style? If you were looking at your own development, would you say, "Ah, I see that all along I was working towards…"

Atwood: I've never written any novels about alligators. I think this is a Ph.D. topic, or possibly an MA topic. I don't think that writers should do their own Ph.D. thesis on their own work. I think it's bad for their souls. And they don't anyway. Kurt Vonnegut has a stamp that he stamps on people's letters: Write Your Own Thesis.

Garron: As a reader—and yes, especially a reader who just got out of University—I'm very keen on asking, "What was unfinished business in this last book?" One thing I particularly liked about the work was its focus on female relationships—females being females together. And the issue of being female was not necessarily the primary issue, the issue was friendship. And obligation. And loyalty. And the characters happen to be women. And what I did see was a kind of development from other works—for example, *The Handmaid's Tale* in which the issue was female relationships in the context of a dystopia—to what has Zenia provoked in the relationships of these three other women.

Atwood: Yeah, that's right.

Garron: It's about what happens in the relationships among women when forces outside or inside affect those relatiothe macs are all acting upnships. And I did see that as a continual focusing on females…as full human beings. So do you feel, when you've just completed a work, that there is unfinished business that wasn't appropriate to the work in question, but you'd like to explore in another work?

Atwood: If there is never any unfinished business—I think "unfinished business" is actually a term in the book—then there's never anything else you want to write about so there's obviously unfinished business somewhere…but it doesn't necessarily occur in the work you've just written. I mean, hopefully what you want to do with the book is to make it as complete as it needs to be. But it may raise other questions.

I think if I were teaching myself as a course—and if you're very very bad on earth maybe you'll have to do this in Hell, although my feeling is if you're very, very bad what you have to be is eternally in a panel discussion. If you've been a little less bad you have to teach creative writing to first-year university students for a long, long time—so if I were teaching such a course, I would probably say that you can see my first three novels as a unit, and then you can see two others which move out in different directions. You could say that *Life Before Man* prefigures the next trio, which includes *Handmaid's Tale*, *Cat's Eye* and *The Robber Bride*. And you could say *Bodily Harm* prefigures *Handmaid's Tale*. You could say that the first trio has to do with women and men, last trio with women and women, and then two in between have to do with both: one pointing towards *Cat's Eye* and *Robber Bride* and one pointing towards *Handmaid's Tale* and *Bodily Harm*. I think that would be a reasonable way of arranging the course. Of course, I would never teach it, but if we wish to write things on blackboards which I'm quite fond of doing for other people's work—I do a really good blackboard analysis of *Great Expectations*.

Garron: So speaking of your last book—you've now coupled it with other books—do you think its primary inspiration was unfinished business?

Atwood: No. As I say, I don't think the other business exists in the other books. I think unfinished business exists in life. Or in the great potential ideas which kick around on the shelves.

Garron: And what was the inspiring idea for this?

Atwood: There are no inspiring ideas. There are inspiring stories. Writers don't get inspired by ideas.

Garron: OK, then how did you come by this? What was the inspiring "story"?

Atwood: It came from the great place where all such things come from; and that's why we call it a gift. You never know who's going to give you a gift or where you're going to get that gift from, or how it's going to develop. So, let's just say I started thinking about it one day.

Garron: In any specific terms? I mean, did Zenia appear to you?

Atwood: Um, did Zenia appear to me? Well, really, who cares? I mean, who gives a poop, let's face it. What you have is the book, and who cares how it began. Do you?

Garron: As a writer? Yes.

Atwood: Oh, this is an As-a-writer-how-do-other-writers-do-it question?

Garron: Well, I'm curious because I know, speaking with other writers we naturally often wonder…how and why *do* people go about writing? I find that I *do* often start with a very set idea, I say, "This is it," and I find that in the writing it changes.

Atwood: Well, it has to change. And I'm more of a reviser than a writer, because I'll start and get halfway and then I have to go back, because I'll realize that I'm forcing characters or stories to do something that they don't want to do. Exactly.

Garron: But there are people who say, "I knew this was the conception I wanted from the beginning, and I stuck to it."

Atwood: Well, that's them. You're you, and I'm me. I revise a lot. I don't start with It—I know people who have, but they have everything all plotted out beforehand. But that is in a way begging the question, because before that point at which they had everything plotted out beforehand, there was that same area of turbulence and uncertainty that we happened to have displaced to the manuscript so there's always the area of turbulence.

Garron: It's a question of where it comes for each writer.

Atwood: Well, it comes out of something that looks like the back shelves of the museum or an apartment building that's exploded. That's where it comes from. It comes out of a lot of broken fragments that then get collected together and come to life.

Garron: Let me ask you a final question to wrap it all up: with this last book—I don't know if you tend to read your work after it's finished—

Atwood: I will when I'm eighty. They've got big-print editions.

Garron: OK, then are you able to say at this point that you have a favorite part?

Atwood: Do you mean, of this book?

Garron: Of this book.

Atwood: No.

Garron: I mean, have you, or do you read through a part now and think, This is a part that really intrigued me in the writing?

Atwood: The thing is, if the whole book were climax, there wouldn't be any development. Some of the parts are the parts in which you can get to that point where the book's really terrific and it works really well, but if you have not put in the other work, that thing that you think is so wonderful wouldn't work. I mean, everything in a book should be organically related to everything else in the book, I mean, structurally related. So I could tell, Well, I think this part is particularly wonderful, but if it's towards the end of the book and I show it to you, and you haven't read the rest of the book, you wouldn't know what I was talking about…it wouldn't be a climax of anything. A favorite part is favorite because you know what comes before it.

Letting the Words Do the Work

Evan Solomon

The following conversation was aired by CBC on 10 December 2000. Printed with the permission of the Canadian Broadcasting Corporation

---

Solomon: How do you keep track of all the characters in a long novel such as *The Blind Assassin*?

Atwood: If you're covering any length of time, you have to know when the person was born and then go on from there, just as you would with a real person. You find out when they were born and then you find out what year it was when they were ten years old, or twenty…

Solomon: Then you live with a person. It's kind of like having new companions in your life.

Atwood: Yes, you do, but they're not like a roommate.

Solomon: What are they like?

Atwood: They're not nearly as tidy as you would wish your roommate to be. And they talk all the time. You wouldn't want that in a roommate.

Solomon: You wrote, on page 283 in the book, "The only way you can write the truth is to assume that what you write down will never be read, not by any other person, not by yourself at some later date. That's the only way you can write to get at the truth." Now do you actually take that approach yourself?

Atwood: Well, the absolute truth, the absolute truth. Even if you're writing a letter to somebody, you're still writing to that person. So, what the letter has in it is what you want to say on that occasion to that person, which may not necessarily be the truth. Just think about it for one minute. "I'll love you forever." "You looked terrific last night." Just think about it.

Solomon: When I think about it, it's true. We never write the brutal truth.

Atwood: Well, we might in our diaries, some of us might. I don't.

Solomon: You don't?

Atwood: No. I wrote, "Today it was raining," and things like that.

Solomon: Just the facts, ma'am.

Atwood: Yep.

Solomon: But what about when you write fiction? Because there's a truth—I guess there's a truth when you're writing, and writing's about finding the truth of the story, right?

Atwood: That's right.

Solomon: Right? So how do you know as a writer when you've found the truth of the book?

Atwood: First of all, it wasn't me saying what you just read. It was Iris. OK. And why is Iris saying that? She's finding it hard at that particular moment in the story to set forth the truth. Of what she herself has done. She has a few things in her steamer trunk that she has never ever unpacked. So the book is really about her unpacking her baggage, which is really difficult baggage for her. So she has to work up to it. And when she first starts setting down her story, she assumes that it never will have a reader, she doesn't know who she's writing it for. She does find out towards the end of the book that she is writing it for a person, a real person. But before that time, she has to assume that it's for nobody or for the eye of God, or for the unknown. Because otherwise she wouldn't be able to set it down. It's too difficult for her.

Solomon: It's a conceit, of course, because the act of writing almost presupposes that there's going to be a witness.

Atwood: This is an interesting question. And one that everybody considers when they are setting down something on paper. You do presuppose a reader. But, you often do not know who that reader will be. If you're writing a novel, you actually never know who that reader will be.

Solomon: So you don't write for anybody?

Atwood: I didn't say that. I said you don't know. You write for the perfect reader. And somebody out there—because writers are eternally optimistic—somebody out there will be the perfect reader. But you don't know who that person will be. Or put it this way. You're on a desert island. You have a message you wish to impart—to somebody. You write your message. You put it in a bottle. You heave it into the sea. You have no idea—number one—

whether anyone will find that bottle of yours, and—number two—who that person will be.

Solomon: Are you surprised that people find the bottles that you're sending out?

Atwood: Not anymore. Some people find them. Some people find other bottles. Or they find the bottle with the message in it and they hold it upside down. Or they can't quite make it out. Or something gets between them and it.

Solomon: However, there is still an anxiety. Once you get to your level, your tenth novel, and you know it's going to be sold, yet is there any kind of fear that you're going to send out a message— and I think in this book, which I consider such a risky choice especially, the book-within-the-book, *The Blind Assassin*, which is a science-fiction tale, and a pulpy one at that—didn't you think, Is this too risky, will people not get this message? Or do you care?

Atwood: By my age and stage, you're going to know a couple of things. And if you don't know these things, where have you been all your life? Number one: some people aren't going to like you. This may come as a big shock. But it is true of every human being. There's some people who aren't going to like you. And there's some people who aren't going to like what you do, no matter what it is. So why not enjoy yourself, and have fun?

Solomon: That didn't bother you. You didn't want to be…was there a point in your life…?

Atwood: Do I want to be universally loved by everyone? It's not possible.

Solomon: Is there a point when a writer wants to be universally praised?

Atwood: No. If you've read any history of literature at all, in your entire life, you know that no writer has ever been universally praised. Ever. Ever.

Solomon: There's a lovely line in this book. And you say, "In paradise there are no stories because in paradise there are no journeys. It's loss and regret and misery and yearning that drive the story forward along its twisted road." I always thought people always wanted happy endings.

Atwood: Even if there's a happy ending, they want a miserable "in-between." But let me put it this way. You are going to write a novel. And it's going to be about…what would you like your characters to be called?

Solomon: I'm not going to reveal…I'm writing a novel.

Atwood: OK, just make it up.

Solomon: OK, Henry and Priscilla

Atwood: Henry and Priscilla are lovely people. They have no character flaws. They're very good-looking. They have a reasonable amount of money, but not so much that we hate them. And they lead lives of perfection and bliss. And they go to their interesting jobs. And then they go on their vacation, which is very nice. Are you bored, yet?

Solomon: I'm getting there. You write in *The Blind Assassin* that stories that are true-to-life have wolves in them. So as a writer, is that what you do, you pursue the wolves?

Atwood: Unless you want to write the story about Henry and Priscilla having a beautiful life on every page, a wolf will arrive in some form, just as they do in real life. No matter what you do, sooner or later, something is going to happen in your life that will not be happy.

Solomon: One of the things you do in this book is unpack clichés. And one of the clichés that I think about is people who go through life saying, No regrets.

Atwood: Yeah. No regrets. That's not in my book.

Solomon: No, but I wonder. Your book is almost about the importance of regrets. That regrets are what make the character.

Atwood: I think people who say no regrets are probably lying, unless they've led the life of Henry and Priscilla, and nothing bad has ever happened to them. And they've never done anything bad. We all have little corners of regret.

Solomon: In the book, Iris has a daughter, Aimee. And Iris is a bad mother.

Atwood: She's a bad mother. Ssshh. She is.

Solomon: And she regrets it.

Atwood: She does.

Solomon: But yet she didn't seem to fight to be a good mother.

Atwood: Well, people can only do what they can do.

Solomon: So my question to you is, Are they worthy of our sympathy, then?

Atwood: Well, it depends what kind of sympathy you've got on hand. *Hamlet* is about bad parenting. You know, every single parent in *Hamlet* is rotten, including the ghost. If he'd been a good father, he wouldn't have appeared to Hamlet at all. And even so, when he does appear, he doesn't say a thing about Hamlet. He doesn't say, You're my son, I love you, I feel very proud of you. He says, What about me? Take care of me. It's your job to get revenge for me. He doesn't think of Hamlet at all; therefore, should we feel sympathetic towards the ghost? We do when we see the play. You know, often we feel sympathetic towards people not because they are models of character whom we should all emulate, but because they aren't.

Solomon: One of the questions that Iris deals with as she writes this book is why she's writing. She writes, "Why is it that we want to so badly memorialize ourselves? We wish to assert our existence like dogs peeing on fire hydrants. What do we hope from it? Applause, envy, or simply attention?" I thought, Is that why people write? Is that the reason we write—for applause, envy, atten…?

Atwood: Just a minute. That's Iris talking. Then we can turn the question around and say, Why do people do TV shows? Why? Why? Why, indeed. If we want to become sociological or anthropological about it, we could say, Because we are members of a social species. And people like nothing better than to communicate with other people, to watch other people, to talk about other people. It's part of what human beings do. But in the book, it is Iris posing that question to herself. She's saying, basically, Why am I doing this? And it is a question that does answer itself. Yes, she does want attention. She wants attention, finally, for who she really is and what she's really done, rather than for what people think she is and what they think she's done.

Solomon: But there is this question that people struggle with of biographical criticism. Trying to understand the book by understanding the author. And in this book, this issue is raised considerably. There's the cult of Laura, who writes this book. And I guess the question is, Is that a fair way to approach fiction, biographically, do you think so?

Atwood: Not always. I used to be very much against it. When I was twenty, I used to be very much against biography and against any kind of biographical interpretation, partly because I was twenty and I didn't have enough of a life for that to apply.

Solomon: So you'd have a thin little biography.

Atwood: Very thin. Then as I got to be a little bit older, I got to be more interested in writers' biographies, but not so much for the connection between them and their work, which often you just couldn't see. I mean, Byron's life is interesting as a life, not so much for the connection between him and the writing.

Solomon: I think about *Red Shoes*, a biography, Rosemary Sullivan's biography about you.

Atwood: Oh, you've been reading the biographies. Oh, oh. I haven't. I was talking to an English television person who had read the biography. And I said, "Oh you shouldn't have read the biographies. (That person had actually read the other one [by Nathalie Cooke]. There's two of them.) That person said, "I did read it, and I didn't believe that anybody could be that nice." And I said, "Don't worry, I'm not." According to these biographies, I'm the most wonderful person that you've ever, ever met.

Solomon: This is practically fiction, is that right? Is that what you're saying?

Atwood: Completely fiction. Wait 'til you find out after I'm dead. Boy, will you be surprised.

Solomon: Then I'll probably say, I shouldn't have asked her about that. She was such a nasty...

There's a line in this book. I mean, what I want to do is just read out my favorite lines, but we would be here for like six hours. It's from page 245: "The phrase 'in the spotlight' has seemed to me ever since to denote a precise form of humiliation. The spotlight was something you evidently should stay out of if you could." Right. This reminds me of the old, sort of WASPish mentality, you should only appear in the paper three times in your life: when you're born, when you're married and when you die.

Atwood: That was for women, yeah. Exactly. But also, it was Iris, who's done her best to stay out of that very same spotlight. And the results are true that we think artists, and we think performers, and we think, how glamourous, et cetera, et cetera, et cetera. But it is, in fact, a humiliating position. Because you are subject to the judgments of others.

Solomon: Now, do you find that a humiliating position?

Atwood: Think of a rock star on the slide.

Solomon: People have said that book tours is a series of humiliations.

Atwood: You want to hear about awful things that happened to me on book tours. OK. Misery. Here you are. I did my first book signing in the Hudson's Bay Store in Edmonton, Alberta, in 1969 in the men's sock and underwear department. Who put it there? Who knows? But there I was with a table which said *The Edible Woman*. And all the guys, in to buy their y-fronts [underwear], they would see this and they would gallop in the other direction. I think I sold two copies. That was an interesting initiation. The absolutely most zero signing I ever did was at a period in which Jack McClelland was trying to put his writers into Coles bookstores. So I ended up in one in a mall on the outskirts of Winnipeg on a Tuesday afternoon, when there was no one in the mall anyway. So there I was with my pile of books. And the only thing that ever happened to me for that awful endless hour was that somebody came and said, "Where's the scotch tape?" I said, "I think it's down there."

It used to be that the writer did not go out on a book tour. John Bunyan did not go out on a book tour. Charles Dickens used to give readings. But he thought of them as theatrical performances. In fact, he thought that if he hadn't reduced everybody in the audience to tears by the end of his reading, he had failed.

Solomon: Why do you bother going on book tours? I mean, you must get something out of it?

Atwood: I was brainwashed by the Brownies when I was very young…

Solomon: You're a do-gooder…

Atwood: And I was told, Always lend a hand. And you know who we have to lend a hand to these days? It is our publishers and our booksellers, most particularly the independents. You worry, there'll be an end to that. Pretty soon I'll be too old to hobble on to the plane and other people will have to do that.

Solomon: I see. This is one of the benefits of aging. Speaking of how selfless you are, let's talk about selflessness. The other side of selflessness is its tyranny. There's a tyranny to selflessness.

Atwood: Only when you're exercising it on another individual.

Solomon: In the book I thought the relationship between Iris's mother and father was such a unique, such a tragic description.

Atwood: Iris herself says none of this rubbed off on me.

Solomon: When he came back from the war...

Atwood: When Iris's father came back from the war minus an eye and a leg, the mother, who was quite an old-style model—very selfless—devoted herself to being selfless in his direction which he found somewhat intolerable because part of her selflessness was to forgive him for all the things he might have done when out of her sight.

Solomon: And forgiveness as a form of tyranny—when I think of forgiveness in our present-day society...

Atwood: Think about it.

Solomon: It's supposed to be the ultimate good.

Atwood: That's your relationship with yourself. If you can crank yourself up to forgiveness, I'm sure you will have a less bile-filled day. But when you're exercising forgiveness on another person, it can be intolerable for the other person to be constantly forgiven.

Solomon: And he ends up just locking himself in the turret, silently drinking.

Atwood: Well, he drinks rather noisily, in point of fact. And he alley-cats around. Do you blame him? Some people say, Oh, how badly behaved he was. I personally don't happen to blame him. Do you? Do you think he should have been better behaved?

Solomon: No, I don't actually. They are victims of the idea of selflessness. I found this line fascinating: "No one is born with that kind of selflessness. It has to be acquired only by the most relentless discipline, a crushing out of natural inclination." A bit cynical.

Atwood: No, it's not. It's simply what religion has always said. Think about it.

Solomon: Selflessness requires...

Atwood: Seven Deadly Sins. Those are what you're supposed to stamp out in yourself. Can you name them? Pride, envy...

Solomon: Greed.

Atwood: Avarice, greed, lust, anger and...

Solomon: Sloth.

Atwood: Sloth. Yeah, this is what we're naturally inclined to be like.

Solomon: I like how those are just on the tip of your fingers, by the way. You carry those around with you.

Atwood: Well, you helped me out with sloth.

Solomon: Yes, I did. That's right.

Atwood: Usually I can remember six. There's always one missing. So, sloth is obviously the one which bothers you.

Solomon: No, but what a Christian view. In the Jewish view we don't begin with a state of sin and crush out the sin to be good. It's the opposite.

Atwood: Ten Commandments. OK. Thou shalt not. Thou shalt not ten times.

Solomon: No, the first one is Thou shalt.

Atwood: OK. The other nine.

Solomon: We're crossing theological swords here. But, but it is interesting that…

Atwood: You know the joke.

Solomon: What's the joke?

Atwood: Moses comes down from the mountain. And he says, "There's good news and there's bad news." And they say, "Well, what are they?" And he said, "Well, the good news is I got him down to ten. The bad news is adultery stays."

Solomon: Adultery stays, yeah. There's this great sentence about Laura's book. "And they say there's nothing like a shovelful of dirt to encourage literacy."

Atwood: I read that at a reading that I was giving, and a woman came up afterwards, who works with a literacy program, and said, "You know, that's so true."

Solomon: If there's dirt.

Atwood: No, she says, "We give people a selection of books to practice on. And the ones that are always the most in demand are the ones with lots of sex in them."

Solomon: Dickens did readings as performance. Now, I've seen you read. And you read in that deadpan voice. Do you think of it as performance? What is your thesis behind how you read? As opposed to Dickens. Is that performance? Is that how you're trying to let the world think of you?

Atwood: OK. An actor is a person who is trained to impersonate people. And, also trained to project in pre-microphone days to the back of an auditorium. An actor is always pretending to be other people. I'm not up there pretending to be anybody other than who I am. I like to read slowly enough so that people can hear the words. And then I like to let the words do the work. It's not just that I like to. I don't have a choice. I'm not an actor.

Solomon: When you write, do you ever take on the voice of your character…

Atwood: A little bit. I adopt a tone, but not necessarily a voice because, as I say, I am not an actor. I used to do puppet shows, and I would take on all the voices. But that's quite different.

Solomon: Now, let me talk about this idea of you as a do-gooder. You say the Brownie in you that forced you to get out…

Atwood: It was a joke. It was a joke.

Solomon: I know. But, you have a side of you which is…

Atwood: It's because I'm Canadian.

Solomon: What does that mean? Another joke? But you're very politically active outside of your writing. Do you have to write from an ethical position?

Atwood: This is a topic which will be thoroughly discussed in my next book which is not a novel, which is not a book of poetry. It is the book form of six lectures which I gave in Cambridge, England, last April. And one of these lectures is about that very same thing. Should we be doing art for art's sake? Or should we be doing art for the sake of some other thing? And what are the consequences of each one of those positions? Because there are consequences to each of them. If you just do art for art's sake, you're in danger of ending up in the amoral corner. And, if you devote yourself instead to being the propagandist for a cause, what you will turn out will be propaganda. So what do you do? Wait for it.

Solomon: Oh, come on.

Atwood: Would I tell the ending?

Solomon: Why don't politicians value art? Or culture? Why are we in a constant struggle to…

Atwood: Because artists are dispersed throughout the society. They're not just in one space. Therefore, they don't have a riding where their vote is crucial to anybody being elected. That's probably the reason.

Solomon: What about Plato's idea? In Plato's perfect Republic, there were no artists, because artists undermine authority.

Atwood: There were no poets. There were no poets because they told lies, said Plato.

Solomon: You think you'd slip in as a fiction writer, not as a poet?

Atwood: No, no, I'd be among liars. Licensed liars. What Plato didn't recognize was that a certain amount of lying is absolutely necessary to the conduct of a civilization. Somebody said Voltaire was a hypocrite. And somebody else replied, That is the tribute he pays to virtue.

Solomon: In the book, the really beautiful description of Iris aging, the betrayals of her body were so precise. I guess this is a question that you really have to have read the book to appreciate, but so many of the metaphors that she uses are domestic metaphors. My skin was bloodless like meat soaking in water. The air was like skim milk. Are you conscious of using language that she would have understood?

Atwood: You can't use language that would be very far out of character for that person. Iris is not going to immediately start talking like somebody out of a Roddy Doyle novel with strings of four-letter words. It's not her. It's not what she would do.

Solomon: We all feel our mortality, even when we're young. But there's a difference between feeling your mortality and feeling you're getting older and aging. What's the difference?

Atwood: Well, when you're in your twenties, you usually think you're not going to make it past thirty, that you'll go out in some sort of spectacular motorcycle accident or burst of flame.

Solomon: Really? I'm out of my twenties, but I never had that one before.

Atwood: You didn't. Oh, well, most people who I knew who were writing in their twenties never thought they would…and it's partly just to make you write faster. You know, I don't have enough time. I've got to get this done before I'm thirty, or else it's curtains.

Solomon: Here comes…

Atwood: Yeah, here it comes. And I remember writing a story when I was seventeen about a very, very, very, very, very old person whose life was over, she was past it, all washed up, no hope. She was forty. So your perspective does change a bit. But if you're asking me how I have access to all this material, by this age, you have known quite a few people that age.

Solomon: But Iris has this sense of "do not go gently into that good night"?

Atwood: Oh, she's quite an angry old lady, yeah.

Solomon: Was the secret that she kept her whole life the thing that was keeping her alive or the thing that was killing her? What was it?

Atwood: It could be both. But you know, old age happens no matter what, as long as you don't die first. It's nothing that you did that makes it happen. It just happens. As long as you remain alive, you will get older.

Solomon: But there is a passage in the book that secrets corrode us as we get older.

Atwood: Iris is of two minds about that. In fact, she has a little riff on how talk shows seem to be all the thing today. And that people get onto these talk shows and they just spill these outrageous beans that nobody once upon a time would have thought of ever revealing about their own lives and their families and the awful things they've done. And here they are, it's entertainment for other people, people watching it. What are they left with at the end? They're empty. They've spilled all the beans. There's no beans left. So is it better to keep some beans, or to spill them?

Solomon: Well, what is it?

Atwood: She doesn't know. She doesn't know.

Solomon: Now, quickly, let me just ask you something. There's a wonderful scene where Iris writes letters back to people who are writing to Laura.

Atwood: Nosy Parker academics who want the stuff on Laura, because they want to make academic papers and biographies out of Laura, and Iris is foiling them.

Solomon: Not just foiling them

Atwood: She's writing rude letters to them and taking a great deal of pleasure out of doing so.

Solomon: I like this one: "I believe you are suffering from auto-intoxication. You should try an enema."

Atwood: As I said, rude letters.

Solomon: Are these fantasy letters you would like to write to some people?

Atwood: These are letters written by Iris on a particular occasion within the context of the book. I would never, ever write a letter like that to anybody.

Solomon: Now that's a lie. Now, let me tell you…because writing is an act of revenge to a certain extent, isn't it?

Atwood: In this book, yes.

Solomon: But in general, as well.

Atwood: No, remember what I said. I was brainwashed by the Brownies. I'm incapable of doing such a thing.

Solomon: Have we changed in the last thirty years in terms of the maturity of Canadian fiction and the themes that we deal with?

Atwood: The relationship between the writer and the publisher has changed a lot. I think we are now in a place in which people don't go galloping off to read a book just because it's Canadian. They read Canadian books in Canada because they're interesting—books that people want to read. And when you look at new writers coming along, the standards have become quite a lot higher, the bar has been raised. It's now possible for a young writer to come onto the scene, have an international publisher, etc, etc, which would have been unthinkable in 1965.

Solomon: There's a complaint that there's a tyranny of the new literary canon, the Atwood, Ondaatje, MacLeod…

Atwood: No. The same people that say that we're "new" are also saying that we're teetering on the brink of the grave.

Solomon: Do you feel you're part of a canon, a Canadian canon?

Atwood: Well, what does the word *canon* actually mean? What it meant originally was this was acceptable doctrine. We are not in a religious situation here. Canadian literature is not a religion. Literature is not a religion in itself. So canon usually just means, what people are choosing to teach, or what people are choosing to read. Those are all choices made by people. There isn't some demigod up there saying, "This shall be the canon." And there's no longer even anything you can call a closed establishment. I would say it's very permeable, people are coming and going all the time. So really you're just talking about choices people are making.

Solomon: So you're saying it's a meritocracy.

Atwood: No, I'm not even saying that. It's an open situation in which lots of people are making lots of choices, and those choices can be very diverse.

Solomon: All right, I have two last questions for you.

Atwood: Those kinds of things are usually formulated by people who feel that they're not getting into the so-called canon, and that there's a reason, that somebody's barring the gate against them.

Solomon: Sometimes there is, but sometimes there isn't.

Atwood: But who might those people be that are barring the gate? Because when you've got about ninety gates, one of them is going to be open if the person has anything that other people will be interested in reading about.

Solomon: Now, you ended *Survival* with the question, "Have we survived?" So, have we?

Atwood: No. It's a gerund. We are in the process of surviving, but we don't know whether we've done it yet.

Solomon: Did you catch a real thrill when you won the Booker?

Atwood: It was a big surprise. Because my English pals had been on the phone for weeks telling me all the reasons it wasn't going to happen.

Solomon: But it must have been a real thrill. Because it was electric here.

Atwood: It was, it was a real thrill. It was a real thrill and then it was followed by an immediate anxiety, because he said, "Three times a bridesmaid and now the bride." And my first thought was, Who's the groom?

Fifty-Two Ways of Making Butter
Ann Heilmann and Debbie Taylor

This interview took place during the 2001 literature festival in Hay-on-Wye in which Margaret Atwood featured prominently. Here she talks about her work as a writer, with particular reference to her latest, Booker-Prize winning novel, *The Blind Assassin*, which was also nominated for the Orange Prize and which won the International Crime Writers' Association's Dashiell Hammett Award. It originally appeared in *European Journal of American Culture*, 20.3 (2001). Reprinted with permission of Intellect Books, Ltd.

Heilmann: When you discussed the narrative structure of *The Blind Assassin* yesterday, you said that the innermost layer is a reversal of the Scheherazade situation.

Atwood: Because of the situation of the man telling the story to hold the woman's attention. The difference is that if he fails, he doesn't get his head cut off—but he may lose the woman.

Heilmann: Would it be possible to say, as the story of the stories is told by a woman who is an unreliable narrator, that it is really Iris who invents the "blind assassin" stories?

Atwood: Well, of course, in the text that we have before us, Iris is its narrator so you could say that she is its controller. But she's not the controller of, for instance, the newspaper excerpts. She is, however, the selector of them. So what you really have is a book in which there are at least five types of narration, at least five types of representations of reality, if you like. One is Iris's own story. One is the newspaper excerpts which act vis-à-vis Iris's story like the newspaper bits that used to be glued on to canvas and then painted over by the early collagists. You know, two forms of representation: each contradicts the other, each comments on the other, and each reinforces the other in an odd way, call it counterpoint in music. Point counterpoint. So you have Iris's story and the newspaper stories, then you have the *Blind Assassin*, the novel within the novel, which contains two narrative threads—the story of the woman and the man and their affair, and in addition to that the story that he is telling her. And then you have a fifth one—the graffiti narratives in the washroom, which are anonymous, and commented on—you know, they are added to by other visitors to that particular washroom cubicle. So you have a text, the commentary on a text, a commentary on the commentary on a text, a sideways addition to a text, and all of those little ongoing narratives you might say are communal efforts. They are all by women, we assume, unless a man is going into the washroom. This too is a core narrative. So you've got five different kinds of narrative, not just the story of Iris. She's reporting some of them, but she is not necessarily creating them—for instance, the ones in the washroom—unless she is lying to us all of the time. She's copying down what she has found in the washroom cubicles, some of which are the very same things that I myself have copied down out of washroom cubicles. They can often get very interesting, especially on repeated visits, when you see what people have added. So there you have it: five different kinds, and they weave in and out amongst the other narrative strands. Carol Shields has a novel in which the main character thinks her husband is having an affair, and she gets very suspicious of him because he's been very secretive about something, but what she finds in the end is that he's been weaving a tapestry meant to represent the plots and strands in Milton's *Paradise Lost*, using different colors of wool. So, interweaving—we often speak of narrative "threads," we also speak of "fabric-ation"—another word for lying.

Heilmann: And this is a feature of your writing, isn't it?

Atwood: Interweaving? Sometimes.

Heilmann: Interweaving, and also interweaving interconnecting threads between different texts?

Atwood: Sometimes it is and sometimes not. It is something that happens very much in this book. In *Alias Grace* there aren't actually texts as such. There are some letters, but really it's an oral story, and like all such, it has to do with the person it's being told to as well as the person telling it. When you have an oral storyteller, when you have anybody actually using the speaking voice and addressing somebody who's there in the room, what is said is going to be influenced by the person who is listening. When a writer is writing a book, on the other hand, he or she is using a piece of paper and something that makes marks on it, and doesn't know who's going to be reading it. So it is a different existential situation. I am sitting here talking to you and what I say is in answer to things you want to know; if I were off in a room somewhere, writing an essay, it would be a different situation. I would not actually know which individuals were going to be reading that piece of writing.

Heilmann: Do you have a reader in mind?

Atwood: No, I don't because you can't. If you want to hear about all this, you can get the book that's coming out in Spring 2002, called *Negotiating with the Dead*, based on the lectures I gave in Cambridge on the subject of writing: what is this "writing," how does it differ from other things, why do people say they do it. Six lectures—now chapters—on the subject of writing. And this illustrates my point, which is that when I was giving the lectures I knew who the audience was, I could see them right in front of me, and I knew there was a mix of students, academics, and general public. So if I used an esoteric reference, I had to elucidate it, OK—but not too much because some of the people would already know, because they would be professional scholars. When you put such a thing into a book, you don't actually know who's going to be reading it, and that's what footnotes are for. I can't ad lib in a written text, I can only do it in a situation such as the one we are in right now.

Heilmann: Your texts reflect a metafictional concern with storytelling and writing as a masquerade. When writing, aren't you constructing a reader with whom you are playing a game?

Atwood: I'm constructing a particular listener within, for instance, *Alias Grace*. She's telling the story to a man in the story. But the reader can also eavesdrop on what she's really thinking. // And we have the possibility of seeing what other people say both to her and about her. Thus we see her interacting with other people and we see them thinking about her, apart from what they say to her or how they interact with her.

Heilmann: It's also that you are taking on a past point of reference.

Atwood: In *The Blind Assassin*, we are in the present with Iris when she's 82—every step along the hallway, every bowl of breakfast cereal, that's what she has to deal with, every huge doughnut that she can't actually finish: those are what's in her life now as it diminishes, and as more and more things become impossible for her to do. So that's the now. And then there is the story of her past, which she is setting down for reasons that become apparent in the book.

So you might say her listener within the book is the person to whom the written text is addressed, and both the reader and Iris figure that out at about the same time. When Iris figures out to whom she is writing, she lets us, the reader, know. But there are other things she doesn't tell us. She never actually lies. So it's like any conversation with anybody that you might meet for the first time. // What we choose to say has a lot to do with why we are saying it and whom we trust. As a writer, of course, you have to trust the reader, but it's mutual: the reader has to trust the writer not to be completely lying to them all the time and doing things to no purpose.

Taylor: How did you write *The Blind Assassin*?

Atwood: I started it three times, but only the third time was it the correct start.

Taylor: How far did you get each time?

Atwood: Reasonably far.

Taylor: Did you then throw the false starts away?

Atwood: I never throw them away, but I go through them for what can be used, as you might go through your rubbish heap, finally discarding everything. Some of what I wrote was usable, and some of it wasn't, the usual story, it's nothing new. I started writing about a dead old woman who was of interest to another person, and the controller of the narration was therefore the other person, and she found that this dead old lady had a hat box in her house, and in the hat box there were some letters. So those were the layers. And that didn't work out, so out it went. I then had the old lady be alive, but in the third person. She was meeting two younger people for the first time, and the old lady's story was discovered through them. But then their stories took over the narrative and they started having an affair with each other, even though he was married with new-born twins, so off they went into a drawer. That old lady had a suitcase, and inside the suitcase there was a photograph album: this was the layer within the layer. She began to speak for herself, and that was when the novel really got off the ground. There was always an old lady, there was always a container, there was always a sister, the thing inside the container always had to do with the sister, and there was always a hidden side to her life which was going to be discovered in this containerish way. That's how it all began to go forward. But the other thing I did—which I do for any of my characters—is I always have to know how old people are, because by knowing how old people are you can tell when their tastes were formed, what they went through. So I take a piece of squared paper, and across the top I put the years, and down the side I put the months, and then I put their birth dates, the month, the year, and then I put zero in that square, and then I move across, using that line, 1-2-3-4-5-6-7-8, so that I know that on, say, May 27th, 2001, that character will be that old because they haven't had their birthday yet that year, so we have to wait until October for them to turn a different age. You have to be able to know exactly what age the character is at any given time.

Taylor: When do you do that?

Atwood: I fiddle around with that quite a bit. It always happens at the beginning. I knew the interval of the years I wanted between Laura and Iris, but it was a question of getting the two of them conceived, given the fact that their father was off involved in the First World War. Luckily we have a ton of military histories, including histories of Canadian regiments, and I was able to look up and find among the regiments one that went off to Bermuda for a year or so and then made a stop at Halifax to get new uniforms, winter ones.

Taylor: Is this what you use your researchers for?

Atwood: I use them to check things, by and large. Sometimes I send them off and say, "Tell me how you color-tinted black and white photos." Off they go, they find it, here is how it was done, you had little bottles, you had little tubes, you used a brush, you did this, you did that—so I now know how to color-tint a photo if I ever need to have that information. But a lot is just stuff that I either already know because I've read about it and it's in my head, or that I've seen. For instance, the architecture, the interior decoration of restaurants did not change between the 1930s and, say, 1950 because nobody had any money, it all stayed the same. So all of it was still there for me to see as a child, which I did. I didn't have to go off and research those things; they are in my memory. But when I need things checked up, then I send the researchers off to the library and they look about amongst the microfiches. With *Alias Grace* we had quite a time finding things out because Susanna Moodie, my first source, had not been very accurate. So off we went to try and find when and where this crime actually took place, because she was wrong on both counts. And we narrowed it down, and then we started looking through the newspapers. I took a compass. And she had said 50 miles or so, so I drew a radius around and then looked at the towns inside that and looked at the areas on either side, and we found it. And once we had found it, it led to all kinds of other things, but that was a real research job. Then I sent a person off to the Kingston Penitentiary to see what they had in their archives, and off to the lunatic asylum, and off to the Legal Society. The original judge's notes are still there. They're illegible: nobody has yet deciphered them, his handwriting is unreadable. He made notes to himself, you can pick out a word here and there; they're useless, but they're there. //

Taylor: I'm just thinking of the process of research and your interest in detail.

Atwood: Well, I write first and research later. For instance, in *The Blind Assassin* I knew I needed buttons. The buttons came first. I knew quite a bit about the small Ontario towns that had factories in them, I knew the kinds of things they made and amongst the things they made were buttons. So then how the buttons were made was the next question, what were they made from and when did it change over to plastic and rubber and all of the things we have now. Quite early on, believe it or not.

Taylor: So what you have is like a skeleton that you write…

Atwood: No, I have a very dense text, the details of which need to be checked. Let me give you an example. *Cat's Eye*, set in a time I lived through, contemporaneous with myself. I thought I remembered the song that the little Brownies sang as they danced around the cardboard mushroom, so I wrote that down. Then I sent somebody off to check to see if I'd remembered correctly; as it turned out, there were a few mistakes, so those I was able to correct.

Taylor: So do you then make up some stuff about buttons?

Atwood: I wouldn't say I make up, I would call it informed speculation. But then you have to check to see whether your informed speculation has been as informed as you thought it was. And usually you're wrong about this and that. For instance, I had a great scene in which Grace is present at the hanging of McDermott. But then I found out through the archives that by that time she was actually in the Kingston Penitentiary, they'd shipped McDermott off first. She wasn't there so I couldn't describe that scene.

Taylor: That's one of your rules, that's your rule of writing?

Atwood: For things that are based on real, historical events. I cannot write the life of Napoleon and have it come out happily, with him still married to Josephine and reigning as the Emperor of France. That didn't happen.

Taylor: Yes, but that's your decision, isn't it? Somebody could write that.

Atwood: They could, but if they presented it as reality, they would be telling a huge lying whopper. So I try not to lie about things that are part of the fabric of reality, if you like. I can't have people using pop-up toasters in 1910. They did not exist then, just simple things like that. When did women start wearing underpants—later than you thought. Because you know that if you get it wrong, especially if you write about an 82-year-old woman, some real 82-year-old woman is going to write you a letter that tears your head off. So you have to be quite careful, and then you get a blistering letter from a woman who said that the way Grace made butter was a disgrace. Which it probably was, she should have cooled the cream first. My problem was: they did have a cellar, but in the real documents pertaining to the case the cellar was unused. So she was making cream, making butter in this way, with the cream too warm. But my granny didn't have a cellar and she didn't make butter in that proper way; it was a little granular, it wasn't the best butter, but that's how she made it. Anyway, Mrs. Beeton said there's fifty-two ways of making butter.

Taylor: It's very interesting that you talk about all the information and the detail.

Atwood: Well, it's actually a hazard. In *Alias Grace* there's an entry in a warden's journal that says, on such and such a day, Tuesday the what not of what not, I drove Grace Marks with one of my daughters—obviously as the chaperone—to the United States, where there was a home prepared. OK. I get a letter from a guy who says, "You say this says it's Tuesday"—let's say May 27th—"well that wasn't a Tuesday, it was a Wednesday." So that's when I have to xerox the historical document, send it to him and say, "This is what the warden wrote down. It's obvious what happened; he'd made the trip, and then a week later he'd written it all up, and he'd made a mistake about the day of the week. But was I going to falsify what he'd actually written? No, because the parts of the beginnings of chapters are all true, they're real excerpts from real newspapers and really what Susanna Moodie said and what the warden said and what all these people said— right or wrong. But some guy will actually look up the day of the week.

Taylor: It's the penalty of having so many readers...

Atwood: ...of different kinds. This man happened to be a music teacher, and they are very interested in numbers. And there are now functions on your computer, you can type in any date, and it will tell you what day of the week it was. Very useful for me, but I better get it right, because other people can do that too.

Heilmann: So your work is a combination between Tony's and Zenia's in *The Robber Bride*?

Atwood: Absolutely, it is. And Tony, the historian, knows that her work is like the work of Zenia the fabricator: it's arbitrary and an invention. And Zenia knows that her lies have to be like Tony's histories, or else she won't succeed—she has to get the details right in these fraudulent stories she tells about herself or she won't be believed. So that's exactly right. People have often said, So who's the character in *The Robber Bride* that you identify with most? and I say, "Well, obviously, it's Zenia because she's the one who does the storytelling. Tony controls the narrative, but Zenia is the liar, the professional liar."

Heilmann: Yes, that's what you said in "Murder in the Dark," that's what the writer is.

Atwood: The writer is a licensed liar. The difference between the writer and a real liar is that the writer puts on the front, "Fiction," and usually people then believe it's really disguised autobiography, whereas with autobiographers they believe that the person is telling fibs. So you have an interplay, but you know, you always have had such an interplay: Daniel Defoe, one of the first novelists, did not present himself as a spinner of fictions; he presented himself as a person telling true histories about real people. You know, a lot of people thought that Richardson's *Clarissa* was a real account of a real young lady's awful ordeal. And they still do. There are tons of people who think a novel must be disguised autobiography: who are you in this book? I've even had a man say that *The Handmaid's Tale* was autobiography and I said, it couldn't be, it takes place in the future, and he said that was no excuse, it had to have happened to me in some form. A friend said, "Oh I loved this book, it was just like girls' boarding schools."

Heilmann: In "Spotty-Handed Villainesses" you suggest that the allure of villains resides in their capacity to possess forbidden rooms. Do you have forbidden rooms?

Atwood: Everyone has. They transgress, and their transgressions are hidden in those rooms, and we all have within ourselves a little child-transgressor, that child who once took the forbidden cookie and either did or didn't get caught. But the innocents who enter such rooms are also transgressing.

Taylor: Do you think you are transgressing anything in *The Blind Assassin*?

Atwood: You know, I will not tell; I will let you figure that out.

Heilmann: How would you define your relationship with academics and critics?

Atwood: I'm not there in the room when they're doing whatever it is they do. It is a function of the written text that the author is never present during the reading of it. In fact, you can never ever talk to the author of a book. You think you are talking to me, but actually I'm a different person by now and not the person I was when I was composing *The Blind Assassin*. Time has moved on.

I'm now thinking about other things. If you'd tried to talk to me while I was writing the book, I wouldn't have let you into the room because I wasn't finished yet.

Taylor: That means it's an exploration for you at the time it is happening.

Atwood: Of course. The other truth is that an author can never read his or her own book in the way that a reader can. In a way you are like the cook who never actually gets to sit down at the meal. You've made this thing, other people get to see it in its finished form, with all of the icing and decoration, but they haven't been there when you've been mixing up the eggs, and in a way you can never know your book in the way your reader can. You know it in a different way but not in that way. You never have that delightful feeling that you get when you begin a book: "Here's the first page. Oh, I like this page. What's going to happen on the next page?" You can never have that feeling with your own book.

Taylor: So when you start writing, you don't have a sense of, Oh, this is going to be fun?

Atwood: I may, but suppose I write the first page and then go on and finish the book, I cannot then pick it up and read it the way you can. In a way the writer is always Moses excluded from the Promised Land: you can stand on the hill and look across the border, but you can never have a reader's experience with your own book. Luckily you can have it with other people's books.

Taylor: Are you the sort of person who writes very fast to get it out and then look at it?

Atwood: I write very fast and then look at it, yes.

Taylor: And how far do you get before you say, "I've run out of steam"?

Atwood: You get maybe thirty pages of handwriting, which is very hard to transcribe because my handwriting is difficult to read. I start transcribing that, which may go quite slowly. There are always a lot of errors all over the page, stars, marks, additions, things scratched out. I start transcribing that onto a computer; at the same time I will be continuing to write at the other end of the text.

Heilmann: Do you write by hand because it's all a collage?

Atwood: I write by hand because I never learnt properly to touch-type. At the time I had the chance to learn, I didn't know I was going to be a writer. If I'd known that, I would have taken the typing course, I would have taken secretarial sciences and learnt to touch-type. I didn't do that; instead, I know how to set in a zipper and make choux paste.

Taylor: The stuff that's on the computer, then, is that pretty finished?

Atwood: No, it's a first draft. How many drafts? About six. Then there is the editing and the line editing. My manuscripts are, by publishers' standards, usually what they call quite "clean"—I used to be an editor—but there are always things you miss. And the new programs that they have, with squiggly lines: the red ones are always worth looking at, the green ones are sometimes wrong because what they want to tell you is "sentence too long" or other idiocies of that kind, but I leave the program on, just so I can look at all those things, and they do catch the double *the*s and the places where you leave out a word when you are typing, and all those things you can usually catch. But I don't even do that until I have got to the end.

Taylor: When you've got, as you have in *The Blind Assassin*, several parallel stories, different narratives, do you write them separately?

Atwood: No, I didn't, I wrote them as I went along, and very much in reference to a time line, because again I had to know what was happening in history at the time of these events. There were a couple of key dates—well, more than a couple, I needed to know quite a few dates. I needed to know, for instance, when the maiden voyage of the *Queen Mary* was, where it went, how long it took, who was on it, and then I had to know how old Iris was in relation to it, and how old Laura was, what was going on in the economic life of this or that part of the country, what was going on in the political life. I had an historian read the book for these very reasons.

Heilmann: So you put in the newspaper articles contemporaneous with the story?

Atwood: Yes.

Heilmann: But that must mean you must spend a very long time working out the story.

Atwood: No. Because, you see, I'm quite old and I just have a lot of this stuff in my head.

Taylor: What about characterization? It's particularly Laura I'm interested in.

Atwood: There is a condition in some children which makes it difficult for them to handle metaphor. It's probably a mild form of autism. Laura's not the usual sort of child. She cannot handle metaphor. You can't say to her, "Go jump in the lake," because she might do it. // I knew a child who was like that. Laura's a fairly clear case—but then it goes all along the continuum to children, or adults, who may have trouble with poetry. They don't get why "my love is like a red red rose"—a person isn't a flower—and it's these people who tend to be literalists, especially in religious matters. They just skip over the Song of Solomon: they cannot handle "my love is a garden enclosed"—a person is not a piece of property. //

Taylor: She's a very beguiling character.

Atwood: Well, yes and no. She would have been a complete pain in the butt, especially if you were the older sister and told that you were responsible for her. The things she says—like "Does God lie?" A legitimate question—we may think they're funny, but the people that she said them to would have found them extremely annoying.

Heilmann: Could you say something more about your use of metaphor?

Atwood: Or similes. What can I say about it? That's what writers do.

Heilmann: And you don't think it would be possible to include metaphors in a film script?

Atwood: Well, you can't, because a metaphor says this is that. You know, "Your eyes are periwinkles." If you chose somebody with blue eyes but show their eyes turning into periwinkles, unless it's surrealism, unless it is a Dadaist film of great peculiarity, you couldn't do it.

Taylor: They use allegory instead, don't they?

Atwood: Or just suggestion, description, atmosphere, sound-track, all of those things that films can do so well—effects of light and many suggestive things. You can show a picture of somebody turning and looking over their shoulder with an unfathomable expression: it's not a metaphor, it's a depiction, it's a different thing.

Heilmann: But in *The Piano* you've got different points of view and you've got the fingers and the keys of the piano...

Atwood: Yes, but that's depiction. It's not saying the piano was a great lion that I had to master; the piano does not turn into a lion. Metaphor equates one thing with another. Simile says, This is like that, and film has trouble even with that. We the readers supply all that: "She looks like my aunt." Film has a lot of trouble with that. It can play with all sorts of things that would be a bit hard to play with using words; it can play games with illusion just as magicians do. There are sleights of hand, there are visual transpositions, but they are not metaphors as such.

Taylor: Do you see the scenes in your books as you are writing them, or do you hear them?

Atwood: I see them, I hear them, but I'm not hallucinating. It's like walking through life: you have to go see the headmaster, but your child has tonsillitis. You rehearse it in your mind: I will walk up the stairs, I will go to the door, I will say, "Miss So-and-so, here I am for the interview, but my child has tonsillitis." "Oh, do come in." What shall I wear, etc.?

Taylor: But you know exactly what your characters look like, do you? Could you sketch them?

Atwood: Oh yes, certainly I could. But my idea of what they look like would be somewhat different from yours because you've made up an inner image based on the text.

Taylor: But the voices are very strong in your work. The sort of things that Reenie says.

Atwood: Reenie says lots of things that people of that time said.

Taylor: But Iris has a strong voice as well.

Atwood: Yes, she does, she's a crabby old creature: mean, rather mean. She doesn't like being patronized, and helped; but she's weak, so she accepts but doesn't like the well-meant efforts of other people. She's an ungrateful old thing.

Taylor: Did you research old people?

Atwood: Who needs to? I know a lot of them. Come on, you don't live to my age without knowing people older than yourself. You don't need to research them. You don't need to go and ask them what they think, because believe me, they'll tell you. //

Taylor: You were deciding to do a book about an old woman and a container. Were there other ideas floating around at that time?

Atwood: I usually have about three to choose from, and the one that ends up being chosen is usually the most impossible and crazy of the three.

Taylor: Do you start the others at all?

Atwood: I usually start them, I think about them anyway, or I make little pictures of them or I jot down notes about them, and then the other one takes over.

Heilmann: Are they developed later on?

Atwood: Sometimes they are, indeed. I started *Cat's Eye* before I wrote *The Handmaid's Tale*—had the notes for *Cat's Eye*. I had notes for *Surfacing* at the same time as I was writing *Edible Woman*, but I didn't develop it until some years later.

Heilmann: And *Wilderness Tips* recurs in *The Robber Bride*, from a different perspective?

Atwood: Does it?

Heilmann: Yes, "Hairball" is the femme fatale, and "Isis in Darkness," the man's perspective.

Atwood: Oh, a "man's perspective"—well, there isn't just one man in the real world, though. Men don't come in a homogeneous lump; they are different from one another. No, I wouldn't necessarily have thought of it that way. There is a man's perspective in *Life Before Man*: a third of the book is a man, and most of the women commenting on that book or interviewing me would say, "Where can I meet this man?"and a couple of them said, "I just wanted to shake him and say, 'Get some spine'."

Heilmann: How important do you find the uncanny and the Gothic?

Atwood: It's part of people's lives. You question anybody for more than half an hour about odd experiences they've had, and believe me, they've had some and usually these are part of their dream life, but they may have heard a voice at some important part in their life or, strange coincidences. Everybody's got their little stash of these things, so it's part of how people live, and the Gothic, developed in its most full-blown Mrs. Radcliffe form, is just that element—you know, the creaking footstep on the stair which isn't really there—it's just that developed to its extreme. *Dracula* is our feeling that some people are secretly malicious and may not be who we think they are, and are sucking our emotional blood. And it's those common experiences taken to an extreme. All novels anyway are "what if": they all start with an hypothesis and the hypothesis can be ordinary: "What if there's a girl called Bridget Jones who is overweight and smokes too much and is having an ordinary but dramatic life? Let's follow what happens to her." Or it can be, "What if I'm Dr. Frankenstein and have discovered the secret of life and have created a person out of body parts? What happens then?" All novels begin with something like this: what if Robinson Crusoe gets shipwrecked on an island and all he has at his disposal are limited amounts of supplies? Suppose the island is a tropical one. What happens then?

Heilmann: But *Frankenstein* wasn't in your mind when you were writing *The Blind Assassin*—I mean the box-in-a-box structure?

Atwood: You could say that it's very similar to *The Turn of the Screw*. It was a commonplace in nineteenth-century fiction to enclose stories within other stories. It's a commonplace even of certain kinds of eighteenth-century fictions, it's a thing that happens in fiction. It is essentially the Scheherazade notion anyway: the story of the King and Scheherazade, and all the stories she tells, which reflect one another and have something to say about her own position—a very precarious one. Most of the people in the stories she tells are at risk of losing their lives. It's just one of those things about storytelling: I was sitting by the fireside with the person I had just met and I said, "What brings you here to this inn?" and he says, "Long ago, twenty years ago I …" etc. Do you know *A Hero of Our Time*, Lermontov's novel: the events in the order in which they really happened are quite different from the order which the author tells them in, so it's a real exercise in complex narrative interweaving. I'm doing nothing more than practicing the art of the novel as it has long been practiced.

Taylor: When you are plotting it, there's a lot of clues. Do you put them in afterwards, thinking the reader needs a bit of help here or I need to give them a bit of mystery there? Does that just happen naturally, as you are writing it?

Atwood: I'm afraid so. All novels are mystery novels: at the beginning there's something that's going to happen and you don't know what it is, or if you do know, then it's a very predictable novel. One of the pleasures of reading is that surprise—in the characters, in the turn of events. We find out something we wouldn't have suspected. We find the fatal letter—always a good device in such stories: "Oh my God, he's having an affair with Jane, who I always thought was such a plain girl and no threat at all."

Taylor: Do you know it all before you start?

Atwood: No, I don't, no, I'm finding it out as I go along, and I'm often just as surprised as you are; otherwise it wouldn't be fun, it would just be painting by numbers.

Taylor: So you use your kind of chronology to keep focused.

Atwood: But I also have to invent the chronology as I go along because there can be something that hadn't occurred to me at the outset. For instance, how fortuitous that the King and Queen came to Canada and had such a bizarre garden party in 1939, with all of those doves released out of a cake. How nice for me that Iris could be there! As for the cellophane hat you'll find in those social notes, it was real—a detail I noted with great interest. Cellophane must have been a new material at that time, and somebody had made a fashion statement.

Taylor: What about your productivity?

Atwood: I'm just old! Take all the years I've been writing and take my ten novels—a mere nothing compared to Joyce Carol Oates— and divide it into my enormous length of years, and I'm actually quite a slow writer. // *Surfacing* came out in '72, and so did *Survival*, a very quickly written book. *Lady Oracle* came out in '76, the year I had the baby, but I had been writing the book meanwhile, and then there is a pause, there isn't another book until 1980, I think.

Taylor: So the baby did sort of interfere?

Atwood: You lose your brain, it grows back, your hair falls out, ditto. I can say to young people who've just had babies, "It's all right, your brain comes back," they say, "When?" I'd say, "Two years." Well, the other awful thing—though it's not that awful at the time—you don't care! "I've lost my brain, oh well, who cares, didn't need that, I don't need to write books."

Taylor: Do you still work at night?

Atwood: No, too old.

Heilmann: But you used to?

Atwood: Yes, all the time. Had a day job—had to—had to work at night.

Taylor: So what do you do now?

Atwood: Go to bed.

Taylor: What's your pattern?

Atwood: More like ten to twelve in the morning, and then sometimes in the evenings, but sometimes in the afternoons. I try to work in the morning. Morning is good, I'm awake.

Heilmann: And do you have to be at home or can you write anywhere?

Atwood: I can write anywhere if I have solitude. I can be in a room full of people, it doesn't matter, as long as they're not talking to me. Jane Austen wrote all her books in the sitting room with hordes of people around her. I grew up doing my reading and homework around a kerosene lamp, with other people using the same lamp, so you just learn to build a little mental cubicle and do it within that cubicle. Very useful to me when I was going to school, I didn't actually have to listen to anything that was happening, or I could listen, I could be tuned in with one ear and then be leading a completely different kind of life. I only got caught out at it on the rare occasion when I had completely drifted off.

Taylor: And is the process pretty similar for all of them?

Atwood: In a way. You've seen juggling acts. First, he does two plates in the air and you think, that's pretty neat, maybe I could do that at home. Then he adds three more so the tension is higher when all those objects are in the air rather than just the two. So with a book like this, the tension is very high. It's like when Hitchcock puts a bomb under the bed: how are you going to get out of this? The heroine is in a perilous situation, being chased down the deserted abbey—as in one of Mrs. Radcliffe's, probably in all of Mrs. Radcliffe's novels, I read them all, come to think of it. There's the heroine in a perilous situation, the tension is high. The heroine as author in the perilous situation is about page 200. When you've written yourself into the book and you don't actually know how to get out of it, that's when the tension is high.

Awaiting the Perfect Storm

Martin Halliwell

Margaret Atwood spoke with Martin Halliwell of the Centre for American Studies at the University of Leicester, 3 June 2003. Printed with permission.

Atwood: I am going to read from my new novel *Oryx and Crake*, which is a book set in the not-so-distant future. It is not a prediction. You can't predict the future. There are too many variables. Think of it sort of like a *Christmas Carol*, and Scrooge has a dreadful experience, but then he gets to wake up the next morning and say, "It hasn't happened yet, I can still change my ways." So it is not inevitable what happens in this book: it's a rather cheerful, joke-filled book about the end of the human race, as we know it. [She reads three passages from *Oryx and Crake*.]

Halliwell: At the beginning of the novel, Snowman/Jimmy wakes up and seems to have no clear memory of the past, and no real idea where he is. Can you say something about why you started at that point in the story of *Oryx and Crake*?

Atwood: Let's see: he wakes up, he climbs down from his tree, and he does various other things while eating. He doesn't have much left to eat. That's not usually the point in the day where you go back over your entire past life. And anyway, you cannot go over your entire past life on the first page of a book. If you go back to the *Iliad*, Achilles is sulking in his tent. What tent? You will find out about that later. Why is he in front of the walls of Troy? You will find out about that later, too. But you start at the point at which the character is with you at a moment in time. There are other ways of starting a book. You could start "Jimmy was born" or you could even do "Before Jimmy was born." And then you can go in a linear fashion like that. So really it's a question of picking how you are going to start a book.

Halliwell: Many of your other novels have been critically appraised for the ways in which you explore the inner life of women. Why did you choose to tell this story through the eyes of a male character: Snowman/Jimmy?

Atwood: Actually, sometimes the novels have been trashed for going into the inner life of women! "Why do we want to go into the inner life of women? This is rubbish!" So it just depends on the critic's predilections. Why did I decide to do a man this time? You couldn't have told this story from the point of view of a woman.

Halliwell: Why not?

Atwood: Well, I think it really comes home to you when you get to the part where Jimmy and his pal Crake are adolescents and they spend a huge amount of time playing computer games on two computers with their backs turned to each other. How many girls do you know who have ever done that! In fact, I read in the paper the other day that they are trying to do a study on whether computer games enhance your visual capabilities and they could only find one girl who had done this enough to be in the study. Now visually girls play relational games and if they do play stuff on the computer it might be something with a different type of narrative structure. The interest in strategy and tactics—it tends to be boys who play those kinds of games. So that's one reason. The other reasons become apparent as we go through the plot. If it had been a woman up in the tree in the bed sheet with the sunglasses with one lens it would've been quite a different history of how she'd got there.

Halliwell: Women seem to be not totally absent, but largely absent in the narrative, except for Oryx, who is this strange female character…

Atwood: Well, there are some female people. There's Jimmy's mother: although she is absent, she's this very big part of it. And there's Jimmy's pet, which is female. His pet is quite important to him. It's a blend of skunk and raccoon. I think this would be quite a good idea myself—the good features of both: it doesn't smell, it doesn't grow up and tear your house apart the way that raccoons do. And very cute. Skunks are very cute animals. So he has got one of those and its name is Killer. How many girls would have named their pet "Killer"? Well, these days maybe quite a few! But, that's a female.

Halliwell: Oryx is a kind of hazy character who never seems to be fully fleshed out.

Atwood: Now remember we are hearing everything from the point of view of Jimmy. Now name ten men of your acquaintance who are fully conversant with the inner lives of women who are the objects of their affections! Yes, she is partly how he wants her to be, of course, because that's what love is. And so is Crake, but because Crake is a boy he understands more that goes on in his head than he does in Oryx's. He does have a long selection of girlfriends, so we do hear about them, but not individually. You hear about them generically, as it were. It's not that he's not fond of women. He is. He just has a short attention span.

Halliwell: It seems as if Oryx is a digital image that never reaches the realm of reality.

Atwood: Oh no, she's a real person. She turns up. She's in the flesh. She first appears as a digital image because he first encounters her on a porn show because these two lads spend a lot of time watching programs like the Nudey News and various porn sites. This may be atypical but not according to the statistics that I have come across. Some people have said to me, "Did you have to do much research yourself on this?" and I said, "Actually no, because the range of motifs is limited." They are mostly all in *Police Gazette* in the '50s. So this time it is with moving images.

Halliwell: Do you think this world could be narrated from the perspective of Oryx?

Atwood: You could do another whole novel from the perspective of Oryx, but it would be a different novel. So certainly you could. We do have her story, but it is a story she has told to Jimmy. Partly because he has nagged her so we don't know how much of her story is tailor-made, according to what she thinks he wants to hear. Of course, women never do that.

Halliwell: Do you think it would be a more interesting story than this one in which Jimmy discovers how he has got from the past to here? Or just a different story?

Atwood: It would be a different story. You read stories like this in the papers a lot. Child prostitution is with us in quite a massive way and so is ordinary, run-of-the-mill prostitution and so are lots of stories like that.

Halliwell: To go back to "toast" [this refers to one of the readings from *Oryx and Crake* in which Jimmy ponders the origins and meanings of the word "toast"]. Toast is probably not one of the running themes of the novel—but certainly language and words are aspects of one of the major themes. Jimmy is preoccupied by "odd words," "old words," words that seem to remind him of the past and give him that connection.

Atwood: Jimmy is out of step with his times. He's not a math genius. He grows up in a world of science and math where top points go to people who are good at those things and he is not gifted in that way. He's a word person. So when they have got through high school (Jimmy with some coaching in the math department from his friend) they go off to two different kinds of institutions. Jimmy goes to the falling-apart, liberal arts institution known as the Martha Graham Academy where there are silver fish in the rooms and the food is horrible. And nothing has been repaired for some time because this is not the kind of institution that is getting major funding—in the future: unlike now! And Crake goes off to the Watson-Crick Institute, which is very well funded and where they're playing with the great big toy box that we have now opened, namely gene-splicing. So they go in two different directions at that time. And Jimmy, almost as an act of stubbornness, focuses his attention on words—words that are becoming of less relevance in the so-called "real world." I have to say that I put nothing into this book that we don't have or are not on the way to having. It's like *The Handmaid's Tale* in that I didn't invent. I just extrapolated.

Halliwell: On the words versus numbers issue: there seems to be a development of the "two cultures" debate from the '50s, that somehow science and arts are going their separate ways, and there is no dialogue between them.

Atwood: It's not an argument! There are some attempts being made to put them back together—Stephen J. Gould and E. L. Wilson have been talking about this, and it usually is biologists, rather than your chemists and physicists, who are interested in this area because biology at least is a life science, so people can be included in that. They took different stands on that question. Wilson felt that the humanities could somehow be subsumed and incorporated into one giant overview, which would in essence be scientific. Stephen J. Gould took a somewhat opposite point of view. So there is a dialogue that is ongoing.

Halliwell: Do you work through that dialogue in this novel, then?

Atwood: Not really, no. For Jimmy it's just the way the world is. It is not an argument; it's just how things are. You know, you don't have an argument about whether or not there are trains—there are trains. You can then talk about how well they run, but that's a different conversation.

Halliwell: A lot of films shown at the Cannes Film Festival last week (May 2003) dealt with what you might call "the post-human condition"—language and identity on the verge of extinction, people surviving from what might be a holocaust or war, or waking up in the way that Snowman seems to wake…

Atwood: I wonder why we all feel this way!

Halliwell: Some critics have commented that your book seems to fit in with a "post-September 11 zeitgeist."

Atwood: Yes, except I started writing it well before September 11. No, I think it's probably the "twentieth and twenty-first century zeitgeist." The first novel of this kind that I can remember reading is something called *The Purple Cloud*, and I think its date is around 1900. We weren't even told what the "purple cloud" was; it was just something that wiped everybody out, except for a couple of people. So I think there was a turning point. Before that time, people were very interested in writing utopias, how everything could be made better, and they did continue writing some of those. But there is a definite tip-over into a darker view of sudden attempts to change everything around. And I think that was partly because two utopias were tried: in the U.S.S.R. under Stalin and in Nazi Germany. Both said, "We're going to make things so much better, everything will be just blissful…except there is this bumpy part at the beginning…during which we have to kill tens of millions of people…but after that it will all be great." And the mythical model of that, if you like, is the Book of Revelations. First there will be all of these awful catastrophes and events and after that you will get the New Jerusalem. So that will be the—I hate to say it—"roadmap" (I will not say roadmap!). That is the model for that kind of utopian thinking: first catastrophe, then blissful wonderfulness. The typical utopias/dystopias of the twentieth century are Evgenii Zemiatin's *We*, Aldous Huxley's *Brave New World* and George Orwell's *1984*. So none of them are really good news for the human race.

Halliwell: You pick up on the issue of eugenics, going back to the Nazi experiments.

Atwood: Yes, there is always this catch. What do you do with the people who (a) don't fit in or (b) don't agree with you? Well, usually it involves an unfortunate end for those people.

Halliwell: When you were preparing the novel did you go back to the utopia/dystopia examples you cited or was it mainly scientific research you did in terms of genetic engineering and techno-science?

Atwood: It was mainly the scientific. I just clipped things out of newspapers and magazines, and I have to say a number of the things put in the book as being theoretically possible but not yet with us have since happened. For instance, a man has just put together a virus from scratch. He chose the polio virus. When people asked him why he did it, a question you or I might have thought to mean, "Why did you do such a dangerous thing?" he answered a different question, he said "because it's quite a simple virus." In other words, "I'll make a more complicated one next time!" So it was mostly that. The other stuff was something I've been familiar with for quite some time, I didn't need to go back and look at it.

Halliwell: Your brother helped in mapping out the scientific debates for you?

Atwood: My brother? Oh, he occasionally sends me weird clippings. Yes, I did grow up amongst the scientists. I guess we should explain that my father was an entomologist, my brother is a neurophysiologist specializing in the synapse, and two of his sons are also scientists—one is a physicist, he does the universe, and one of them is a materials engineer, and does crystal modeling on computers. So they're all conversant with these kinds of things and to keep up I've continued to read pop science all my life. By pop science I mean the stuff without the math. I don't want to do the math. I just want people to tell me what they found out! I also, however, want somebody that's good at it to check the math so we know it's just not another bogus scientist—of which there have been quite a few.

Halliwell: When *The Handmaid's Tale* came out people were saying it was a "science-fiction novel," but you resisted that label.

Atwood: When people think "science fiction" they usually think *Star Trek*, or they think *Star Wars*, or they think *War of the Worlds*—you know, talking squid...talking cannibalistic squid. And I saw a huge range of sci-fi B-movies in the '50s: the glory days, those low-budget ones with names like *The Creeping Eye*, which was quite good until you actually saw it! You could see the tractor tires underneath as it crept along! So that's what people think of when they think "science fiction." And *Oryx and Crake* is not that because, as I said, there's nothing in it that we can't do. The location is Earth. The characters are us. There are no Spocks with pointed ears. This comes out of the period of my life: "safe TV programs you can watch with your ten-year-old," it was one called *Murder She Wrote* in which you knew that Angela Lansbury would have it all tidied up at the end...you wouldn't see too much actual blood.

Halliwell: So the conventions of science-fiction are too tight for the kind of fiction you want to write?

Atwood: It is not that I don't like it. I just can't write it. I start laughing. But I like reading it. And a lot of the things that classic writers have explored have come pretty close to coming true in many ways. *Fahrenheit 451*, for instance. I was very keen on Ray Bradbury as a teenager. So, nothing against it, but I prefer to call *1984*, *Brave New World*, *The Handmaid's Tale* and *Oryx and Crake* "speculative fiction."

Halliwell: Is there something novelists can tell us about the future that scientists cannot?

Atwood: Well, it depends how motivated the scientists are. A lot of them are problem-solvers. They want to solve the immediate problem of how you get a jellyfish gene into a fish, which we've got now, too. It's blue. It lights up. And it is selling like hotcakes in the States. Said to be 90% sterile. So, who is worrying about the other 10%? They should have a little sign on: "Don't flush it down the toilet, kids!" I think this is what novels can do that non-fiction cannot.

If you want the really good non-fiction book about gene splicing and what it may do for you, me, and your grandkids the book is called *Enough* by Bill McKibben. He quotes people who go further than anybody in my book, who are saying in all seriousness, "Why shouldn't we have two mouths, because it's so inefficient to have one, to do all these things like eating and talking. If we had two we could eat and talk at the same time. Wouldn't that be a blast! Or why shouldn't we have eyes in the back of our heads?" But they don't consider the hair-do problems! Anyway, they tend to be single-issue, single-focus thinkers—how to solve the immediate problem of what they're doing. What a novel can do is take an individual, because novels are always about individual characters, and "go there" with that person.

Halliwell: Would you say that your vision of the future—or the Atwoodian fictional world—is getting bleaker? Is there hope for the world of *Oryx and Crake*?

Atwood: Well, as I said, it is like *The Christmas Carol*. You can wake up after reading the book—supposing it has put you to sleep!—and say to yourself, "It hasn't happened yet," and nobody can predict the future because there are too many variables. However, if nothing changes and we keep doing what we're doing, we are heading for the perfect storm. The perfect storm, if you recall, was what happened when various forces came together all at once and here's a couple of them: one, the human population will peak at ten billion in the year 2050; two, we are running out of stuff—we happened to have run through 90% of the ocean fish stocks in the past fifty years; and, number three, we've just opened the great big gene-splicing toy box and people are going to be playing with that for years. So put it all together and what have you got? We are not sure yet! They are also working on nano-technologies, which may enable you to, for instance, put your dirt in one end and out the other end comes your potato. That technique might solve the food shortage for a while but then what happens when you run out of dirt?

Halliwell: Well, George W. Bush seems to have the answer with his advocacy of GM food and it's being used in Africa!

Atwood: I wonder how many dollars and campaign contributions he got for that! Science isn't the bad thing; the bad thing is making all science completely commercial, and with no watch-dogs. That is when you have to get very nervous. We already know that pharmaceutical companies have been suppressing their own research for years. We know how the cigarette companies behaved. You are in a world in which "Buy a scientist" is not out of the question at all.

Halliwell: *The Handmaid's Tale* was set in a specific year, 2010 I think…

Atwood: No, it wasn't. I don't know how these things get there. I think they creep in through students' term papers.

Halliwell: I've been reading too many of them then! Anyway, *Oryx and Crake* seems to step aside from making a critique of the U.S.A. Was that deliberate?

Atwood: Well, it is set in roughly the same spot. But there isn't any what you may call "government" anymore. That's completely caved. The movement towards small government has finally succeeded and it has vanished—everything is being run by corporations now…in the future.

Questions from the Floor

Questioner 1: Can I ask you about the ending?

Atwood: No, no, no, no, no!

Questioner 1: I heard you talking on the radio recently about writing up to the point where you don't know what happens next. Could you talk a bit more about that?

Atwood: I hate talking about endings of books when it's a new book and there may be lots of people who may not have read it. I think it kind of spoils it for them, but I can talk about the ending of *The Handmaid's Tale*. That's a book that's been around for a while. *The Handmaid's Tale* actually has two endings: one, the ending of the narrative involving the character and, two, the postscript, which takes place in a future beyond the future and you find out that the regime we've been following is over. Which is a somewhat hopeful way of ending that book. But endings in general are always a bit hard because any ending in life is artificial. Life doesn't end. People's lives end. But other lives keep going from that and the dance goes on. So whenever you come to a point in the book where you have to say "the end," it is always like snipping off a piece of ribbon. It's always a bit arbitrary. I like to leave the endings open enough so the reader can make some choices, because readers in fact make choices all the way throughout books in any case. If you tie up the characters' lives too neatly, people may feel somewhat tricked—that you've just kind of ended things happily. Anthony Trollope's *Barchester Towers* has a lot to say about the conventional ending and how expected it is, and how artificial it is.

Questioner 2: Do you approach writing poetry in a similar way to writing novels, or is it a very different experience?

Atwood: Writing poetry and writing novels, a very different experience, unless I was writing, for instance, *The Divine Comedy*, which is a very, very long poem with a narrative thrust. If you write a novel, you know that you're going to be writing very hard for a minimum of a year and a half. You know you're going to get pains in your arms. You know you're going to get pains in your neck. You know you're going to get headaches. It is hard, physical work. And you know you're going to become an obsessive and wake up in the middle of the night and write things down on pieces of paper that will be illegible in the morning! All of these are experiences that you will have, and you also know that you are going to be unable to travel anywhere without mailing copies of your…you don't want to know! With a poem, on the other hand, you can have the whole experience in half an hour! It's a much shorter-term thing. Not that you don't go back and rewrite and revise and throw things out and do all of those things, but the actual physical labor is not the same. It's also not an experience I, at any rate, can "will." You know that once you have started a novel a lot of willpower is going to go into it. You may have had the idea, but then you are going to have to work it out, which means getting up in the morning, sitting down at your desk and working. Somebody said, "one part inspiration, nine parts perspiration." That's about right. So it's quite different for me. Poets annoy people because they spend a lot of the time looking out of a window and when people say, "Why aren't you mowing the lawn?" they say, "I'm working." With a novelist you can see them working…it actually looks something like work.

Questioner 3: Are you an activist?

Atwood: I separate my life as a citizen from my life as a writer. Writers often get shoved into the front lines of things for a very simple reason. They don't have jobs. Therefore, they can't be fired. A lot of people say things that they are thinking, but they know that they would be looked at with suspicion at work if they did those things. That isn't a consideration that comes into it if you're a writer. So you often get asked to be the spokesperson. I have done that on various issues quite a bit, but do I lick the stamps? Actually, no. Not much. I have done some stamp-licking in my earlier days…with a few other stamp-lickers. We started PEN Canada, which is the poets, novelists, editors and essayists group and I took that on, on the condition that it not be a tea party and it put most of its energies into the operation known as Writers in Prison—which doesn't mean going to teach creative writing in prisons; it means trying to get people out of prison in other countries who have been put there for writing things. So we can go down the list and it's actually probably much more than I should have done and if I were leading another life I might be Thomas Pynchon and never show my head above water or let my picture appear on a book jacket. In that way you can lead a nice, solitary life as a writer, but being Canadian had something to do with it. We had to practically build the publishing industry for our generation ourselves, and a lot of us worked for small publishing companies, and you learn a lot of things that way. I don't actually throw stones through windows. I leave that to the young.

Questioner 4: Which in your own view are your most successful and least successful novels?

Atwood: That is a question I never answer. The reason I never answer it is that the others will hear and they'll be very annoyed. And in any case, don't you think each one of them has something special that only they have?

Questioner 5: Do you think (a) the structure affects the readability of the book, (b) it doesn't affect the readability of the book, or (c) "what do I care about the readability of the book"?

Atwood: (a), (b) or (c)? How about (d)? (d) would be the one in which each reader is different, and therefore we cannot really speak about a quality called readability because what may be readability for person X may be facile and boring for person Y and completely unintelligible for person Z. So the only thing that you can do as a writer is to do the best with the book that you can. Do the best you can with the book, considering what sort of book it is and what sort of parameters exist, then you send it off into the world and perhaps reader R will have a jolly good time with it, reader T will not be able to get past page 2 and reader Q will think it's pretty horrible when they're 16 but when they're 50 they'll come back to it and say, "I appreciate this book now!" So all of these experiences have been had, in fact, by me! With different books. And that's the way it is. If you want to read more about these experiences and the writer's relationship with the book and the book's relation with the reader, there is a cunning book I wrote called *Negotiating with the Dead*. And you will find it in the chapter on the reader: it is called "The Eternal Triangle"—reader, book, and writer. The writer actually never has any relationship with the reader at all. It's the reader who has the relationship with the book. Readability is actually in your hands, not mine.

Contributor Notes

Rudolf Bader has taught at universities in Switzerland, Germany, Australia, and Canada. He is currently a professor of English at Zurich University of Applied Sciences, Switzerland. He has published seven books and over 100 scholarly articles in the areas of Canadian, Australian, and other international literatures in English as well as in Shakespearean studies.

Jo Brans is the author of four books of nonfiction: *Mother, I Have Something to Tell You*; *Take Two*; *Feast Here Awhile*; and *Listen to the Voices*, in which the interview with Atwood was previously published. Formerly a member of the Department of English at Southern Methodist University, she is now retired and living in New York City.

Rebecca Garron was born in the Chicago area, graduated from The Johns Hopkins University, and traveled throughout Germany on a Watson Scholarship, working in various theaters. At the time the interview was first published in *Clockwatch Review*, Garron was living in Berlin and working as a freelance writer.

Graeme Gibson, who has travelled around the world in search of birds, is the acclaimed author of *The Bedside Book of Birds*, *Five Legs*, *Perpetual Motion*, and *Gentleman Death*. He is the past president of PEN Canada and the recipient of both the Harbourfront Festival Prize and the Toronto Arts Award. He is a council member of WWF Canada, and chairman of the Pelee Island Bird Observatory. Graeme Gibson lives in Toronto, Canada, with Margaret Atwood.

Martin Halliwell is Professor of American Studies at the University of Leicester. He is the author of five books, including *Transatlantic Modernism: Moral Dilemmas in Modernist Fiction* (2005) and *Images of Idiocy: The Idiot Figure in Modern Fiction and Film* (2004). He is currently working on a sixth book on American culture in the 1950s.

Karla Hammond has spent ten years full time in the literary field—publishing in over 180 journals (poetry, fiction, book reviews, articles, essays, interviews, etc.) in the US, Canada, Australia, England, Japan, Italy and Greece.

Geoff Hancock was the editor-in-chief of *Canadian Fiction Magazine*. He is the editor or author of numerous books, including *Canadian Writers at Work: Interviews* (Oxford, 1987), from which his interview has been reprinted.

Ann Heilmann is a senior lecturer in English at the University of Wales, Swansea. Her specialities are gender in 19th-century literature and feminist studies. She is the author of *New Woman Fiction: Women Writing First-Wave Feminism*.

Beryl Langer is in the Sociology and Anthropology Program at LaTrobe University, in Melbourne, Australia. Her PhD in Sociology is from the University of Toronto, and she maintains an active research interest in Canadian literature and cultural politics. Her essays on Canadian literature are published in Australian-Canadian Studies and in a number of edited collections.

James McElroy teaches at the University of California at Davis. His previous publications include pieces in the *New York Times, San Francisco Review of Books* and the *American Poetry Review*. McElroy is also editor of *The International Journal of Irish Studies*.

Gabrielle Meltzer received her doctorate from the University of Tübingen and presently teaches at the University of Education in Freiburg. In addition to two books she has published articles in diverse areas such as international relations, Canadian politics, gender studies, and creativity, along with her own short fiction and poetry.

Bruce Meyer is author of twenty-three books of poetry, short fiction and non-fiction including the national bestseller, *The Golden Thread*. He teaches in the Laurentian University BA Program at Georgian College and in the St. Michael's College Continuing Education Program at the University of Toronto. He is artistic director of the Leacock Summer Festival of Canadian Literature.

Mary Morris, Professor of English at Sarah Lawrence, is the author of a number of novels, collections of short stories, and travel books, including *Revenge, The Lifeguard: Stories*, and *Angels & Aliens: A Journey West*.

Joyce Carol Oates, Roger S. Berlind Distinguished Professor in the Humanities at Princeton University, is the author of the novels *Blonde, I'll Take You There, The Falls*, and *Missing Mom*. She has been a member of the American Academy of Arts and Letters since 1978 and is the recipient of the 2005 Prix Femina.

Brian O'Riordan is co-editor with **Bruce Meyer** of two books of interviews with Canadian writers, *In Their Own Words* and *Lives and Works*. He is also a published poet and book reviewer, and currently works in a senior capacity for the Ontario government in the Ministry of Health and Long-Term Care.

Evan Solomon is the co-host of the two weekly news and current affairs shows, CBC News: Sunday and CBC News: Sunday Night. Solomon is the co-editor and writer of the best-selling book *Fueling the Future: How the Battle Over Energy Is Changing Everything* (2004) and *Feeding the Future: From Fat to Famine, How to Solve the World's Food Crisis* (2005).

John Stone is a PhD candidate and Associate Lecturer in the Department of English and German Philology at the University of Barcelona. He has edited and helped translate a Catalan edition of Samuel Johnson's Preface to Shakespeare; published work on Johnson, seventeenth-century university drama, modern British cinema, and contemporary Canadian novelists; and is currently engaged in a study of Johnson's reception in eighteenth-century Spain.

Debbie Taylor edits *Mslexia,* reputed to be "the fastest-growing literary magazine in the UK." Her book *My Children My Gold: A Journey to the World of Seven Single Mothers* (1995) was short-listed for the Fawcett Prize.

Index

MARGARET ATWOOD is the author of a dozen novels, most recently, *The Penelopiad* (2005); over a dozen books of poetry; and a dozen or more collections of short fiction, nonfiction, and children's books. Among her many honors and awards is the Booker Prize, for her novel *The Blind Assassin* in 2000.

EARL G. INGERSOLL is a distinguished university professor at the State University of New York at Brockport. He is the author or editor of eleven books of interviews and literary criticism.